THE LOCAL HISTORIAN'S GLOSSARY OF WORDS AND TERMS

JOY BRISTOW

D1353182

COUNTRYSIDE BOOKS
NEWBURY · BERKSHIRE

Produced through MRM Associates Ltd., Reading
Typeset by Techniset Typesetters, Merseyside
Printed by Woolnough Bookbinding Ltd., Irthlingborough

CONTENTS

ACKNOWLEDGEMENTS

Acknowledgement is given to all who have assisted in the preparation of this publication. In the first two editions thanks must go to the University of Nottingham at whose instigation it was published, and particularly to Dr David Marcombe, Director of the Centre for Local History, for his help and advice.

I must also express my thanks to my husband Ralph, and to my daughter Wendy Bateman, for their patience, understanding and helpful comments on these three editions.

Every effort has been made to ascertain copyright permission, and if any infringement has occurred, sincere apologies are offered, and correction will be made during any reprinting.

I commend the publications listed in the bibliography for the knowledge and information they contain. I am very grateful to the following sources:

Royal Historical Society for permission to reproduce material from *A Handbook of Dates for Students of British History*, C. R. Cheney, revised by Michael Jones (2000).

Macmillan Press Ltd for permission to reproduce material from *The Macmillan Dictionary of Historical Terms*, C. Cook (1990).

The Society of Genealogists, for permission to reproduce material from *The Dictionary of Genealogy*, Terrick V. H. FitzHugh (1988).

Cassell plc for permission to reproduce material from *The Dictionary of Phrase & Fable*, E. C. Brewer (1988).

The Derbyshire Record Society & D. Kiernan for permission to reproduce material from *The Derbyshire Lead Mining Industry in the Sixteenth Century*, D. Kiernan (1989).

Dr. J.H. Rieuwerts for permission to reproduce material from *Lead Mining in the Peak District* (1983).

Spink & Son Ltd for permission to reproduce material from the *(Spink) Standard Catalogue of Coins of England*.

INTRODUCTION

This Glossary was compiled from a collection of words unfamiliar to me while studying for the Advanced Certificate in Local History at the University of Nottingham. The first edition was published in 1990, was enlarged in 1994 and reprinted with amendments in 1997. This current edition has been modified slightly and will, it is hoped, be of help to a wider selection of students of local and family history.

The local history students should find it helpful when transcribing Manorial and Estate papers and other old documents, as the book contains many of the words and phrases they will encounter. Probate documents and wills give many family details, stating relationship, and sometimes throw light on any family feuds. Care has to be taken in interpreting words whose meaning seems obvious, but which might have had a different meaning in the past.

Family historians can obtain useful information if they study inventories which often go with a will. These can be found in local archive offices, and inventories contain many details which may be unknown about a person. For example, what kind of dwelling they lived in, how much money was in their purse, as well as what goods and chattels they owned. They list the articles in each room, the acreage held, what crops were grown and also the crops being stored in the barn. Inventories are the most useful and interesting of documents. They give a marvellous insight into the way of life and the standard of living of the ancestor.

The Latin section will be invaluable when reading the early parish registers, in particular those of the seventeenth century, and of course, *The Oxford English Dictionary* should never be excluded as a work of reference.

A

abred. Spread out or 'abroad'; outdoors.

achyyt. Hatchet.

acled chest. Meaning obscure. Possibly a cupboard for crockery, as in 'acobil' or 'acobgill' (Oxfordshire dialect).

acolyte. Lowest of the four orders of priesthood; a boy who had taken the first tonsure with a view to becoming sub-deacon, then deacon, then priest.

acquavite. *See* **aquavite.**

acre. Unit of area standardized by Edward I at 40 rods x 4 rods. However, it varied in different parts of the country. A statute acre today = 4,840 sq. yards.

acre tax. Drainage tax — 1787.

act book. Register in which the minutes of a court were written. Some entries are very cramped and difficult to read because the same page spacing was allowed under each heading.

addice/ades/adze. Tool with the cutting edge at right angles to the handle, used by coopers for shaping the concave sides of timber boards.

adit. *See* **sough.**

advent. Four weeks before Christmas set aside to commemorate the first and second coming of Christ: the first to redeem, and the second to judge the world. The season begins on St. Andrew's Day, 30 November, or the Sunday nearest to it.

adventurer. Shareholder in a lead mine or **sough** *q.v.*

advertisements. Series of injunctions issued to the clergy in 1566, pursuant to the Act of Uniformity, 1 Elizabeth, c.2 (1558), 2 & 3 Edward VI, c.1 (1548), 14 Car. II, c.4 (1662).

advowson. Right of presentation to an ecclesiastical benefice.

aelevan. *See* **aleven.**

affeer. To settle the amount of an **amercement** *q.v.;* to assess.

affeerer/afferatore. Officer of the manorial court whose duty it was to assess monetary penalties.

affinity. The entourage of a lord.

aftermath. Herbage remaining after hay harvest.

ager/eagre/eger. High tidal wave of the rivers Trent and Ouse. Also called the 'Bore' in the Severn.

agist. To pasture; to pay for pasture.

agistment/gysting/joisting. The pasturing, on payment, of one's animals on someone else's land.

agnate. Any male relation on the father's side.

agnatic. Related entirely through the male line of ancestors. *See also* **cognate.**

agnus dei. Cake of wax or dough stamped with the figure of a lamb supporting the banner of the Cross, distributed by the Pope on the Sunday after Easter as an amulet.

aicent/aiecent. Adjacent.

aid. Tax in medieval times paid by a vassal to his liege lord either:
1. as a ransom after capture;
2. on the occasion of the lord's eldest son being knighted; or
3. on the occasion of his eldest daughter being married.
Feudal Aids were abolished in 1660.

ails. *See* **hales.**

alamode. Thin, light, glossy black silk.

albacio. Whitewashing.

alcuin/alkemy. Antimony.

ale conner/finder/taster. A manorial officer whose duty it was to assess the **assize and goodness of bread and ale** *q.v.* within the precincts of the manor.

alehouse. A public house distinguished by a long pole in front; if wine could be obtained, a bush was placed on the pole.

alembic. *See* **limbeck.**

aleplay. Mystery or miracle play in aid of church funds. *See also* **church ales.**

aleven/aleaven/alevan/aelevan. Eleven.

alienation. The transfer of a holding by sale rather than by inheritance. A feudal tenant was unable to alienate without licence from the lord who would collect a fee from granting the transfer.

allotment. The allocation of lands parcelled out under an enclosure award.

almain rivets. Kind of flexible light armour of German origin made of overlapping plates sliding on rivets.

almer. Alternative form of **ambry** *q.v.*

almerye. Cupboard.

altarage. Mortuaries, surplice fees, and other minor ecclesiastical offerings.

alum/allam. Potassium (or sodium or ammonium) aluminium sulphate, used in dyeing as a mordant, and also in tanning.

ambry. 1. wooden cupboard containing provisions, usually prepared foods rather than stores, kept in a cool place, e.g. the buttery.
2. niche in a church for holding books and sacred utensils.

amerce/amercement. Fine in a manorial court.

amphora. Large heavy earthenware vessel used for storing and carrying oil and wine.

anabaptist. One who denies the validity of infant baptism and maintains that re-baptism of adults (by immersion) is necessary. A member of a fanatical sect of Protestants in Saxony in the sixteenth century. Sometimes used derogatively, as a loose term for a Baptist or Quaker.

andirons. 1. pair of iron bars with hooked brackets for supporting roasting spit.
2. moveable iron plates used to contact the fire area in a grate.
3. large fire-dogs or **cobirons** *q.v.*, with hooks at various levels from which cooking spits were supported.

angel/angelle. Old English gold coin, originally called 'Angel-Noble', having as its device the archangel Michael and the dragon. Its value varied from six shillings to ten shillings.

angwite. Fine paid to compound, i.e. to settle out of court, for bloodshed. Also called **blodwite**.

anilepiman. A man, usually unmarried, who held no land in a village; he could be boarded or given a cottage on the tenement of a man who did hold land, and he could keep a few cattle or sheep on the village pasture.

annel seed. Aniseed; seeds of *Pimpinella anisum*. Used as a carminative, and in oil of anise. Sometimes confused with dill.

annuity. Grant made by a lord to a retainer, either for life or for a specific number of years.

annus luctus. The period during which a widow was supposed to maintain chastity. If she married within about nine months from the death of her husband and a child was born, a doubt

1. Open chimney fitted with a Sussex fire-back and *andirons*. From a drawing made by J.J. Hissey in 1887.

might have arisen as to the paternity of the child. Such a marriage was not illegal, but was thought to be inexpedient.

aperne. Apron.

appanage. Landed estate of a royal prince, often accompanied by extensive legal privileges.

apparator/apparatour/apparitor. Servant, attendant or official messenger of a civil or ecclesiastical court, entitled as such to customary fees. These fees, which had been a grievance for centuries, were regulated by the Canons of 1604. *See also* **visitation.**

appendant (common). Common land attached to an arable holding, and used only for grazing of animals.

appenne/apptence. *See* **appurtenant.**

apple mill. *See* **cider press.**

apple roaster. Iron utensil used for roasting apples over an open fire.

appropriate. Ecclesiastical benefice whose tithe is annexed in whole or in part to an ecclesiastical body or individual other than the incumbent.

appropriator. Ecclesiastical body or person, other than the parish priest, having (usually) the right to great tithes in the parish. *See also* **impropriator.**

approvement. Enclosure of common, especially by the lord of the manor, under the Statutes of Merton 20 Henry III, cc. 4.9. (1235) and Westminster II 13 Edward I, c. 46 (1285).

appurtenant (common). Common land which was in fact, though not quite in legal theory, attached to a house, rather than to ancient arable land. Known also as **appenne.**

aquavite/acquavite. 'Water of life', used to describe any form of distilled spirits, such as brandy.

archdeacon. Ecclesiastical dignitary ranking above the incumbent but below the bishop. In many matters the bishop's principal officer, *oculus episcopi.*

Arches, Court of. Provincial court of the Archbishop of Canterbury.

arders. The process of ploughing and manuring; in inventory usage meaning the valuation of the work put into the land. *See also* **clod, tile land.**

ardyn. Harden.

ark. Wooden chest or bin for dry stores. *See also* **ambry.**

arles. *See* **earles.**

armed field chair. Possibly a portable chair.

arras/arrice/aryse. Fabric originating from Arras, Flanders. Later identified with the tapestry hanging.

arretine. Type of fine pottery made at Arrezzo, Italy, in the first century B.C., of pinkish clay coated with dark red slip. Made in a mould and decorated in low relief.

arroy. Harrow.

artileine. Possibly 'artillery', i.e. implements of war.

arvill supper. Feast made at funerals, in part still retained in the North of England.

ascertaciones sedilium. Pew rents.

ash spitt. Ash-pit.

assart/essart. Enclosure or clearing of forest or waste land.

assize of bread and ale. Statutory regulations or settling of price of bread and ale with reference to that of grain.

attainder. The parliamentary act of attainting, literally 'corrupting the blood', whereby a person guilty of treason loses all civil rights including the right to inherit or hold property.

attorney. One of the two types of legal practice which coalesced in 1827 to form the modern profession of 'the solicitor'.

attornment. Transferral, by ancient law, of tenants' homage and service to new lord after death of the previous landowner. The 'attornment of tenants' is accordingly entered on the roll of every lord's first court after acquiring, inheriting or succeeding to the manor.

aubergel. Sleeveless coat of scale armour.

auger. Three-pronged instrument with serrated edges and a long shaft for spearing eels. A similar instrument is called a **leister** *q.v.*, or 'lister' in Scotland.

aulnager. Official in a port or market town responsible for measuring woollen cloth and seeing that it was sold in correct widths and lengths. Approved cloth bore the town seal.

aver. Beast; usually a beast of burden.

average. Lincolnshire term for land that is fed with animal manure, lime, seaweed or thatching from houses, in common by the parish as soon as the corn is harvested.

avowry. Protector or guardian, such as the lord of the manor, in relation to the manor's tenants. A stranger outside any tithing could purchase a lord's **avowry** by paying a fine. May also mean the right of patronage granted to the founder of a religious house or to one who has endowed a church; a term used in distrainment cases where the distrainer avows or openly declares that he has justification for seizing the goods.

award. Judicial decision given after arbitration rather than as a result of court proceedings.

axeltree/axtree. Fixed bar on the rounded ends of which the wheels of a vehicle revolve.

ayes/ayetes/aythe/eyth. A harrow.

ayshes. Coal ashes or soot, used 'above all thing' as manure in south Gloucestershire.

aythe. *See* **ayes.**

B

babbing. A mode of removing the warp or soft mud from drains running into a river. A 'babbing-boat' is dragged along so as to disturb the warp, which is carried by the current out into the river.

backand flyck. (Bacon flick/flitch) a flitch or side of bacon, cured and salted.

backband/backbond. Strap or chain passing over a cart saddle and supporting the shafts of a vehicle.

back board chair. Chair with a solid back which could be turned to lie flat on the arms, forming a table or board.

backbord. Piece of wood placed behind a bench to exclude draughts; also, wooden back for a mirror.

backend/backerend. Probably an extension of a small house, serving as a buttery.

backerhowse/backhouse. Bakehouse, or possibly a general store room, particularly one containing brewing equipment.

back pannes. Baking pans.

backstays *or* **backsters.** Wide flat pieces of board, made like snow shoes, strapped on the feet and used by fishermen when walking over loose beach or soft mud of the seashore.

backston. Slate, hung in an iron frame over the fire, on which cakes are baked.

badger. 1. term derived from the 1697 Settlement Act, under which paupers were obliged to wear a capital 'P' on their clothing. At certain hours they were allowed to beg for victuals. They were also known as **badgemen**.
2. buyer and seller of grain and other commodities; later also a pedlar or chapman.
3. licensed beggar.

badstaff. Possibly a staff used in a butter churn.

bag. Measure, particularly of hops, usually 2½ cwt.

bait. To break a journey for food, or to give food and drink to an animal. A 'baiting place' was where cattle gathered for feeding.

baked on the sole. Of bread: baked on the oven shelf without being confined in a tin.

baker weight. Weight used in transactions between a baker and a miller for assessing the amount of flour milled from a given quantity of grain.

bailiff. Agent of the lord of the manor, who collects rents etc.

baldric. *See* **bautrick.**

balk. 1. untilled boundary strip either between adjacent **selions** *q.v.* in a common field furlong or, more often, between two adjacent furlongs in a common field. Hence a grass way over an open field. 'Sidebalks' are those running parallel to the **selions**, 'waybalks' those running at right angles to them; headlands.
2. beam of wood; the beam of a balance.
3. *see* **gallow balke.**

ballance clock. Clock controlled by a rotating balance wheel.

balles/ballows. Bellows.

ballys. Small rod.

band. Band of straw used to tie up sheaves.

band-kitt. Kind of large can with a cover.

banksman. Person who superintends the business of the coal pit.

banneret. Knight entitled to bear a banner, of higher status than a bachelor; a young or junior knight.

bannikin. Small drinking cup.

bannut. Fruit of the common walnut; the growing tree is called **bannut**, but the converted timber is called walnut.

bantamwork. Very ornate kind of painted or carved work.

barbican. Outer defence protecting castle entrance.

barebone parliament. Parliament convened by Cromwell in 1653; so called from Praise-God Barebone, a fanatical leader, who was a prominent member.

barefoot wheel. Wheel without an iron rim.

bareing mantle. Christening robe.

bare leap. *See* **leap.**

barfam. Horse collar.

bargh. Narrow way up a steep hill used by pack horses or horse riders.

bark. Candle box made of tin.

bark bing. Implement for beating bark in the tanning industry.

barker. Person engaged in peeling bark for tanning.

bark howse/house. House in which bark is stored; also called a tan-house.

barking iron. Chisel-like metal implement used to strip bark from cut timber.

barley drawers. Shafts for the **barley roll** *q.v.*

barleymow. Stack or **rick** *q.v.* of barley.

barley roll. Roller or 'hummeller', a wooden cylinder rolled across a heap of barley, to separate the grain from the awns.

barmaster. Representative of the Crown responsible for administration of mining law, measuring ore, and measuring out meers along a length of vein.

barmoot/barmote. The lead miners' court, usually held twice a year in each liberty, with a jury, once 24 in number now 12, charged with judicial duties continuously from the sitting of one court until the next. The jury is called the 'Body of the Mine'.

barmskin. Leather apron.

barn-barley. Barley which has never been in **rick** *q.v.*, but has been kept under cover from harvesting, and is therefore perfectly dry and of high value for malting purposes.

barnstable oven. Type of clay bread oven manufactured in potteries around Barum and Fremington in North Devon. The high proportion of Barnstaple Grit used in its manufacture enabled the oven itself, first heated by wood or furze fires, to bake spontaneously the bread or meat later placed inside. Their capacity varied from 1½ to 12 **pecks** *q.v.*

barrateen. Kind of woven fabric.

barratry. Lawyer's term for any of a number of disorderly activities, especially those committed by women.

barrow. Conical basket in which salt is drained, containing six **pecks** *q.v.*

barth. 1. warm place or pasture for calves and lambs.
2. lean-to shelter.

barton/barten. 1. farmyard or enclosed area of ground used for some specific agricultural purpose. *See also* **corn barton, rick barton**.
2. demesne lands of manor.

bartrees. The wooden frame on which the warp is placed during warping; a term found in weavers' inventories.

barvel. Short leather apron worn by washerwomen.

barytes. The mineral barium sulphate, commonly called cawk, calk, caulk or heavy spar.

bason. Bench with a fitted plate of iron or stone flag on which the first part of the felting process in hatting was performed. A fire was lit beneath the **bason.**

bass. A vegetable fibre. The word may be applied to an article made from **bass,** e.g. a cloth or carpet.

bass bottam chair. Chair with a bass or rush seat.

bass chair. Possibly a low chair.

basset. Outcrop of a vein or stratum.

bastard. Properly the base child of a father of gentle or noble birth, but more generally any illegitimate child.

bastard stile. Small gate, above a stile, set at such an angle that it will close by gravitational pull.

basterino. Bastard.

basterly-gullion. A bastard's bastard.

battin. The straw of two sheaves folded together.

battlement. Parapet with defensive indentations.

battle royal. 1. fight between 3, 5 or 7 cocks engaged together, so that the cock which stands longest wins.
2. unruly fight between several persons.

battles. At Oxford or Cambridge, commons or board.

battlings. The loppings of trees, larger than faggots, and smaller than timber.

battril. Batting staff used by washer women.

baurghwan. Horse collar.

bautrick. Alternative spelling of **baldric,** a leather thong inside a bell on which the clapper is hung.

bawks. Hay loft.

bay. 1. division in a barn.
2. any colour from light gold to dark brown, but most probably a dark mahogany shade.

bayle. Ladle for beer.

baze/baize. Coarse woollen fabric, with a long nap.

beadle. Parish officer with various duties such as messenger, town crier, assistant to the constable, mace bearer. Often had a special dress together with a whip or 'wand', which was not only a symbol of his authority, but also enabled him to drive dogs from any vestry meetings.

beakment. Measure containing four quarts.

beame. 1. crescent-shaped piece of smooth iron raised at one end, over which a tanner placed a hide to remove the hair and flesh. 2. transverse bar of a set of scales; sometimes known as a **weighbeame** *q.v.*

beame knife. Long, heavy, curved knife, used by tanners for removing hair from skins.

bear/bere. Pillow case.

beare hose. Stand on which beer barrels were placed.

bearing land. Probably land in crop.

bearing sheet. Sheet used to carry a child to church for baptism.

bear leap. *See* **leap.**

beast gate. *See* **gate.**

beath. To heat unseasoned wood in order to straighten it.

beating. The operations involved in the reduction of raw materials to the fineness required for papermaking.

beating hurdle. Possibly a frame on which carcasses were hung; an obscure term.

Beating the Bounds. It was the custom in Ascension week to walk and re-define the boundaries of the parish. The ceremony was carried out by the Incumbent, Churchwardens and parishioners. The custom is known to date from the end of the ninth century at least.

beckhorn. Small anvil, or the pointed end of an anvil.

beckstone. *See* **hippins**.

bed. Foundation woodwork or body of a cart.

bede house. Alms house.

bedell. Like the **reeve** *q.v.*, a manorial officer, but one of lower rank.

bede roll. List of benefactors to the church, for whose souls the faithful were asked to pray; it was read from the pulpit each Sunday and at Christmas and Michaelmas, usually by the parish priest but occasionally by clerk or sexton. A small payment from the parish accounts was made usually to the 'bedeman' for this service. It is now replaced by the Bidding Prayer.

bed licken. Bed linen.

bed staves. Staves or sticks laid across the **bedstocks** *q.v.* to support the bedding.

bedstock(s). Bedstead, or its front and back parts.

bee-pot. Bee hive; also called **skep** *q.v.* if the hive is made of straw.

beest/beestings. The first milk after a cow has calved, particularly used in Lancashire and Gloucester. This varies according to county.

beetle. Small heavy-headed hammer used for ramming down a **pavement** *q.v.*, hedge-stakes or wedges but sometimes covered with nails and used for splitting wood.

beggarly. Of land: exhausted from want of manure.

beldered. Bellowed.

belfray/belfrey/belfry. North Lincolnshire term for a temporary farm building, which provided a raised area for crop storage, and a shelter for cattle and farm implements. In East Yorkshire and parts of North Lincolnshire the term used was 'helm'.

Belgium. Type of heavy horse; possibly a Shire.

belland. Finely powdered lead ore. It could cause poisoning in animals and humans if allowed to flow in to streams or on to grass. Animals so poisoned were said to be 'belland(ed)'.

bell, book and candle. Ceremony in the greater excommunication introduced into the Catholic Church in the eighth century. After reading the sentence a bell was rung, a book closed, and a candle extinguished. From that moment the excommunicated person was excluded from the sacraments and divine worship.

bell metall. Alloy of copper and tin.

belly pooce. Belly piece; a triangular stiffening of buckram or pasteboard — one sewn each to the lining on either side at about waist level, with the base of each triangle placed vertically along the front border to form a corset-like ridge down the 'belly'.

ben. *See* **but and ben.**

bench borde. Plank placed on two trestles to make a seat.

bend leather. Section of the **butt** *q.v.* Used for sole-leather.

benefit of clergy. The system under which the clergy and, later, certain literate persons, could claim immunity from trial in a civil court on a felony charge. Abolished in 1827.

bere. Pillow-bere; a pillow case.

berewick. Subsidiary or outlying estate.

berry. To thresh out corn.

besom. Broom, usually made by tying a bunch of broom, or similar, round a handle.

betany. Bottle-shaped basket placed at the end of a spigot to prevent the malt and hops from getting into the spigot. Called a 'tap-wisk' in Leicestershire, and also a 'strumme'.

beverett. Small beaver-fur hat.

biat. 1. leather strap worn over the shoulders, a sort of drag-harness used by miners to draw the produce of the mine to the shaft.
2. kind of British coarse garment or jacket worn loose over other apparel.

bibb. Small tankard.

bick. Wooden bottle or cask in which beer is carried into harvest fields.

bidreaps. Days when the lord of the manor has the right to call upon the villagers to come and reap his corn.

bill. 1. crescent-shaped agricultural cutter with a long or short handle, especially a **hedgebill** *q.v.*
2. heavy knife or chopper with a hooked end.
3. a pickaxe.
4. an axe with two sharp pointed spikes mounted on a long staff, carried by the village watchman.

billard. A type of fish, possibly a coal-fish (a variety of cod).

billet (metal). Soft white or yellow metal cast in sprays and stamped in a 'die-billet' to make the 'shields' of knives on which the owners name is cut.

billet (wood). Piece of wood cut to a proper length for fuel.

billhouse. Probably the cupboard in the church in which the **bill** *q.v.*, carried by the village watchman, was stored.

billman. 1. man who cuts faggots.
2. formerly a soldier who was armed with a **bill** *q.v.*

billycock. Type of bowler hat said to have been originally designed for William Coke c. 1850.

binch/bink. Shelf or bench common at the doors of cottages, often made of stones or earth and planted on the top with camomile.

binding day. The second Tuesday after Easter, also called Binding Tuesday.

bing/bin. 1. large pieces of ore drawn from the mine and requiring little further dressing. 2. receptacle for corn or meal; a manger.

bird-bolt/burbot. Short arrow with a broad flat end, used to kill birds without piercing, by the mere force of the blow.

birding piece. Long-barrelled sporting gun.

birds eye. Pattern on fabrics derived from small weave and colour effects resulting in rectangular ornamentations.

bird spit. Spit for cooking poultry or game birds.

birny. Cuirass; a coat of mail.

biscan. Finger glove.

bi-scot. Fine imposed on the owners of marsh land for not keeping it in proper order.

bisgee. Kind of mattock, with a short handle, which served both for a pickaxe and a common axe.

bitt bridle. Mouthpiece of a bridle.

bittle rings/beetle rings. Iron rings used to strengthen the heads of **beetles** *q.v.*

Black Monday. Easter Monday; so called from the severity of the weather that day in 1360. Many of Edward III's soldiers, on the outskirts of Paris, died from the cold.

black wad. Manganese in its natural state.

blacksmith. A smith who works in iron or black metal, as distinguished from a **whitesmith** *q.v.* who works in tin and white metal.

blackthorn winter. Cold weather which is often experienced at the latter end of April and the beginning of May, when the blackthorn is in blossom.

blancher. Anything set round a wood to keep the deer in. Various articles were employed for the purpose, and sometimes men on this service were so called.

blanch farm. Annual rent paid to the lord of the manor.

blanktable. Plain, scrubbed kitchen-table.

blanquit. Blanket.

blash coke. Soft coke, made at the coal pits near Sheffield for steel smelters.

2. Blacksmiths.

blend corn. Mixture of wheat and rye.

blew pease. 'Blue peas' — the common or garden pea, *Pisum sativum.*

blinds. Blinkers on horse harness.

blocks. Sections of a mould consisting of variously shaped pieces of wood placed together for shaping hats to a required style after they had been sewn and stiffened.

blodwite. *See* **angwite.**

blood strike. Probably some kind of blacksmith's tool.

blunderbuss. Flintlock gun with a wide bore.

board/bord. Flat wooden surface, such as a table top. The supports are usually mentioned separately.

board cloth. Table cloth.

bocardo. The old north gate at Oxford, taken down in the eighteenth century. It was formerly used as a prison for criminals, drunkards, prostitutes and poor debtors.

boddle. Small iron instrument used for peeling oaks and other trees.

bodle. Scottish coin; one-sixth of a penny.

body-girts. Belly-bands of a saddle.

bofett/buffet. Early form of sideboard which incorporated shelves at three levels. The top and middle shelves or, alternatively, the middle and bottom shelves were usually open for the purpose of displaying household plate or food.

boggart. Spectre; 'to take **boggart**', said of a horse that starts at any object in the hedge or road.

bole/boles. 1. bowl.
2. primitive smelting hearth, often on a hilltop, hence 'Bole Hill', as a common place name, where the miners smelted or ran their ore, before the invention of mills or furnaces.

boll. An old grain measure of two to six bushels or 140 lbs *avoirdupois*. In Northumberland, a **boll of salt** equalled two bushels.

bolster. Solid lump of steel or some other material between the tang and the blade of a knife. In the better knives it is forged as part of the blade.

bolster stone. Used by grinders in grinding the **bolster** *q.v.*

bolt. Sale bundle of rods of willow made up of two wads. A wad is about two feet seven inches (79 cm) circumference.

bolter. Cloth used for sifting meal or flour.

bolting house/boltying. Room used for preparing food, in particular for **bolting**, i.e. sieving of flour, before making bread.

bolting vessel. Receptacle for sifting of flour.

bonch. Bench (many variations).

bond of indemnification. Device adopted to secure the parish against pecuniary liabilities, and often demanded
a) from relatives or friends of potential paupers who might gain a settlement;
b) from masters engaging servants for twelve months, whose service would gain them a settlement;
c) from putative fathers of illegitimate children, in order to secure the observance of covenants for their maintenance.

bone. Bobbin for making lace, probably first made of bones, hence 'bone-lace'.

bone grace. Veil or shade attached to a hat to protect the complexion. Also a large bonnet or straw hat.

bonet. Kind of small cap, worn close to the head.

bonnaght. Formerly, in Ireland, a tax paid to the lord of the manor.

bonting. Binding; curved bars of iron connected together by hooks and links and put round the outside of ovens and furnaces to prevent their outward swelling.

boonmaster. *See* **waywarden**.

boonwork. Seasonal labour services on a medieval manor, such as ploughing, haymaking or reaping, performed by tenants on a daily basis.

boor. In Cumberland, the parlour, bed-chamber or inner room.

boose/bowse. Stall for cattle.

bootcatcher. Person at an inn who pulls off the boots of passengers.

boot hose. Separate overstockings, worn inside boots to protect the undersole from becoming soiled or rubbed.

booting house. Possibly a workshop.

bordar. Villager holding less land than a **villein** *q.v.*

borden bedstead. Bedstead which had panels or wainscot either at the head or at both ends.

bore franke. Enclosure for boars; a pen.

bore tree. Elder tree. Children would commonly bore out the pith from the young branches in order to make potguns or pea shooters.

borier. Auger.

borlyng/burlyng. Yearling ox or heifer.

Borough English. Custom of inheritance in certain ancient boroughs and manors where the youngest son, and not the eldest, was considered the heir to his father's copyhold tenement. The custom died out with the ending of copyhold tenure. *See also* **fee**.

borsholder. Parish constable.

bose. Ox or cow stall.

botchet. Liquor made from honey and mead.

bote. Common right of taking timber from the **waste** *q.v.* of the manor for the repair of hedges and fences, for house repair, for firewood, for the maintenance and repair of the tools of husbandry, etc. Often as haybote, housebote, firebote, plough-bote, etc.

botews. Large boots, reaching above the knee and sometimes covering the whole leg.

bothem. Watercourse.

bottle jack. Spring-driven mechanical jack. A roast was suspended from a wheel under the bottle-shaped brass cylinder which contained a clockwork spring. The roast would revolve for an hour or so as the spring unwound.

bottle (of straw). As much straw or hay as a person could carry.

bottoming tool. Narrow concave shovel.

bouch/bouk. Bucket.

bough house. Private house allowed to open during fairs for the sale of liquor.

boulting mill. Bin used for sieving flour to separate it from the bran.

bound waggon. Waggon with sides.

bound wheel. Wheel with an iron rim.

bounty, parochial. Payment to militia volunteers.

bouse. Lead ore, as raised from the mine before dressing.

bouted bread. Bread made of wheat and rye.

bovate. The law Latin equivalent of the English term 'oxgang', or as much land as one ox could plough in a year; one-eighth of a **carucute** *q.v.* or ploughland; varied from 10-18 acres, or 10-30 acres in Lincolnshire.

bow. 1. catgut string which was stretched on a **bow hurdle** *q.v.* 2. loop in front of the yoke of a harrow which passed round the necks of oxen.

bowhawler. Man who manually draws barges or small vessels along rivers or canals.

bow handle/hurdle. Pole about six feet long on which a catgut string was stretched. The material from which hats were made was opened out on this construction.

bow pann. Possibly a pan with a 'bow' or handle.

bowse. *See* **boose**.

box iron. Flat iron with a cavity for some form of heating, usually hot coals.

boy bishop. Boy chosen from the cathedral choir or congregation, according to an ancient custom, to be Bishop on St. Nicholas' Day, December 6th. The boy possessed episcopal honour for three weeks, and the rest of the choir were his prebendaries.

boyler. 1. cooking vessel of iron, tin or copper, an early form of saucepan.
2. large kind of kettle.

bracer. *See* **wardbrace.**

bragget/braket. Compound drink made with honey, spices etc. Commonly drunk by country folk at their feasts or wakes.

brake. 1. implement for crushing hemp.
2. large heavy harrow for breaking clods in rough ground.
3. hook or sickle used for uprooting or tearing out grass. 'Break' in the sense of 'tear' is a recorded local dialect usage.

brande yron/brandiron. Gridiron *q.v.*; used also of **andirons** *q.v.*, a stand for a kettle or trivet.

brandreth. Metal gridiron or trivet for supporting cooking vessels directly over the embers of the open fire; also wood frame, e.g. for supporting barrels.

branduts. Four wooden arms fixed to the throat of a spindle in an oatmeal mill.

brank. 1. an instrument formerly used for punishing scolds, consisting of a framework of iron that fitted over the head like a knight's helmet. The mouthpiece was made so that an iron tongue was inserted into the mouth and the rest of the instrument clamped the jaw shut.
2. kind of halter or bridle, used by country people on the borders of England.

brant. Steep hill.

brassarts. Armour pieces between the elbow and the top of the shoulder, fastened together by straps around the arms.

brasses. The sockets in which the axles of a bell work.

brass pieces. Counters for the **shovelboard** *q.v.*

brauchin. Collar for a horse, made of old stockings stuffed with straw.

brazen. Made of brass. This alloy was stronger than **latten** *q.v.*, which it replaced in the fifteenth century for cooking utensils. Brass pots and pans could be repaired, whereas iron ones could not.

brazen dish. The standard dish or measure by which the wooden dishes used for measuring the lead in Derbyshire were gauged.

bread corn. Grain for making bread.

bread grate. Wooden slatted crate suspended from the ceiling for bread storage.

break. Land that has long lain fallow, or in sheep walks, the first year after it has been ploughed or broken up.

breakditch. Term originally applied to a cow that will not stay in her appropriate pasture; and generally, anyone in the habit of rambling.

breast plate. 1. metal plate or piece of armour for protecting the chest, still part of the full dress uniform of the Horse Guards. 2. coffin plate. 3. square of embroidered linen worn by a Jewish high priest. 4. leather or canvas strap running across a horse's breast as part of the harness.

breastwork. Low defensive earthwork or masonry.

brecks/breaks/breeches. Temporary enclosures which in fact often became permanent ones, especially from forest land.

brewhouse. Room for brewing, and containing brewing equipment.

brian. In Northumberland, to keep fire at the mouth of an oven, either to give light or preserve the heat. Elsewhere this fire is called **spruzzing**.

bride ale. Function organised in the parish by church wardens, to raise money to help a newly married couple to set up home.

bride wain. Carriage loaded with household furniture and utensils, which travelled from the home of the bride's father to the bridegroom's house. The event caused much celebration. The **wains** *q.v.* were drawn by oxen, whose horns and heads were decorated with ribbons.

bridewell. Early form of 'county gaol' or 'house of correction'.

brief. Letter from civil or ecclesiastical authorities, commending a charitable appeal.

brigg/brigge. Wooden frame placed over a tub to support the 'tems' or strainer used in brewing, and the **sile** *q.v.* in dairy work.

briscote. Brisket (of beef).

brite/britt. Of hops: to become overripe and fall out or shatter.

broach/broche/brooch. 1. narrow tapering iron rod or pin, especially the rod on a spit. 2. church spire.

3. wooden spindle, from which a **cop** *q.v.* of yarn is wound upon a **clew** *q.v.*

broadcloth. 1. weave of two yards width.

2. fine, densely woven woollen cloth used in the making of men's clothes and much valued because of its hard-wearing qualities. By 1660 it was well established as a West of England speciality.

broad oxgang. Yardland.

broad peeces (broad gold). 'Broadpieces'; hammer-struck gold coins, especially Jacobean and Caroline sovereigns, superseded after 1663 by the guinea. They were still legal tender until 1733.

brockfield. Field which was ploughed in the spring, having been left fallow all the previous year.

brod. Round-headed nail made by blacksmiths.

brode. Broad (as opposed to narrow).

brode chamber. Broad chamber; probably the chief living and dining room of the house.

broiling iron. Support for a cooking pot, like a gridiron.

bromhook/broom hook. Tool for clearing undergrowth, particularly brooms.

broome. Brome grass (*bromus*); a variety of grass with a strong resemblance to oats.

Brownists. Alternative name for the Separatists, the earliest sect of Puritan dissenters. Named after Robert Browne who established a group in Norwich c. 1580. It rejected Episcopacy and Presbyterianism and any form of state association with religion. Browne himself eventually accepted Church of England ordination in 1591 and was a rector in Northamptonshire until his death.

bruinge cowle. Brewing cooler; possibly a tub, with two ears on the upper edge, in which beer was left to ferment before being tunned.

brushing hook. Sickle-shaped hook on a long handle, for cutting tall hedges.

brushing the road. Repairing the road by filling up the worst holes with brundles of brushwood.

brusse. 1. possibly an iron-toothed wool card, or

2. crushing hammer, a 'bruiser'.

Brydgytt satten. Probably 'Bruges satin', sometimes corrupted to 'Satin of Bridges'.

buck. 1. term used by Derbyshire miners for beating or reducing ore to a small sand. 2. washing tub in which to steep clothes in **lye** *q.v. See also* **bucking baskett.** 3. to wash linen in **lye** *q.v.*

bucken pott. Wash-tub or possibly container for **lye** *q.v.*

bucker. Broad-headed hammer with which lead-ore is broken, consisting of a flat piece of iron about the size of a man's open hand; at the back of it is a broad ring, through which is thrust a piece of wood for a handle.

buckey cheese. Sweet cheese made in Hampshire. Possibly from its rank, goatish taste.

bucking baskett. Washing-basket.

bucking stand. Table on which linen was either beaten or washed.

buckram. Linen cloth stiffened with gum or paste.

buckswanging. Punishment used by grinders and other workmen for idleness or drunkenness. The offender was jostled against a thorn hedge or a wall; this required four men, two to hold the offender's arms and two his legs. Grinders generally **buckswang** a man against the wall of the grinding wheel.

buddle. Vessel made like a shallow tumbrel, where the sand and earth is washed from the tin ore by water running over it.

budget/budgett. Haversack worn by a rider on horseback or alternatively a bucket or similar utensil.

budget kettle. Small portable flask or billy-can.

buffet stool. Stool to be used with a table.

bugle cuffs. Cuffs adorned with tube-shaped beads, usually black, made of glass and resembling bugles.

buhrsilver. Medieval tax on whole village for upkeep of manorial hall or 'bury'.

buk iron. Buck iron; a grooved iron used for making horseshoes.

bull. 1. seal affixed to a Papal edict; by extension the edict itself. Papal **bulls** have statutory authority within the Roman Catholic Church. 2. village **bull** used to inseminate all the cows; it was exchanged every year with a neighbouring village to avoid inbreeding. 3. **buyll** *q.v.*

bullimong. Usually oats, peas and vetches sown together.

bull seg(e). Bull castrated when full grown.

bull week. The week before Christmas, in which it was customary in Sheffield to work night and day.

bunnel. Dried hemp-stalk, used by smokers to light their pipes.

bunny. Brick arch or wooden bridge, covered with earth, across a 'drawn' or 'carriage' in a water meadow, just wide enough to allow a hay-waggon to pass over.

burbot. *See* **bird-bolt**.

burial in woollen. Burial of a corpse covered in a woollen shroud or in a coffin lined with woollen fabric. The Acts of 18 & 19 Car. II, c.4 (1666); 30 Car. II, c.3 (1678) and 32 Car. II, c.3 (1680) stated that 'no corpse of any person (except those who shall die of the plague), shall be buried in any shirt, shift, sheet or shroud or anything whatsoever made or mingled with flax, hemp, silk, hair, other than what is made of sheep's wool only, or be put into any coffin lined or faced with any other material but sheep's wool only'. The Act provided that within eight days of the funeral, an Affidavit must be drawn up stating that the law had been complied with. Penalties were ordered of £5 on the estate of every person not buried in woollen. *See also* **information**.

buried, partly. Expression meaning that the heart of the deceased was buried separately from the rest of the body, usually to conform with a will or dying wish.

burleyman. Officer appointed to the manor court for various local duties; also **constable** *q.v.*, or **tithingman** *q.v.*

burling. 1. process of picking knots, loose threads etc. off finished cloth.

2. as **burling iron**, pinchers to remove knots.

burlyng. *See* **borlyng**.

burning on the hill. Curious method of punishing a thief, formerly practised by miners on the Mendip Hills. The culprit was shut up in a butt, around which a fire was lit, whence he made his escape in the best way he could. He was often severely injured; he was not allowed to work on the hills again.

burn stick. Crooked stick on which a large piece of coal was carried daily from the pit by each working collier over his shoulder, for his own private use.

bush. Bunch of broom, **besom** *q.v.*, used to stir up fermenting liquor in mashing, and hung up to be kept from one brew to the next. Because it was impregnated with yeast, it would start the fermentation process more quickly. Hung out to dry, it was for centuries the **bush** of an alehouse.

bushel. Measure of capacity; the standard **bushel** contains four **pecks** *q.v.* or eight **gallons** *q.v.*, but regional variations occur. In North Lincolnshire the **bushel** represents one-fourth of a quarter of corn, and not one-eighth as elsewhere. Also used to describe the vessel used as a **bushel** measure. The Shropshire **bushel** of wheat or barley was sometimes expressed as 9½-10 gallons.

bustain. Fabric, a coarse type of **fustian** *q.v.*

but and ben. Small two-roomed dwelling. The **but** was the kitchen or outer room; the **ben** was the parlour or inner room.

butt. 1. the thickest and best quality part of a hide or skin.
2. cask or pipe; a wine measure usually containing 126 gallons.

butteris. Farrier's tool for paring a horse's hoofs.

buttery. 1. room where ale was brewed and kept.
2. storeroom for provisions and tableware; a cool room as opposed to the kitchen with its cooking implements.

buttmaund/butter maund. A hand-basket fitted with two lids and used to convey butter and eggs.

butts. 1. lands in a common field abutting more or less at right angles upon another **selion** *q.v.*, or lands which because of the irregular shape of the field fall short of the full length.
2. mound with targets where shooting was practised.

3. Practising at the *butts*. The illustration shows archery practice at a range. The man standing in front appears to be instructing five others and a bull's eye has already been scored.

butty. 1. chum or pal.

2. one who contracts the right of working a certain section of a mine.

butty-gang. Men who, as co-partners, work a section of a mine.

buyll/bull. Bar or beam of a harrow.

byeblow. Bastard.

bylawman. Variant of **burleyman** *q.v.*

byre. Building in which cattle are kept tied.

Parish chests can still be found in many churches. Originally, they would contain vestments, parish plate, alms and registers of baptisms, etc. They usually had three keys: one held by the incumbent and one each by the two churchwardens.

C

caddice/caddeaux/cadour. Shortened form of **caddice ribbon**; a worsted tape or binding used for garters etc.

caddows. Bedding or blankets.

cage. Cupboard with an open front.

cakerd. Bound with iron, as are clog shoes.

calamanco. Glossy woollen material originally from Flanders, twilled and chequered in the warp, so that the checks are seen on one side only. Much used in the eighteenth century for waistcoats and breeches.

calbot. Cobirons *q.v.*

calendar. Catalogue of documents, with summaries of their contents.

calico. Plain, often white, unprinted cotton, coarser than muslin. Originally imported, but by 1600 also made in England. By 1680 it was also printed and glazed.

caliver. Light sort of musket.

calldron. Cauldron.

caltrop. Instrument with four spikes so contrived that one of the spikes always stands upwards, no matter in what direction it is thrown.

cambrell. *See* **gambrell.**

cambric. Kind of fine white linen originally manufactured at Cambrai in France, although the term was also applied to a hard-spun cotton yarn imitation.

cameril stick. Curved piece of wood, with several notches in it at each end, used to put through the hamstrings of animals when dressed, and by which the carcase was suspended.

camlet/camblet/chamlet. Originally a costly oriental fabric. Later a fabric made of various combinations of wool, silk, hair, cotton or linen. From the sixteenth and seventeenth centuries onwards the hair of the Angora goat was used in its manufacture, the product being known as mohair.

camperknows. Ale pottage, made with sugar, spices etc.

campers/camping. Football game. Sixteenth century farmers believed such activities on their fields improved the quality of the grass.

campipars. To pay the rent of land in the form of a proportion of the crop.

candle. When there was a dead body in the house it was believed that a candle should always be burnt in the room to keep away evil spirits. Wax candles were considered much more efficacious for this purpose than those made of tallow. If this candle fell out of the stick it was said to be an indication of another death within 12 months.

candlebranch. Socket for the provision of a candle.

candle, sale by the. Method of limiting the time of an auction sale by lighting a candle when the bidding commenced. At the expiration of the flame, the last bidder was the successful buyer.

candlestick/canstck/canstycke. Stick for holding candle, originally with 'stock' or 'pricket' rather than socket. Inventories may have both 'nailed' and 'pillar' candlesticks recorded.

candlewoake/candle-wick. Cheap fabric, probably with a tufted texture.

cann/can. Vessel for holding liquids, not necessarily of metal.

canon. 1. law of the church. All clerics were subject to canon law.
2. cleric in a group observing a definite rule of life, for example an Augustinian Canon.
3. cleric possessing a prebend for his support in a cathedral or collegiate church.

cantaloon. Woollen fabric manufactured in the West of England. A wide range of quality.

cantell/cantle. Fragments or remnants of anything, especially the **holy loaf** *q.v.*

canvas. 1. coarse, unbleached cloth made of hemp or flax. Often used for sheets and window curtains.
2. unbleached cloth woven on regular meshes for tapestry work, called 'cushion canvas'.
3. cloth made in imitation of nankeen, a natural yellow cotton from Nanking.

cap/cop. Cover for a waggon.

capital messuage/mansion. Manor house.

caplin. Leather hinge on a flail.

cap money. Fine levied on a township and paid by the constable for breach of the 1571 Act concerning the wearing of woollen caps on Sundays and Holy Days.

capo. Working horse in Cheshire.

capon. Castrated cockerel intended for eating.

caponcall/caponcoop. Wicker cage in which fowl were confined for fattening or transport.

capp paper. Form of wrapping paper, sold and used to wrap other goods.

caps. Hood-sheaves of **rick-staddles**. *See* **rickstavel**.

cap staff. Capstan or crane.

caqueteuse. Conversion chair with arms and low seat; from the French *caqueter* (to chatter), late sixteenth-century.

car. Low unenclosed land, subject to flooding.

caracute. *See* **carucute**.

carbine. Gun, shorter than a musket, used especially by cavalry-men.

card. Tool for combing wool or flax before spinning.

carlings. Grey peas steeped in water, fried and eaten on the fifth Sunday in Lent, which, in the north of England, is called Carl Sunday.

carpet/carpet-cloth. Cloth invariably used as a covering for tables etc., and not on the floor; also known as a **board cloth** *q.v.*

carr. Common, especially marshy common.

carre. Hollow place which is moist and boggy. Also a wood of alder or other trees in such a place.

carriage. Water-course; a meadow drain. In South Wiltshire carriages bring water into and through the meadow; the **drawn** *q.v.* takes it back to the river.

carrow seeds. Probably caraway seeds; the seeds of *Carum Carni*, used as a carminative and for flavour.

cart. Two-wheeled farm vehicle as opposed to a **wain** *q.v.* which had four wheels.

cart, parish. A device consisting of a farm cart to which paupers were harnessed in the early nineteenth century.

cart strokes. Section of rim of wheel.

cartulary. Collection of charters relating to a particular estate.

carucute/caracute. Measure of land, as much as could be ploughed by one plough and eight oxen in a year, the amount varying with soil, etc; a **ploughland** *q.v.* Generally taken to be about 120 acres. A basic fiscal unit in the Midlands, comparable to the **hide** *q.v.* in other parts of the country.

caslin. Inferior type of calf skin.

cast back. Iron fire-back.

caster/castor. 1. best quality beaver fur. 2. small utensil with a perforated top, used to contain pepper and drugs.

caster hat. Hat made of beaver fur (in the sixteenth century); later used for one of rabbit skin.

castor. Small wheel.

catchpole acre. An acre or strip on a parish boundary, the tithe of which belonged to the first incumbent who arrived at the spot to collect it.

Catherine, Saint. Virgin of royal descent, in Alexandria, who publicly confessed the Christian faith at a sacrificial feast appointed by the Emperor Maximinus; for this confession she was put to death by torture, by means of a wheel like that of a chaff-cutter, hence Catherine Wheel. 25th November is her Saint's Day.

catmallison. Cupboard round or near a chimney where dried beef and provisions were kept.

catshid. 'Cut shide', a sawn plank. *See* **sheyd**.

cattlegate. The right to graze a single beast on land in which one has no legal interest.

caudle cup. Posset *q.v.* cup; used for drinks of hot milk curdled with wine or ale.

cauldron/cawderon/cawdern. Large container for hot liquids, suspended over a fire.

causey. Causeway, path or pavement.

cawdern. *See* **cauldron**.

cawfoy/cawsey/cawsoy. Coarse woollen cloth which probably took its name from the village of Kersey in Suffolk where a wool-trade was once conducted. *See also* **kersey**.

cazzons. Dung of cattle dried and used for fuel.

cellot. Small metal cooking pot with a handle and three short feet which enabled it to stand in a fire. Also known as a **skellet/skillet** *q.v. See also* **posnet**.

census returns. These were taken on the following dates:
1841 — Sunday 6th June
1851 — Sunday 30th March
1861 — Sunday 7th April
1871 — Sunday 2nd April
1881 — Sunday 3rd April
1891 — Sunday 5th April
1901 — Sunday 31st March

cepe/kip. 1. the hide of a young beast, from which was derived a supple leather suitable for making goods such as boot and shoe uppers.
2. usually as **kip**, bundle of hides of young beasts, usually a specific number, but the number varied from place to place.

cerecloth. 1. cloth smeared or impregnated with wax or some other substance, used as a plaster.
2. cloth in which dead bodies were wrapped.

certificate. 1. **of good conduct**: In the middle of the eighteenth century a certificate of good conduct from the minister was needed by a parishioner desiring to perform any one of a wide variety of actions, from leaving his employment in husbandry for labour in another parish, to opening an alehouse, or even a slaughterhouse.
2. **of settlement**: Written admission by a parish that a certain pauper or potential pauper was legally settled in it, and undertaking to receive him back, or otherwise to indemnify any other parish to which he fell chargeable. The Settlement Act 8 & 9 William III, c.30 (1697) debarred strangers from entering a parish unless they had a Settlement Certificate to prove they would be taken back by their home parish if they became in need of poor relief. Where these certificates exist, they are held in archives offices.

cess. Rate, tax or assessment.

cettle. Kettle.

chadfarthing. Farthing paid as part of the Easter dues to hallow the font for christenings.

chafer. Small dish with a lid used for containing hot ashes or charcoal for heating food.

chaff bed. Mattress filled with chaff.

chafing dish. Dish containing food to be placed on a **chafer** *q.v.*

chair, back board. *See* **back board chair**.

chairman. The head of the family. Furniture to sit upon was of the rudest sort in most dwellings. Even by 1603 nearly everyone sat on stools. The single chair was the prerogative of the head of the family — though there may have been a second chair for the chief guest. The phrase 'to take the chair' derives from the same prerogative.

chaise mayrez. Cart for transporting of fresh fish (French, *chassemaree*).

chaldron. Measure of volume of coal equal to 25½ cwt, 36 **bushels** *q.v.*

chamber. 1. any room excluding the hall or the kitchen; principally a bed chamber; less often a parlour.
2. financial office of the royal household; the system of managing royal finances from the chamber rather than the Exchequer.

chamlet. *See* **camlet.**

champaigne/champion. Land divided into strips under the open field system, as opposed to land held in **severalty** *q.v.*

Chancery, Court of. Court of the Lord Chancellor (now the Chancery Division of the High Court of Justice), the chief executive and secretarial office of the crown, housed at Westminster. Chancery records date from 1199.

changerwife. Itinerant female *huckster.*

chantry. Endowed chapel where masses for the dead were sung.

chaplain. Priest of a chapel. An unbeneficed priest existing on a stipend at the pleasure of his employer.

chapter. 1. governing body of a cathedral or secular collegiate church, consisting of a dean, archdeacon, precentor, chancellor, treasurer and canons.
2. periodic assembly of a religious community, originally so called from the custom of reading a chapter from the Rule of the Order (e.g. of St Benedict) in such an assembly.

char. 1. to reduce to charcoal; to burn to a cinder.
2. job; work done by the day; to do small jobs, as a charwoman who does cleaning by the day.
3. long cumbersome vehicle pulled by five horses. The top was often made of painted canvas over hoops.

charcoal, load of. Equivalent to 30 sacks of three bushels.

charger. Large flat dish for serving meat, the largest in a **garness/ garnish** *q.v.* of pewter.

charking brick. Curved brick used for lining walls.

chattels. Moveable goods or belongings including animals; any kind of property except a freehold and things appertaining to it. A more extensive term than 'goods' or 'effects'. In early wills it is sometimes written 'cattel', causing some doubt as to its true meaning. Both 'cattel' (beast) and 'chattels' come from the Old English and Old French words meaning 'property', and the Latin *cattalum* served both meanings.

chattle lease. Leasehold farm or holding.

chayne rod. Curtain rod.

cheeks. The sides of a grate.

cheese board. Table for cutting up cheese.

cheese cowl/chesecoule/chess cowl. Tub or pail in which the milk and rennet were mixed in the early stages of cheese making.

cheese grene (green). New cheese is not called green because of its colour, but because it is unripe when the whey is only half pressed out.

cheese heck/heckle. Rack on which cheeses were both stored and dried.

cheese ladder. Support for a milk-sieve over a pot of cream.

cheeselle. Chisel.

cheese paise. Weight for cheese.

cheese press. Press used for compressing cheese-curd to expel moisture and whey.

cheese rake. Chesewreck etc., rack for storing cheese.

cheesetack. Clasp or metal band.

cheminage. Toll charged on roads in royal forests during the month when hinds were dropping their calves.

cheney/cheyney. Kind of woollen or worsted material.

cherchesed. Offering of wheat to parish church at Martinmas.

chest, Flanders. Originally a carved oak chest, usually of Rhinish origin, imported to England through Flanders.

chest, sugar. Chest used for storing sugar, which was a luxury.

chestub/chesvat/cheswit. 1. cheese tub or vat.
2. wooden mould in which cheese-curd was placed prior to being placed in a **cheese press** *q.v.*

4. Churning butter. In Tudor times dairy farming was best suited to domestic producers. Although much milk had to be converted into butter or cheese before it could be sold, the necessary butter churns, *cheese presses*, etc. were inexpensive.

chevage. Annual payment to lord of the manor by each non-free tenant.

chevill halter. Horse halter.

cheyeer mill/shear-mill. Small apparatus for producing either plough-shares or shears.

chiching. Kitchen.

chief lord. Lord of **fee** *q.v.* under whom inferior lords hold lands.

Childermas Day. Innocent's day — 28 December.

chimney. Chimney had the meaning of 'hearth', not 'flue'. 'Iron chimney' was therefore either a fire back, or more probably a flat iron base for the hearth.

chimney board. Board used to shut off a fireplace during the summer months.

chimney glass. Mirror hung on a chimney-breast.

chine. Backbone and immediately adjoining flesh of a bacon pig which is left when the sides are cut off for bacon curing.

chinks. Loose coins.

chiping/chopping. Knife; alternative name for **randing knife** *q.v.*

chirchelofe. Bread given to the poor in church at Christmas.

chirograph. Legal document written more than once on the same sheet of parchment, as an indenture, then torn in half with irregular edges. These should tally to prove the authenticity of the copies.

chit. The third swarm of bees from a hive. *See also* **smart**.

chogs. Refuse cuttings of hop plants when dressed in spring before being polled.

chopin block. 'Chopping block'; a piece of tree trunk on which wood was cut prior to finer shaping with an axe.

chopine. High patten or wooden shoe, iron shod, worn by women.

chore. Narrow passage between two houses.

chorn. Churn.

chosen sentences. The sentences, generally the Lord's Prayer etc., set up in church 'in convenient places' in accordance with Canon 82.

chrism. Mixture of oil and balsam consecrated by the bishop on Maundy Thursday and used throughout the succeeding year in baptism, confirmation and extreme unction. The mixture was kept in a **chrismatory** *q.v.*

chrismatory. Silver or silver-gilt box used for holy oil.

chrism cloth. Silk cloth used for covering the **chrismatory** *q.v.* in transit from its aumbry to the font. Not to be confused with the **chrisom cloth** *q.v.*

chrisom cloth. White linen cloth placed on a child at the time of baptism. The child continued to wear it until its mother was 'churched', at which time the cloth was presented to the church for use in ablutions. If the child died before its mother's churching, the cloth became its shroud. Such a child would be entered in the burial registers as a **Chrisom Child**, **Chrisomer**, or **Innocent**.

church ales. Medieval-Stuart prototype of the present day parish tea meeting, garden fête or church bazaar.

church commissioners. Body of commissioners established in 1948 by the amalgamation of Queen Anne's Bounty (1703) and the Ecclesiastical Commissioners (1836).

church hacke. Shovel, or a pick axe.

church hay. Churchyard.

church headlands. Lands in the open fields, the crop of which was sold for the benefit of the church, by consent of the whole parish.

church house. Medieval prototype of the parish hall.

church reeve. Churchwarden.

church scot. In Anglo-Saxon England, payment of grain and hens to support parish priests, levied on all free men according to their holdings; originally known as 'food rent'. It continued after the development of the **tithe** *q.v.*, but gradually declined to a modest payment of eggs and hens.

churchwarden. Annually elected representative of parishioners.

churchwardens (tied). Wardens compelled to serve the office by virtue of their occupation of certain houses or land whose turn on the rota had come round.

churchyard rails. Churchyard fence, often repaired by the parishioners in respect of their ownership of a particular house or farm.

cider press. Properly a press which squeezed out the juice of apples previously crushed in a cider-mill. The terms press and mill were used virtually synonymously. Also known as an **apple mill**.

cine. Variant of **kine** *q.v.*

cistern/sewstern. *See* **lead**.

citch. Lump.

civil parish. *See* **parish, civil**.

clags. Dirty clots which adhere to the wool of sheep.

clams. 1. nippers that shoemakers and saddlers put between their knees.
2. iron braces for binding together stone work.

Clarendon, Constitutions of. Laws made by a general council of nobles and prelates, held at Clarendon in Wiltshire, in 1164, to check the power of the Church, and restrain the prerogatives of ecclesiastics. These famous ordinances, 16 in number, define the limits of the patronage and jurisdiction of the Pope in these realms.

clavy. Beam of wood which served as a lintel over a fireplace; forerunner of the modern mantlepiece.

clay lane. Unstoned parish road which had a strong clay surface. If this kind of road had grass on the side it was called a green-lane.

clerical titles. Clerk — a scholar or clergyman.
Curate *q.v.* — one who has the cure of souls.
Rector *q.v.* — one who has the parsonage and great **tithes**.
Vicar *q.v.* — one who does the 'duty' of a parish for the person who receives the tithes.
Incumbent *q.v.* and **Perpetual Curate** *q.v.* are now termed Vicar.

clevis. U-shaped piece of iron used with tackle for lifting.

clew. 1. ball of thread or cord.
2. ball of thread used as a guide through a maze.
3. lower corner of a sail.

clift. Probably 'cleft' or cut timber. Also wedges.

clincquant. Brass thinly wrought out into ornamental leaves.

clippet. Small brass or iron cap for the toe of a shoe.

clipping the church. An old Warwickshire custom on Easter Monday. The charity children, joined hand-in-hand, formed a circle round each church.

clock. Possibly a timepiece, but more likely a clockwork mechanism for operating a **jack** *q.v.*

clock lines. Cords carrying weights in a pendulum clock.

clod/clot. Clod of earth or patch of cultivated ground; probably meaning the valuation of the work that has been put into cultivated ground. *See also* **arders**, **tile land**.

clod salt. Cake of salt which sticks to the bottom of pan.

close. Hedged, fenced or walled piece of land, now usually, but incorrectly, called a **field** *q.v.*

close bouke. Bucket or pan for placing under a **close stool** *q.v.*

close parish. Parish which took stringent precautions against the gaining of settlements by strangers.

close rolls. Mandates, letters and writs of a private nature, addressed in the Sovereign's name, to individuals and folded or closed and sealed on the outside with the **great seal** *q.v.*

close stool. Commode, with a pan.

clot. *See* **clod.**

clothes hussey. Box for containing clothes.

clothing boots. Cloth or button boots that reached to the calf of the leg.

clouted/clowted. Nailed or patched.

cloves. Dried flower buds of *Caryophyllus aromaticus*. Used as a pungent spice and to make oil. The spice came from the Molluccas which was still a Dutch monopoly in 1700.

clowt leather. Leather for patching.

club men. Irregular force of armed men who rose in the West of England in 1645 about the time of the battle of Naseby.

clume buzza. Earthen pan from Cornwall.

clunch. Chalk, usually soft chalk for making floors.

clustered column. Group of slender shafts joined to form a single column.

co-aration. Communal cultivation of open fields.

cob. Wicker basket to carry on the arm. A seed-cob or seed lep is such a basket for sowing. Still used in Gloucester and Wiltshire in 1902.

cobble. Small flat-bottomed fishing boat. *See* **inwiver/inwaver.**

cobirons. Pair of long iron supports with hooks at frequent intervals for roasting-spit, simpler than **andirons** *q.v.* Usually two iron bars with knobs at one end which rested on the back of the grate. Sometimes a kind of cradle for firewood. *See also* **dogs.**

cock. Small conical heap.

cockers. 1. kind of rustic high shoes, or half-boots, fastened with laces or buttons.
2. old stockings without feet.
3. rims of iron round wooden shoes (also called **cokers** in Cumberland).

cockhead. That part of a mill which is fixed into a stave of the ladder on which the hopper rests.

cocking fork. Large hay-fork, used for carrying hay from the **cock** *q.v.* into the summer **rick** *q.v.*

cockle hat. Pilgrim's hat. As the chief places of devotion were overseas, or on the coast, pilgrims used to put cockle-shells on their hats to indicate that they were pilgrims. The polished side of the shell was scratched with a drawing of the Blessed Virgin, the Crucifixion, and being blessed by the priest, they were considered amulets against spiritual foes, and the cockle shells might be used as drinking vessels.

cockloft. Space between the uppermost ceiling of a house and the roof; sometimes used loosely to mean an attic or garrett.

cockstang. Hand barrow for carrying hay, etc. It was carried by two men, like a sedan chair.

codding. Gathering of peas, beans, vetches.

cod glove. Thick glove, without fingers, used on Exmoor to handle turf.

coe. Small shed, usually of stone, above or near a mine, in which the miners kept their tools, and sometimes a change of clothing. The climbing shaft was often under a trap door in the floor of the **coe.** Those who pilfered or stole from **coes** were termed 'cavers'.

coffer/cofare/coffare. Wooden box or chest used for storing clothes and other valuables. The most specific meaning was 'money box'.

cog. One of the short handles on the pole of a scythe.

cog(e). Small fishing boat.

cogbell. Icicle — ice candle.

coggers. 1. half boots made of stiff leather, strong cloth or even of worsted, buttoned at the side, and strapped under the shoe. 2. pair of old stocking legs worn over the shoes to keep out the snow.

cogler. Hook, with cogged rack-work for lifting or lowering, by which pots and kettles were formerly hung over open fireplaces. Later superseded by **hanglesses** *q.v.*

cognate. Allied by blood or birth; from the same origin, formation, a relation on the mother's side. *See also* **agnatic.**

coif. Close-fitting cap.

coker. *See* **cocker.**

collar-lander. *See* **hogger.**

collation. Nomination of a clerk to a benefice by the bishop either as patron or because of the failure of the real patron to present within six months. Strictly speaking the benefice is collated to the man, not the man to the benefice.

collectioner. Relieved pauper.

collector of the poor. The prototype under the 1572 Act 14 Elizabeth I, c.5 of the officer later known as the **overseer of the poor** *q.v.* The term is also used in later years as a kind of assistant overseer.

collraker. Coal rake; an implement like a hoe used for raking together coals, ashes etc.

colls/coles. Coals are probably in every case charcoal; mineral 'sea-coal' was not satisfactory for cooking on an open hearth. The inventories regularly show wood and coals together. Leases which mention tenants' duties to supply coals to their landlords in rural areas usually show that charcoal and not mineral coal was intended.

coloured. Sometimes it meant 'as opposed to white', but more often it meant patterned or of more than one colour.

combe. Corn measure of four bushels or one sack. The weight of a comb or sack varied according to variety of corn: oats 12 stones; barley 16 stones; wheat 18 stones; beans, peas, tares 19 stones.

comb-rippling. Comb for flax or hemp, i.e. a wool comb.

comen well. Well which all the village inhabitants could use.

commissioners. Any body of persons given formal authority to act. *See also* **Enclosure Commissioners**.

common appendant. *See* **appendant**.

common appurtenant. *See* **appurtenant**.

common fine. Fine payable to the lord of the manor. In medieval rolls sometimes termed 'cert money' or 'head silver', it originated as a contribution by the tenants towards the lord's cost of maintaining the **court leet** *q.v.*, thus relieving them from attendance at the **Sheriff's Tourn** *q.v.*, with the privilege of having their disputes adjudged locally.

common in gross. Common right detached from both house and land.

common lands. Term usually applied to manorial **waste** *q.v.*, but applicable also to open fields over which common pasture rights existed.

common of shack. Common right of grazing upon land after the crop has been lifted, e.g. **lammas lands** *q.v.*

common of turbary. Common right of cutting turf or other fuel.

Commonwealth. Incipient Christian-radical party of the mid-sixteenth century.

communion token. *See* **token, communion**.

compurgation. Practice by which an accused person could be acquitted if 12 or more persons took an oath testifying to the validity of his statement. Later incoporated into common law as a defence in both criminal and civil cases and widely used in ecclesiastical courts. Retained in certain actions until 1833.

conduct. Hired man, usually applied to a singing man, whether lay or cleric; the term is still in use at Eton College for a chaplain.

consistory court. Court of the bishop, presided over by his chancellor.

constable. 1. the **High Constable**. The official of the hundred to whom petty (i.e. parish) constables were responsible for some of their duties.
2. the **Petty Constable**. Official who had to report and take action on a great many matters such as supervising **watch and ward** *q.v.*; ensuring the upkeep of local means of punishment and imprisonment, such as stocks and cage; inspecting alehouses; apprenticing pauper children; supervising the settlement or removal of itinerant strangers or beggars; the welfare of the poor; collecting county rate; caring for the parish bull; and many more. It was not a position welcomed by the parishioners. There was a widespread practice of paying someone else to do the job. It is thought that the office is more ancient than that of Churchwarden. While the manor courts were strong he was appointed by the **court leet** *q.v.*, but later the vestries made the nominations and the J.P.s confirmed the appointments. The vestries officially received this responsibility in 1842. A **constable** appointed by the leet had authority only in that leet's manor; in the rest of the parish, other constables were responsible.

constablewick. Area of a constable's jurisdiction, generally more or less equivalent to township or tithing.

constant man. Agricultural labourer working regularly for the same employer.

cooche handed. Left-handed.

coofer binch. 'Coofer bench'; a **coffer** *q.v.* which could also be used as a seat.

cookle. Pair of prongs with an aperture through which spit with meat is thrust.

cooler. Oval tub, particularly one used in brewing to cool the **woort/wort** *q.v.*, or in the dairy to receive the warm milk from the pail. *See also* **turnell**.

coop/coupe/cowpe. Cart or waggon with closed sides and ends, for carting dung, lime etc.

coopery/cooperie. Goods like barrels etc., made by a cooper.

cop. 1. a measure of peas; *viz* 15 sheaves in a field, and 16 in a barn.
2. tuft; a conical mass of yarn wound on a spindle.
3. *see* **cap**.

copatain. Conical hat; a type of 18th-century hat in the form of a **sugar-loaf** *q.v.*

cope. Duty paid by miners to the owner of the mineral liberty, by virtue of which they may sell their ore to whoever they wish, and which may be a fixed price per load paid by the miners by agreement with the mine agent.

copper. Large cauldron.

copper clout. Kind of **spatterdash** (*see* **fearnought spatterdashes**) worn on the calf of the leg.

copsole. Wedge for keeping the **coulter** *q.v.* of a plough in its place at the proper angle to the beam.

copson. Fence over a dam laid across a ditch in order to prevent sheep from crossing the dam.

copyholder. Tenant who held his land by copy of court roll, and belonged to a class which derived from the medieval **villeins** *q.v.*

cord. 1. measure of sawn wood 8 feet long by 4 feet in width and thickness. The word is generally used in conjunction with **plock** *q.v.*, so called because the length was originally measured with a cord.
2. webbing underlying a **mat** *q.v.*

coracle. Small wicker boat, light enough to be carried on a man's head, covered with hide, oilskin or canvas. It is worked by one paddle.

corf. Small waggon used in coal pits. *See* **corve**.

cork. In oak bark, the thick spongy dead layer of outer bark which had no value in the tanning industry.

corne barton. Enclosed area of ground where corn was grown or stored.

corn rent. Cash annuity, varying in amount according to the ascertained and vouched price of corn in the area; hence a safeguard against any future fluctation in the value of money.

coronation tape. Carnation-rose coloured tape. It was fashionable for haberdashery.

corrack. Rake used when making charcoal.

correction, house of. Type of county gaol. The term is more correctly applied to the gaols established under Act of Parliament 18 Elizabeth I, c.3 (1575–76).

corrody. Originally the right of free accommodation to be provided by a vassal to his lord when necessary; later the term was applied to the boarding provision made by monasteries to their living benefactors.

corselet. Alternative word for 'body armour'.

corve(s)/corf/corfe. 1. originally a basket made from coppiced hazel, used in mines to haul both miners and coal up the shaft. 2. crude wooden sledge used to convey ore underground, sometimes along wooden rails. 3. later, a waggon.

costrall/costrell/costril. Small keg, barrel or wooden bottle for carrying drinks to the fields. Often had projections on either side with holes through which a cord or strap was passed. They were then hung around the necks of their carriers.

cottager. Occupier, sometimes also owner, of a tenement which often had a croft, a common right and a little land, usually not more than eight or ten acres.

cotteril. Iron wedge put through a bell to secure it.

cottoning. Pieces of napping cotton first imported from India, which (unlike modern cottons) had a long fleecy nap.

cottrel. Piece of iron with a hole.

couch chayre/couch-chair. Sofa with an arm or rests at each end; a long wooden settle.

couching floor. Floor on which grain was spread in order to germinate; used especially in malting, or in the preparation of woad for dyeing.

coulter/culter. Part of the plough supporting the **share** *q.v.*

counter/cownter. Table or desk used for counting.

counterford/countersat. Counterfeit; an item made of a base metal but looking like a precious one.

counter point. Counterpane; quilted cover.

coup. *See* **coop.**

couple. *See* **cuple.**

court baron. Assembly of the freehold tenants of a manor under the presidency of the lord or his steward usually held every three weeks to state customs of the manor, whether relating to land tenure or land use, and to enforce payment of all dues and performance of all services owed by the tenants to the lord. The court appointed some local officials, such as the **reeve** *q.v.*, **bailiff** *q.v.* and the **hayward** *q.v.* This was the court to which the free man of the manor owed suit.

courte cubberd. Court cupboard; an early form of sideboard built in two parts, one or both of which might incorporate a cupboard. Linen or plate was usually stored in the cupboard and the flat top used for the display of plate.

courtesy of England, estate by the. Widower's right to hold for life his deceased wife's dower land held in **fee simple** (*see* **fee**) or 'estate tail' (*see* **entail**). He had this right only if he had had by her a child, who was thus the wife's heir or would have been so had it lived.

court leet. Court held usually every six months in lordship, **hundred** *q.v.* or manor before the lord or his steward. It was attended by residents of district, it could not be held unless at least two freehold tenants occupied lands in the manor. It had jurisdiction over petty offences and civil affairs of district, inspected the working of the **frankpledge** *q.v.* and could fine and imprison offenders. It performed a variety of administrative duties such as appointing the **constable** *q.v.*

couttolyne. Covering for a bed.

Coventry blue. Type of blue thread made in Coventry and used for embroidery.

coverlead. Coverlet; cover for a bed. French *couvre-lit*.

cowpe. *See* **coop.**

cows, papers for the. Schedules under an Act 19 George II, c.5 (1745–6) relating to the distemper among horned cattle.

crab mill. Mill for crushing crab apples to make cider.

crab vinegar. Crab-apple vinegar or **verjuice** *q.v.*

crackowes. Long pointed shoes, turned up in a curve. The points were often longer than a finger, cocking upwards, and were said to resemble Devil's claws. The ends were fastened to the knees with chains of gold or silver.

craddle cloth. Swaddling band.

cradle scythe. Scythe with a frame to lay the corn smooth in cutting.

crane/craine. Chimney crane; a rectangular bar of iron moving on a pivot fixed to the back of a fireplace for the purpose of suspending cooking vessels over the fire.

crank cart. Probably a cart in need of repair.

crape. Thin worsted material from which the dress of the clergy was made and used also for woollen shrouds which were compulsory after The Act of Burial in Woollen, 30 Charles II, c.3 (1678).

cratch. 1. rack of any kind; a manger, a cradle.
2. pannier.
3. kind of hand-barrow, a wooden frame used in husbandry.
4. flight of shelves.
5. wooden grating or hurdle.

cravat. Lace, linen or muslin, edged with lace, worn around the neck and tied in a bow. The wearing of cravats became fashionable in France during the seventeenth century in imitation of the linen scarves worn by Croatian mercenaries.

creature. Baptismal name often applied in special circumstances (*Creatura Christi*).

creeper. 1. small iron dog, of which a pair would be placed between the **andirons** *q.v.* in a grate.
2. a small iron frying pan with three legs.

creese/crease. Ridged tile for a roof.

cresset/cressette/cressyt. Iron lamp, or a kitchen utensil for setting over a fire. Could also be an open lamp, suspended on pivots in a kind of fork, and carried on a pole, formerly used in nocturnal processions. The light was a wreathed rope smeared with pitch or rosin stuck on a pin in the centre of the bowl.

crib/cribbe. Barred receptacle for fodder. *See also* **cratch**.

crock/crok/croock. Commonly a small earthenware pan, although in South-West England the word was also applied to metal pots. Today the term survives in 'crockery' or, more particularly, in the Londoners' 'crocks' for cups, plates and saucers.

croft. Piece of enclosed ground for tillage or pasture — usually arable area near house.

crome. Rake with a long handle, used for pulling weeds out of a drain, after they are cut. A 'dung crome' is a hook used to unload dung.

crook lug. Long pole with a hook at the end of it, used for pulling down dead branches of trees.

crooks. Wooden frames used in pairs as trappings of pack-horses. Their size varied according to the size of the load to be carried.

crow. Rotatable form of **trippet** *q.v.*

croze. Coopers tool for cutting the groove or inlet at the ends of a cask, into which the top and bottom of the cask are fitted.

crudcummer/curdscummer. Utensil used for skimming the curd from the top of boiling liquids.

crupper. Part of a horse harness; consisting of a strap of leather fastened to a saddle and passed under the horse's tail.

cubbler. Early form of the colloquial 'cubby-hole'; a small room or closet.

cubeb. Small, aromatic, pungent and peppery berries of a Javanese shrub, *Ar. Kababah.*

cucking-stool. *See* **ducking chair.**

cuckoo gate. Swing gate in a V-shaped enclosure, also called a **kissing-gate** *q.v.*

cues. Shoes made for cattle when taking part in a drove. Made in two parts and affixed by means of nails. In the eighteenth century a smith and his thrower could expect to receive between 10d and a shilling for each beast shod.

cull. Small fish with a large head, found under stones in rivulets; called also a bull-head.

culter. *See* **coulter.**

cumin. Herb with aromatic seed, *cuminum cyminum.*

cumpas. Compost, manure.

cuple/couple. Ewe and a lamb.

curate. Properly not the assistant priest of a parish, but any minister having the cure of souls, especially a deputy in full charge of a parish, but removable at pleasure of his employer.

curfew bell. Bell rung in the reigns of William I and II to give notice to their subjects that they should put out their fires and candles; a requisite precaution in ancient times. Generally rung about eight o'clock; the time of ringing probably varied with the seasons of the year.

curtain. Hanging drapery around a bed; not used for windows until eighteenth century.

curtal. 1. sort of bassoon, a musical instrument.
2. curtal-axe, a short, broad sword; a cutlass.

curtilage. Court or yard or ground attached to a house; also one enclosed within.

cushion/quishan. Form of loose padding used on chests.

custumal. Written collection of customs of manor.

cuts. Carriage used for conveying timber. It consisted of two pairs of wheels with a long pole as a coupling between them so as to place them far apart.

cutwith. Bar of a plough or harrow to which the **traces** *q.v.* are attached.

cypp/kipe/kippe. Bushel *q.v.* basket, broad at the base and narrowing towards the top, with a capacity of 70 pounds.

D

dacian. Vessel used in Derbyshire for holding sour oat cake.

dag. Kind of heavy pistol.

daice board/daisboard. Plank which could be set down to form a temporary trestle seat.

daker. *See* **dicker.**

dale/deal. Softwood; a slice sawn from a log of timber, in Great Britain 9″ wide, not more than 3″ thick, and at least 6′ long. Usually refers to wood of fir or pine.

dallop. 1. patch of ground among growing corn which the plough has missed; a rank tuft of growing corn where heaps of manure have lain. 2. parcel of smuggled tea.

damask. Patterned cloth; a rich silken fabric originally made in Damascus but later applied to figured materials of wool, linen or cotton. In particular, a twilled linen fabric figured in the weaving with designs shown up by opposite reflections of light from the surface and used chiefly for table draperies.

damnified. Damaged.

dane geld. An Anglo-Saxon tax originally imposed to pay for the defence of England against the Danes; it was accounted for as if it had been a settled revenue by the Sheriffs for many years after the Conquest (1066). It was originally a fixed tax on every hide of land.

dasher. Upright board put on the side of a waggon to increase its carrying capacity.

daubing. Mixture of clay or clunch, cow-hair and lime to make walls.

day house. Dairy or room where cheese was made.

day labourer. Labourer selling his work by the day in the open market, i.e. not attached to one employer, or hired yearly.

days lost. The lost days are the 11 days which were omitted when the **New Style Calendar** *q.v.* (i.e. of calculating dates) was introduced in 1752. The day following Wednesday 2nd September of that year was called Thursday 14th.

dead roof. Roof of outhouse or cow shed made of untrimmed brushwood and thatched over.

deads. In a mine, useless stone from a vein or working, usually stacked in abandoned workings, often on timber platforms which became dangerously unstable.

deal. *See* **dale**.

defence, in. Closed to pasture.

demesne. That part of manor not held by tenants, but kept for use and profit of the lord of the manor; later farmed out to one man.

deodand. The personal chattel which had caused a person's violent or accidental death and was deemed to have been given to God as an expiratory offering.

desperate. Of a debt: having little hope of recovery.

desse. 1. rock from which alum is obtained at Whitby.
   2. to lay close together, i.e. to **desse** wool, straw etc.

device to draw leade. Possibly an implement to 'draw' lead into the thin strips for leaded windows.

dew pond. Pond not fed by any spring, but charged or filled by mist, dew and rain. Such ponds rarely fail, even in the longest drought.

dexe. Desk. Its early form was that of a simple lockable box.

deyinge chamber. In the seventeenth century, a room set aside for the delivery of children and for the dying.

diap/diaper/diber. Linen fabric with a diamond patterned weave; by the seventeenth century, often not particularly expensive. Used for napkins, other table linen, and hand towels. The word is a corruption of '*d'Ypres*', the special weave having originated from Ypres.

dibber/dibble. *See* **setting pin**.

dicker/daker. Parcel or lot of ten hides or skins of leather.

dighte. Prepared, dressed, i.e. husks, chaff and rubbish removed.

dimity/dimothy/timothy. Stout cotton cloth, woven with raised stripes and fancy figures. Used undyed for beds and hangings, and sometimes for garments.

dinch pick. Three-pronged fork, used for loading dung.

dintle. *See* **dyntle**.

dish. 1. the smallest size of an ordinary pewter service.
   2. measure for lead ore, either oblong or circular, varying from

liberty to **liberty** *q.v.*, but generally holding between 14 and 15 Winchester pints. A standard dish made in 1512 is kept at the Moot Hall, Wirksworth, Derbyshire.
One dish = about 65 lbs.
Nine dishes = one load.
Approx 3½-4 loads = 1 ton.

dispensation. Licence granted by the Archbishop of Canterbury permitting conduct not contrary to the Holy Scriptures and the law of God, or by diocesan bishops for non-observance of minor regulations, i.e. for non-residence, eating flesh in Lent etc.

disseisin. The act of wrongfully depriving a person of the **seisin** *q.v.* of lands, rents or other hereditaments, such as when a man who did not have the right of entry on certain lands or tenements entered them and ousted the person who had the freehold.

distraint. Seizure of goods or animals for debt or other reason, punishment by seizure; the forcing of a person by seizure to perform an obligation or satisfy a wrong.

distributer. Assistant or deputy **overseer of the poor** *q.v.*

dithe. Lincolnshire term for cow-dung dried and cut into squares for fuel.

docking iron. Tool for docking the tails of horses.

dog. 1. type of clamp.
2. lever used for putting 'bonds' or metal hoops on cartwheels.
3. in plural, bars which supported the end of logs on a wood fire, or on which a spit turned. Originally ornamented with dogs' heads. *See also* **cobirons**.

doghook. Strong hook or wrench used for separating iron boring rods.

dog tongs. *See* **lazy keufs**.

dog wheel. Treadmill wheel revolved by a dog, used especially for working a spit.

dog whipper. Minor official of the church; also known as a **peace keeper**. *See also* **lazy keufs**.

dole. 1. as in **bull dole**, a share of a common meadow, distributed annually or periodically by lot or rotation.
2. charitable donations of any kind.

dolly. *See* **maiden**.

Domesday Book. A comprehensive record of property in England compiled in 1086 on the orders of William the Conqueror (1027–1087).

dommerar. Beggar who pretended to be dumb.

dool. Long, narrow green in a ploughed field, with ploughed land on each side of it; a broad balk, perhaps in a dale or valley, because when standing corn grows on both sides of it, it appears like a valley.

doole. Conical lump of earth about three feet in diameter at the base, and about two feet in height, raised to show the bounds of parishes on farms ᴑn the Sussex Downs.

doom. Judgement or decision made formally by suitors or jury of manor court.

door. Doors and windows were listed in inventories as moveables, and were often taken when people moved house.

dornyx/dornick. Name given to certain fabrics originally manu-factured at Doornick, a Flemish town, and used for hangings, carpets etc.

dorse. Reverse side of a sheet of paper or parchment. Anything written on that side is called an 'endorsement'.

dorsel. Pack saddle, panniers in which fish are carried on horseback.

doss/pess. Hassock, used for kneeling on at church.

double apparel. A term used when at the end of an apprenticeship the master was obliged to provide his apprentice with two sets of clothes, one for Sunday and one for working.

doubler. *See* **dubler.**

doublet. Sort of sleeveless jacket.

double tom. Double-breasted plough.

dough cowl. Tub, generally wooden, used in baking.

dounge/dung. Animal ordure, in contrast to 'soil' relating to human excrement.

dow break. Dough brake; a machine for mixing and kneading dough.

dowlais. Course type of calico which took its name from Daoulas in Brittany.

dowle bed. Featherbed; 'dowle' was the down from feathers.

downecke. Fine down from neck and breast of goose.

dowter. Daughter.

dozen. Measure for minerals, particularly iron ore.

dozener. Burghal official elected by householders in each ward or street to make presentments at the **court leet** *q.v.* in towns. Probably had jurisdiction over 12 houses or families; *see* **tithingman**. In some places the word is used of jurymen, the jury being the 'douzaine'.

dozzle. 1. staff or pole, stuck into the top of a stack, to which the thatch is bound. Often gaudily painted and surmounted with a weather-cock in the form of a fish, bird, fox or man.
2. person oddly dressed.

draff. Brewers grain.

draff ox/stere. Beast used to pull plough or cart.

drage. Mixed cereals.

dram dish. Dish used for serving small portions of spirits or hot drinks. *See also* **caudle cup**.

drape. Sheep or cow culled or drafted from the flock or herd to be fattened for slaughter, especially a cow or ewe whose milk has dried up or has missed being with young.

drashel. Correct term for a 'flail'; a pair of drashells (or dreshols) is more commonly used.

draught. 1. shaft for a cart or waggon.
2. hazel-rod selected for hurdle making. A 'draught' is not a rod, but a bundle of long wood suitable for hurdles or pea sticks, bound with a single withe.

drawer knife/drawing knife. Carpenter's tool for shaving and smoothing wood. It consisted of a blade between two handles set at right angles to the blade and was so called because it was drawn towards the user.

drawing counter. Rent table; it was designed with a sliding top and a well beneath to hold money and papers.

drawn. In a water meadow, the large open main drain which carries the water back to the river, after it has passed through the various **carriages** *q.v.* and trenches.

drawtable. Extending table.

dray. 1. low cart for heavy goods; a timber sledge.
2. as **dray-plough**, a plough made without wheels or feet.

drayblades. Wooden slats beneath a sledge or dray.

draystringe. Rein to haul a **dray** *q.v.*

dream holes. The openings left in the walls of steeples, towers, barns etc. for the admission of light.

dredge. Mixture of grains, mostly oats and barley sown together.

dressing box. Case for toilet accessories and jewellery with a small mirror fitted inside.

dressing stone. Stone table used for 'dressing' meat, removing skin and offal.

dribble. Laborious and diligent servant; a 'true dribble'.

drift. 1. rounding up of animals within a forest on a particular day for determining ownership.
2. the payment of fines etc. held at the beginning of **fence-month** *q.v.* and the beginning of **agistment** *q.v.*

driving (the common). The lord of the manor's privilege of collecting and examining once a year all the beasts on the **common lands** *q.v.* in order to ascertain that only those persons having common right were turning their stock on the **common lands** *q.v.*

drock. 1. short drain under a roadway, often made with a hollow tree.
2. broad flat stone laid as a bridge across a ditch.

drove road. Unenclosed road through a farm leading to different fields.

drowner. Man who attends to the hatches, managing the supply of water, and turning it on and off the meadows at the proper times.

drugget. Coarse, woollen material, or half wool and half silk or linen; also a coarse felted woollen cloth used for floor coverings.

drunkard's cloak. Tub with holes in the sides for the arms to pass through, formerly used in Newcastle for the punishment of scolds and drunkards.

dry. Barren, when applied to farm animals.

dryping pan. Vessel placed beneath meat roasting on spits to catch the fat.

dubbing. 1. kind of paste made of flour and water boiled together, used by cotton weavers to smear the warp. 2. mixture of oil and tallow for making leather impervious to water. 3. suet. 4. mug of beer.

dubbings. Evergreens with which churches and houses were decorated at Christmas.

dubler/doubler. Large sized plate or dish of wood or pewter.

ducape. Plain woven, stout, silk fabric of softer texture than *Gros de Naples*. Its manufacture was introduced into this country by French refugees in 1685.

ducat/duckete. Gold coin of varying value.

ducking chair/stool. Chair or stool at the end of an oscillating plank, in which disorderly women, scolds or dishonest tradesmen were tied, and then ducked or plunged in water as a punishment; also called a **cucking-stool.**

5. *Ducking chair* at a village well. From an old print.

ducking tumbrel. Ducking stool *q.v.* provided with wheels.

duffe house. Dovecot.

dum waiter. Dumb waiter; a serving-trolley on wheels. Early designs resembled cake-stands rather than trolleys and sometimes each shelf had a metal guard around its circumference.

dung put/dung chrib/dunputt. Tub, attached like a pannier to the flank of a pack-horse, in which manure was carried to the fields.

duplicates. 1. **of parish register**, the transcripts furnished annually or triennially to the bishop or archdeacon by the churchwardens.

2. **of land-tax assessment**, the copies furnished each year by the petty constable to the local commissioners and to the clerk of the peace.

dust bed. Bed-tick mattress filled with chaff.

dyall. Alternative spelling of 'dial', as in sundial.

dyntill/dintle. Thin type of leather.

E

eagre. *See* **ager**.

eale. Ale.

earles/arles. Earnest money given to close a bargain or hiring.

earling. Yearling.

earnest. *See* **earles** and **god's penny**.

earwingle. *See* **yarwingle**.

easter. Back of a chimney or chimney-stack.

Easter offering. Customary sum paid to the parish priest, formerly compulsory under both Common and Canon Law. Usually exempted from the redemption of ancient obligations made under Enclosure Acts, but commuted under the Tithe Act 1839.

edder. *See* **ether**.

eddish. Aftergrowth of grass; stubble.

eel scrade. Kind of eel trap.

eelshear. Iron instrument with three or four points, fastened to the end of a long pole, by means of which it was thrust into muddy ponds and ditches to catch eels.

eger. *See* **ager**.

egg and eye. Notch and slot made in opposite walls of a vein in a lead mine to hold a **stemple** *q.v.* or beam.

egress. A going out, or issuing forth from an enclosed or confined space. The right or liberty of going out.

elding. Firewood.

electioner. Person qualified for parochial office but not actually appointed to any.

ell. Measure of length varying between 27 inches (the **Flemish ell**) and 54 inches (the **French ell**). The **English ell**, the original standard for which was the length of King Henry I's arm, was 45 inches, but was increasingly superseded by the Imperial yard measure of 36 inches. A **Shropshire ell** was 48 inches.

elmeing board. Board made from elm.

elson. Shoemaker's awl.

emalyment. Implement.

enclosure. Conversion into **severalty** *q.v.* of open-fields (**champaigne/champion** *q.v.*), common meadow, or common pasture or **waste** *q.v.*

Enclosure Commissioners. 1. were those appointed in the sixteenth century by the Crown to inquire into and/or discourage enclosure.
2. persons named (especially in the eighteenth century) in an Enclosure Act, who were authorized to carry out its provisions.
3. from 1845 Enclosure Commissioners were civil servants entrusted with the duty of administering the 1845 Act (later the Land Division of the Ministry of Agriculture). In 1967 transferred to the Land Commission.

end irons. Two moveable iron plates used to contract the fire place (*see* **andirons**).

enfeoffment. Kind of trust in which land is held by trustees on behalf of its owner, often to escape the effect of **wardship** *q.v.*

engross. To buy up wholesale corn or standing crop, in order to retail it or to hoard it, awaiting higher prices.

engrossing. The accumulation in the hands of one man and his family of agricultural holdings formerly maintaining more than one family.

entail. 1. law restricting inheritance of land to a particular heir or class of heirs.
2. to settle land on persons in succession, none of whom can then dispose of it.

entire. Uncastrated animal.

eorl. Kentish noble in Anglo-Saxon England. The term is peculiar to Kent, and possibly signifies an original nobility by birth rather than by service. The equivalent rank in the rest of England was 'Gesith'.

Epiphany. Church festival held on the 12th day after Christmas (6th January), to commemorate the manifestation of Christ to the Magi, the Wise Men of the East.

equation table. Table for indicating correct time by a clock when the sun is on the meridian.

equity. System of law co-existing with but supplementing or superseding — almost transcending — Common and Statute Law. In England the Chancery administered **equity**, but the Court of Exchequer had also an equitable jurisdiction.

escheat. The legal process, now abolished, whereby tenure of land used to revert to the King in case of freehold property, and to the lord of the manor in copyhold, on the tenant's death without heirs; an estate so lapsing.

escheator. Officer who exercised the powers of **escheat** *q.v.* on behalf of a superior feudal lord.

escorches. Animals that were flayed; an old hunting term.

espringold. Engine used for throwing large stones in sieges.

esquire of the body. Attendant upon a knight, who carried his helmet, spear and shield.

essart. *See* **assart**.

essoin. Lawful excuse; an excuse for failure to attend the king's court when summoned.

essoined. Of an absence from manor court: excused, as being represented by another, or fined for default in attendance. Strictly speaking the **essoin** *q.v.* is the excuse itself and the tenant is the essoiner.

estovers. The Norman French equivalent of the Old English term **bote** *q.v.*

estray. Domestic animal or swan which has strayed on to another person's property, the owner being unknown, and so has become the temporary property of the lord of the manor. By law, waifs and **estrays** had to be publicly proclaimed in the nearest markets and in the parish church. If not claimed by the owner within a year and a day, they were valued and fell to the lord.

estricke. Implement used to strike off all grain above the rim of a measure.

ether/edder. Top band of a fence, the wands of hazel etc., woven in along the top of a 'dead hedge' or wattled fence to keep it compact.

every year lands. Extensive common fields in the neighbourhood of Gloucester, cropped year after year for a century or more, without one intervening **fallow** *q.v.* year.

ewer. Pitcher with a wide spout, particularly for carrying water.

examination. Sworn statement made before one or more magistrates, generally upon the demand of the parish officers, as to settlement (*see* **certificate of settlement**), with a view to removal from the parish.

Exchequer, Court of. Court existing from Henry II's time, originally concerned with the royal revenue, but later attracting legal business of other kinds. It became the Exchequer Division of the High Court of Justice.

excommunication. Censure by most Christian churches, by which someone is excluded from the communion of the faithful according to Canon Law.

executor. Person charged with duty of carrying out the terms of a will.

exercise. Puritan term for weekday sermon.

extent. Formal recital and valuation of lands of a manor and its services, rents, profits etc.

extra-parochial. Outside the bounds of any (civil and/or ecclesiastical) parish, and therefore exempt from the payment of poor and/or church rates, and usually exempt from payment of tithes also, though strictly **extra-parochial** tithe was payable to the Crown. All **extra-parochial** places automatically became civil parishes in 1894.

ey/eye. Alternative spelling of 'eay' and 'eau' — the old.

eyewedge. Small wedge used for securing cart-wheels before the 'band' or tyre was placed over the rim of the wheel, or sometimes for securing the tail-band of a cart. An early form of cotter.

eyre. Court of itinerant justices who travelled in circuit.

eyth. Harrow. *See also* **ayes**.

F

fabrick land. Land given towards the maintenance, building or repair of churches and cathedrals.

faldstool. A portable stool made to fold up like a camp stool. The term is also erroneously applied to the **litany stool** *q.v.*

fallett pole. Pole of felled wood.

fall gate. Gate across a public road.

falling bands. Neck bands worn so as to fall on the shoulders; popular in the seventeenth century.

fallings. Valance; fringe of short curtains attached to the headpiece of a bed or above a window.

fallon. Fallow *q.v.*

fallow. Land ploughed and harrowed, but left uncultivated for a year, so that it may recover its fertility.

fall table. Drop-leaf table.

fallynge gate. Wicket gate; a gate closed by rails falling into a fixed position.

falshead/faucet. Peg or spigot to stop the vent-hole in a cask or in a tap; a vent-peg.

Family of Love. Fanatical sect introduced into England c. 1560, distinguished by their professed love of all mankind, and passive obedience to established authority. Members of it were called Familists, and are mentioned in a list of sects in Taylor's Motto 1622.

fang. Wood or metal pipe used to convey fresh air to the workings in a mine.

fann. 1. winnowing fan; a shallow wicker basket from which the grain was thrown by hand.
2. a mechanical device generating a draught so separating the grain from the chaff.

fardeale. Small bundle or parcel.

farm. Block letting for fixed payment for a number of years; applied not only to land but to tithes, rents, fines etc. First used in connection with the manorial **demesne** *q.v.* let to a 'farmer'.

farthing. Quarter of a penny.

farthingale. 1. as **Spanish farthingale**, a petticoat held out by cane hoops; fashionable until 1580s.
2. as **French farthingale**, a roll of material around the waist which pushed out the skirt almost at right angles to fall vertically to the level of the instep. This was either in the shape of a circle, an oval, or a semi-circle.

farthinghold. Half **oxgang** *q.v.*

Fasting Tuesday. Shrove Tuesday.

fat. Vat or tub.

fathom. 1. measure of six feet, commonly used to express the depth of mines and shafts.
2. quantity of reeds. A man could just get his arms around the bundle. It was about six feet in circumference.

feal heap. Spoil tip from a coal mine.

feal stakes. Some kind of surface equipment at a coal mine, but the exact meaning is uncertain.

fealty. Loyalty; the tenant on taking a holding had to swear an oath of fealty, i.e. promise to conform to the customary practice of services and payments. Continued in use long after the feudal system dissolved.

fearlot. An eighth of a **bushel** *q.v.*

fearnought. A kind of stout woollen cloth.

fearnought spatterdashes. Long protective gaiters made of **fearnought** *q.v.*

fee. The area of jurisdiction of a lord of the manor, subject to feudal obligations. The expression 'in fee' means hereditarily, and 'in fee male' means 'through male descent'. A 'fee simple' was a freehold estate in land which passed at death to the common law heir. For 'fee tail' *see* **entail**. *See also* **fee farm**.

fee farm. 1. fixed annual rent charge payable to the king by chartered boroughs.
2. reservation by the lord on creation of a tenancy, of a portion of the rent to himself.

fee/feying cloth. Winnowing cloth, used in separating the chaff from the grain.

felewote. Velvet.

felloe/felly/filly. Segment of the exterior rim of a wheel supported by the spokes. Also known as **villies** *q.v.*

felony. Serious crime.

feme. Woman. A 'feme covert' was a married woman whose husband was alive. A 'feme sole' was a spinster, widow or a wife economically independent of her husband.

fence month. The time of fawning from 6 June to 6 July, when tenants were forbidden to gather rushes, pick berries, or let cattle wander off the path to graze.

fenestral. Small window. Before glass was in general use, the **fenestral** was often made of paper, cloth or canvas, and sometimes, a kind of lattice-work, or shutter, ornamented with tracery. In the sixteenth century the term 'fenestre' seems to have been applied to a blind or shutter in contra-distinction to a glazed window.

feodary/feodatory. One who held property under the tenure of feudal service.

feoffment. The act of granting a **fee** *q.v.* in trust; a gift or conveyance in **fee** *q.v.*, of land; the deed conveying the gift.

fermable. Sheep fit to be farmed or let out.

ferret. Stout tape, commonly made of cotton, but also of silk, used, amongst other things, for garters.

festing penny. Wage advance given to servants when hired to confirm contract.

fetch/vetch. Bean-like fruit of a leguminous plant (of genus *vicia*), used as cattle fodder.

fetters. Shackles, especially for horse's feet.

field. 1. a large area of open arable land, divided into furlongs, each again sub-divided into **selions** *q.v.*, all the **selions** in a furlong being normally subject to the same crop rotation. Distinct from a modern 'field', which is more properly styled a **close** *q.v.* 2. the space or bay between beam and beam in a barn, as 'a barn with four fields'.

field bedstead. Bed designed for rough use, rather like a modern camp bed.

field jury. Jury of the manorial court regulating the use of the common fields.

fieldmaster/fieldreeve/fieldsman. Communal officer who regulated the use of open fields. The appointment of such officers was regularised by the Act 13 George III, c.81 (1772–3) for the improvement of open fields.

fier panes. Small portable braziers containing charcoal placed within a **chafing dish** *q.v.* Alternatively known as **chafers** *q.v.*

fierskase. Curfew (Fr. *couvre-feu*); a brass or copper hood in the shape of a quarter-sphere with a handle at the top. It was placed over a fire to keep it burning at night, but yet prevented any danger of conflagration throughout the house. In the morning the curfew was removed and the fire resuscitated by bellows.

fifteens. Select vestry.

fifteenth. Occasional tax levied by sovereign for special purpose, e.g. waging war, or royal marriage; one-fifteenth of annual income.

Fill Dyke. The month of February.

filling lace. Possibly a piece of lace to make decent a low-cut gown, or to fill a slashed sleeve. It could also be an abbreviated form of filletting. *See also* **fillit**.

fillit. Originally a headband to keep a headdress in position or a band of ribbon for binding the hair. Later, often ornamental.

filly. *See* **felloe**.

fine. Sum of money payable on admission to a holding; so called because it was 'final', i.e. it only had to be paid once by that person. It was payable by every copyholder on his being admitted through inheritance or purchase. It is not to be confused with **amercement** *q.v.*, or 'fine' for an offence. In nearly all manors the amount was at the discretion of the lord of the manor, or his steward.

fire-bote. Wood granted to tenants by lord of the manor for fuel.

fire hook. Large iron hook on long pole, used for removing the thatch from burning buildings; often stored in churches and, occasionally, still surviving there.

firehouse. The hall or living room of a house containing more than one room.

Fire of London, Great. *See* **Great Fire of London**.

fire, St. Anthony's. *See* **St. Anthony's Fire**.

firescummer. Shovel for removing ashes.

fire slice. Fire shovel.

firkin. Small cask, usually holding eight gallons of ale, nine gallons of beer, or 56 pounds solid measure.

fish garth. Weir or enclosure in a river or pond for keeping fish and aiding in the catching of fish.

fither. Feather.

flackett. *See* **flasket**.

flag. 1. rush, reed or coarse grass.
2. in plural, rush or wicker work.

flagene/flaggon. Flagon; large cask or a large vessel containing a supply of drink for use at table.

flake. Wattle hurdle, e.g. **fold flake** used in building sea-walls.

flambeau. Flaming torch; made with carpenter's chips bound together with a mixture of tow and trimmings from flax and hemp, soaked in beeswax, or resin. It would light a landing stage on a foggy night. The small cup-shaped cages set high on the top of iron firedogs are small holders for **flambeaux**.

Flanders chest. Highly ornamented chest in the Flemish style.

flannel/lanill. Open woollen fabric of loose texture, usually without nap. Possibly from the Welsh 'gwlanen'.

flash kit. Water tub.

flasket/flacket/flackett. 1. long shallow basket with a handle at each end, or an oval washing tub.
2. a small barrel for taking beer to the harvest field.
3. flask or bottle.

flat. One of the large portions into which common field was divided.

flat back. Common knife with its back filed down after it is put together.

flatting trough. Receptacle presumably used for soaking and flattening the rolled-up hands of dried tobacco prior to stripping and fermenting.

flaxen. The produce of the flax plant, *Linun usitatissimum*, which also produced linseed. The quality of **flaxen** cloth was variable, since it depended on the skill of the retter (*see* **retting**) and the energy of the heckler (*see* **heckell**). Much was sold unbleached, when it was called 'brown'. The best quality plain wove was called **holland** *q.v.*

fleam/fleme. 1. stream or artificial channel or drain somewhat wider or deeper than an ordinary ditch.
2. farrier's instrument used for blood-letting horses and cattle.

fleckstone. Small stone used in spinning.

fleeak. Sort of hurdle hung in a horizontal position in a kitchen, just below the ceiling, on which to deposit bread, bacon, dried herbs etc.

fleme. *See* **fleam**.

flese/fleece. Wool shorn from a living animal.

flesh-hook. Long bar with two or three hooks at one end. Used for getting meat out of a pot or **cauldron** *q.v.*

flesh tub. Vessel used for salting meat for preservation.

flitch. Side of an animal, salted and cured. One side of a pig, when killed, minus legs, thighs and ribs, i.e. bacon.

float. Musical instrument; a flute.

float grass. Grass growing in swampy ground.

flock bed. Bed stuffed with wool, bits of cloth etc.

flote. Rough-made river boat formerly used on the Severn.

floted. Skimmed.

flour. Finely-ground meal of wheat etc. Malt, when correctly made from barley, is in the form of a dry mealy flour.

flowers of sulphur. Pure form of sulphur used medically as a laxative and sudorific, and as an ingredient of ointments, especially for skin diseases.

flowting. Process of carding wool (*see* **card**) to spin in the mixture of various grades and lengths of yarn. The wooden instruments used had teeth to straighten the fibres prior to spinning.

6. (*Flowting*) Spinning and carding wool. The woman on the left is turning her spinning wheel by means of a handle, while the one on the right is carding wool with two hand-cards.

fluke. Variety of kidney potato, so called perhaps because of its shape.

foal. Assistant to the **putters** *q.v.* in a coal mine.

fodder. *See* **fother**.

fodge. Small package containing wool fleeces. In packing fleeces of wool, when the quantity was too small to make up a full 'bag' of 240 lbs, the ends of the bag were gathered together as required, and the sides skewered over them, thus forming the small package known as a **fodge**.

fog. 1. second crop of grass or aftermath long grass remaining in pasture till winter.
2. moss.
3. to take cattle out of pasture in the autumn.

foizon. To increase.

fold bar/pike. Iron bar used to make holes in the ground in which to fix hurdles.

fold flake. *See* **flake**.

foldstead/fould. Fold; to enclose.

folkland. In Anglo-Saxon England, land on which food, rent and customary duties were owed to the king. A term denoting an early period in society in which all land bore common burdens.

folkmote. Gathering of the tribe in arms.

fomard/fomiard. Polecat.

font taper. Levy made by churchwardens, originally for the taper used at baptism, but continued long after the Reformation as a customary **fee** *q.v.* at baptism.

food rent. In early Anglo-Saxon England, an obligation to provide sufficient provisions to maintain the king and his household for 24 hours.

foolen. Narrow strip of land between the embankment of a river and the ditch on the land side.

footing. Admission to or fee for membership of a trade or club. 'Foot-Ale' was money spent on ale by a workman on entering a new place of employment.

footing/frill. Ruffle; the narrow strip of lace sewn to the edge of the material, to which the main decorative edging lace is attached.

forcer. *See* **fossett**.

foreign service. Service owed by a tenant to his lord outside of the lord's **fee** *q.v.* Holders of a Knight's Fee were liable to serve with horse and arms for forty days at their own charge.

foreman of the fields. A **fieldmaster** *q.v.*, or sometimes the foreman of the **field jury** *q.v.*

fore room. Alternative term for principal living room or **house** *q.v.*, i.e. the hall.

forestall. To purchase privately any foodstuffs on their way to market or fair.

forestreet chamber. Room facing on to the street.

form. In schools in the past, pupils were seated on long **forms**, one **form** usually accommodating pupils of similar abilities, but widely different ages. This then became the word for a class of school-children.

forthfare. Passing bell which was rung for those *in extremis* as the soul was passing forth on its last journey (in common usage up to the end of Henry VIII's reign).

fosse. Ditch or moat.

fossett/forcer. Small chest, sometimes leather-covered and strengthened with iron bands, used to hold documents, jewellery and other valuables.

fother/fodder/fudder. 1. load; cart-load; a mass; a quantity.
2. **gore** *q.v.* or scrap of land in the open fields.
3. measure of lead or stone. The measure of weight by which lead was sold, normally by volume, occasionally in recent times by weight, varying from **liberty** *q.v.* to **liberty**, from 22½ cwt in Derbyshire to 19½ cwt in London. Two pieces of bole lead usually made up a **fother**.

fotheren heck. Rack for holding fodder.

founday. Space of six days. A term used by iron-workers, it being the time in which they made eight tuns.

founder. First miner to work a lead mine; the first **meers** *q.v.* allocated by the barmaster to found the mine; the first shaft sunk.

four course. Rotation of crops such as wheat, turnips, barley and clover.

four field system. The re-arrangement of lands in an ancient two or three field area to form a fourth field, so that the occupiers might follow the more modern **four-course** *q.v.* technique.

fowling piece. Gun for shooting wild fowl; a light shot gun.

fram/frame. Legs and cross-rails of a table which were always appraised independently of the flat top or **board** *q.v.*

frandell/furendral. Measure of a quarter of an acre.

frankalmoin. Feudal tenure by which land granted to the church by laymen was not subject to the burdens of **escheat** *q.v.*, **reliefs** *q.v.* etc. Usually granted in perpetuity in return for prayers or a **chantry** *q.v.* for the soul, occasionally it was granted for rent.

frankpledge. In old English law, a pledge or surety of freemen; i.e. the pledge taken by all the inhabitants of a **tithing** *q.v.* vouching for the general good behaviour of each free-born citizen over 14 years of age, and for his being forthcoming to answer any infraction of the law; **view of frankpledge** was a meeting held periodically to see that all men who ought to be were in a **tithing** *q.v.*

fraymed table. Joined table, the top being fixed to a frame consisting of the legs, stretchers and top rails. A successor to the loose board supported by trestles.

free bench. Dower of a widow, the income of one-third of the widow's late husband's land; the normal provision and that of inheritance by the eldest son (Borough French) was overridden in manors with the custom of **Borough English** *q.v.*, whereby not only did the widow have the whole of his land for life but the youngest son succeeded. **Widow's bench** *q.v.*

freeing. Act of delivering to the **barmaster** *q.v.* a dish of lead ore to establish ownership of a new vein or mine.

freestone. Any kind of stone that can be sawn or worked freely without breaking; generally limestone or sandstone.

free tenants. Tenants of a **fee** *q.v.* under a superior lord; freeholders.

fregg. *See* **frog.**

french wheat. Buck wheat.

fresch/frisc. Portion of meadow in open field husbandry. Mentioned in **cartularies** *q.v.*, but not traced in books of reference, unless it is to be equated with **frith** *q.v.*

frettes. Old and/or broken things.

frieze. Coarse woollen cloth with a nap, usually on one side only.

frigiam. Possibly an area of woodland, or synonymous with **fresch** *q.v.*

fring. Fringe or ornamental border.

frisc. *See* **fresch.**

frith/fryth. Young whitehorn used for sets in hedges. The term was also generally used for underwood; wooded area or a clearing in a wood. *See also* **frigiam.**

fritter pann. Baking pan for fritters (slices of fruit or meat, dipped in batter and fried).

frodmortell. Free pardon for murder or manslaughter.

frog/fregg. 1. utensil found in fireplaces. Meaning uncertain, but possibly a corruption of furgon, an oven fork or poker.
2. rachett.

frommard. Iron instrument to rend or split laths.

frost nail. Nail with head filed sharp; put in horses' shoes to prevent them slipping in frosty weather.

fruggan/fruggin. 1. curved iron scraper with which the ashes in an oven were stirred.
2. in Lincolnshire, an oven fork used for placing fuel on the fire or stirring the embers.

fry. Pig's liver. The products of lambs' castration are called lamb's fries. Applied locally to various internal parts of animals, usually eaten fried.

fryen pan/fryn pane. Frying pan; these were either designed with very long handles so that the user could stand well clear of the fire, or else with small rings which could be attached to **pot hooks** *q.v.*

fryth. *See* **frith.**

fudder. Load: it relates properly to lead, and signifies a certain weight, *viz* eight pigs, or 16 cwt; as much as a two-horse cart would have contained. *See also* **fother.**

Fufillingday. Day when those newly of age were drafted into **tithing** *q.v.*

full stated. Of a leasehold estate: supporting three specific lives.

furbelows. Derogatory term for elaborate ornaments.

furendel. A quarter of a **bushel** *q.v.* of corn.

furendral. *See* **frandell.**

furlong/flat. 1. measure of length, 220 yards. This was a convenient length in average soil for oxen to plough before enjoying a brief respite, after which they turned on the **headland** *q.v.*
2. sub-division in an open arable field, a block of contiguous

selions *q.v.*, all more or less the same length and all running the same way.
3. an area of land, a furlong each way, containing ten acres.
4. indefinite division of an unenclosed field.

furnace/furnes/furnis. Large metal pot, particularly one used for brewing or boiling.

furniture (bed). The various items needed to go with a bed: mattress, bolster, pillows, sheets, blankets and coverlet.

fustian. Thick coarse woollen cloth usually dyed a dark colour. In the nineteenth century **fustian jackets** was a term used to denote the working classes.

fustick. Dyeing material. **Old fustick**, derived from *chlorpbora tinctoria*, gave yellow with alum as mordant, olive with copper. **Young fustick** from *cotinus coggyria* gave orange-brown with alum as mordant.

futrit. Horizontal shaft or way in the Ironbridge area.

7. (*Fustick*) Cloth being dipped in a dye vat. Note the faggots for keeping the fire going underneath the vat.

G

gad/goad. 1. iron punch with a long wooden handle, held by one miner whilst another, with a great iron hammer or sledge, drove it into the vein.
2. sharp pointed rod for driving oxen.

gair. Strip of verdue on the uplands, generally an outcrop of limestone; a bright green grassy spot, surrounded by bent (stiff, wiry, coarse grass) or heather; an irregular strip of green turf running down the side of a moorland hill.

gait. Gate *q.v.*

galage. A kind of patten or clog, fastened with **latchets** *q.v.*

galash. Covering for the upper part of a leather shoe.

gale/geal. A swing crane over a kitchen grate.

galilee. Porch or chapel at church entrance.

galingale. Aromatic root stock of certain East Indian plants, used in cooking.

gallatrie/gallows-tree. Iron support for a pot over a kitchen fire.

gallon. Standard basic measure of capacity, both dry and liquid, equal to 277.274 cubic inches. 1 **bushel** *q.v.* (dry measure) contains 8 gallons; 8 pints (liquid measure) equal 1 gallon.

galloon. Various spellings. 1. to dress the hair with gold bands or ribbons; this sense goes back to the twelfth century.
2. from the seventeenth century: a narrow, close-woven ribbon or braid of gold, silver, silk or copper, for trimming articles of apparel.

gallow balke/balk. Possibly a gallow brake to stop the gallows over the fire from swinging out of place.

galls. Excrescences on leaves and young twigs of certain types of oak tree, used in dyeing. Aleppo **galls** were the best and contained up to 60% tannic acid.

gally pot. Small glazed earthenware pot.

gamashers. *See* **hoggers**.

gambrell. Bent piece of iron used by butchers for hanging meat. Also spelt **cambrell**.

gange. Set of articles, e.g. 'gange of spokes'.

ganger. *See* **ganner.**

gangue. Waste minerals found alongside or attached to lead ore.

ganner/ganger. Beggar or poor hawker, or a combination of both.

gantrie/gantry. Four-footed wood stand for barrels.

gan-wife. Female pedlar, going about with a basket containing pins, laces and nick-nacks, or with tin ware, brushes and other domestic articles.

garbs, tithe of. *See* **tithe of garbs.**

garde-bras. *See* **wardbrace.**

garderobe/garderoome. Early lavatory or privy; a kind of cupboard with stone or wood seat, with a shute to ground level. Mostly only for night use.

garietes/greaves. Armour for the legs.

garlock. *See* **gavelock.**

garner. Small barn for storing corn.

garness/garnish. Full set of pewter platters, dishes, saucers and chargers, comprising 12 each of the first three items.

garnishing the church. Decorating of a church with appropriate flowers and branches etc. for the major festivals.

garth. Enclosure, yard or garden attached to a house.

gate. Right of pasture on the common for one animal. Often as **beast gate, cow gate, horse gate, sheep gate**, etc.

gated pasture. *See* **stint.**

gate penny. Toll paid by tenants to pass through private gates, for easier passage to and from their own lands.

gate post bargain. Payment of money on the gate post before the stock sold leave the field.

Gateward's Case. Case heard in 1603, in Stixwould, Lincs. (but as a precedent for the country generally), in which it was decided that the word 'inhabitant' was so vague as to be meaningless. This meant that the inhabitants of a rural parish or manor could claim no common right. It was subsequently decided that the ruling did not apply when a district had been incorporated or had, as such, received a Crown grant, which was held to satisfy the technical rule as to incorporation. Sometimes, judges interpreted the law fairly generously, justifying an existing custom by the ingenious theory of a 'Lost Grant'. Inhabitants could exercise 'common rights' while the common remained open, but when it was enclosed they had no legal interest which would entitle them to compensation.

gathering tub. Possibly a tub to collect rainwater.

gaud/gawde. Ornamental trinket.

gauge brick. Brick which shows by its change of colour when the oven is hot enough for baking.

gaun. Ladle, particularly used for dispensing milk, originally one that held a gallon.

gauntry. That on which barrels were set in a cellar, a beer-stall. *See also* **gantrie**.

gauze. Very thin transparent fabric of silk.

gavelcorn. Service of rendering a **bushel** *q.v.* of corn for each half **virgate** *q.v.*

gavelkind. System by which a dead man's property was inherited equally by all the sons, the widow getting half instead of one-third as her dower, and under which a tenant could alienate his lands at the age of 15.

gavelock/garlock. Iron crow-bar, or lever.

gawde. *See* **gaud**.

geal. *See* **gale**.

gear. 1. harness for horses.
2. in a loom, the small wires through which the warp was passed to separate it into two sets to allow the shuttle to pass between alternate threads. Different gears allowed different types of cloth to be woven on the same loom.

geld. 1. payment, tax, tribute or fine.
2. of a barrel etc.: to dry and crack, allowing leakage. *See also* **gizen**.

geldeet. Sun cracked; or in the case of a butt or water tub, cracked through and through, and consequently leaking.

gelding. Castrated horse.

gelt sheep. Castrated sheep.

gersuma. Fee paid on inheritance of freehold land by daughter.

gestum. Guest's portion; allowance of meat and drink.

getherin-coal. Large piece of coal generally put on the fire just before going to bed, so that it may be heated on the under surface. When broken up in the morning, it quickly formed a good fire.

ghenting. *See* **kenting**.

gibbet. Large cudgel, such as those which were thrown at trees to beat down the fruit.

giest/gyste. Pasture let out during the summer for cattle at a fixed price per head.

gill. 1. measure for liquids; vessel holding a **gill**.
2. place hemmed in with two steep brows or banks, usually flourishing with brushwood, with often a rivulet running between them.

gillet. Instrument used in thatching.

gilt. Young female pig.

gimlin. Large shallow tub for salting bacon.

gimmer-hog. A one-year-old ewe.

gimp/gympe. Silk, worsted or cotton twist, with a cord or wire running through it, used for trimmings.

gin/ginn. 1. machine for listing or moving heavy weights.
2. a machine for separating the seeds from cotton.
3. **gin-ring**: the circle traced by a horse turning a **gin**, for the winding gear of a coal pit.

ginger. White ginger, the scraped root, often artificially bleached, from Jamaica. **Black ginger**, the unscraped root from the East Indies.

ginny carriage. Small strong carriage for conveying materials on a rail road.

gipsey. Spring that breaks forth sometimes on the Wolds in Yorkshire. The village of Wold Newton near Hunmanby, in the East Riding, now North Yorkshire, is remarkable for the occurrence in wet seasons of a sudden eruption of cold, clear water, locally called the gipsey or the gipsey-race. These are sometimes called **vipse**.

girandoles. 1. chandelier with several branches.
2. a kind of revolving firework.

girdle. 1. chain, usually with links of precious metal, worn round the waist, knotted or buckled, with the end left hanging almost to the ground; often very elaborate and decorated.
2. round iron plate used in baking.

girdle wheel. Spinning wheel or spindle small enough to hang from the waist.

girse. Horse-girth; leather bands securing the saddle or pack on the back of a horse.

girsome. Fine on renewal of a lease. Lands were leased under annual rents and, by the payment of a fine, called a **girsome fine**, at the end of every 21 years.

girth. Strap of leather or cloth placed round a horse to secure a saddle or pack.

gittern. Stringed instrument.

gizen. Of a butt, water tub, etc.: to split at the joints, allowing leakage.

glauber salt. Sulphate of sodium used as a purge.

glaudkin. Kind of gown, much in fashion in Henry VIII's reign.

glebe. Land assigned to the incumbent of a parish as part of his benefice and the endowment of the church.

glent stone/glenter. Stone inserted at a corner or along the side of a narrow street to prevent the wheels of passing vehicles encroaching onto the footpath.

goad. *See* **gad**.

goaf. A **rick** *q.v.* of corn in the straw laid up in a barn. **Goaf-flap** was a wooden beater to knock the ends of the sheaves, and make the **goaf** more compact. **Goaf-stead** was a division of a barn in which the **goaf** was placed.

goafer. Cake made of batter baked over the fire in an iron instrument somewhat like a pair of tongs with very large ends, usually square, but sometimes round. The inside had many square projections, which formed holes in the cake, which could be filled with butter.

gob. The vacant space which is left after coal has been removed in a coal mine and into which the refuse coming from coal measures is thrown.

god's penny. Small payment made to seal a bargain, or as **earnest** *q.v.* money given on hiring a servant. *See also* **earles**.

gore. A more or less triangular scrap of land, usually between two neighbouring furlongs.

gorget. Armour for the throat; a steel collar.

gormer. Frame or ladder used to extend the sides of a waggon for carrying straw or hay.

gossip/gossib. Godparent.

grafting tool. Long spade used in draining land.

grain staff. Quarter-staff with a pair of short tines at the end, which are called 'graines'.

Great Fire of London. 1666 — broke out at Master Farryner's, the king's baker, in Pudding Lane and after three days and nights was arrested at Pie Corner. St. Paul's Cathedral, eighty-nine other churches and 13,200 houses were burnt down.

8. Great Fire of London, 1666.

Great Seal. Seal used for the authentication of documents of the highest importance issued in the name of the sovereign. *See also* **close rolls** and **letters patent**.

greaves. *See* **garietes**.

green skin. Untanned hide.

Gregorian Calendar. *See* **New Style Calendar**.

grey beard. Brown stoneware spirit bottle. It had a wide belly and a narrow neck, with a curling ear on one side and a man's face with flowing beard on the other. Once a familiar object in cottage homes, it is now a collector's item.

grey parson. Layman who owns or rents the right to collect the tithes of a parish.

grey peas. Runcival or field peas.

grice bag. *See* **grist**.

gridiron. Grid placed on or near the fire, suspended on **andirons** *q.v.* or supported on legs, for roasting and toasting.

grindle stone. Round revolving stone, used for grinding; there were many different sizes, as grindstone, mill stone, groundstone, etc.

grindstone sill. Thick sandstones from which the celebrated Newcastle grindstones were cut. It is on the whole a fine grained moderately hard, light yellow stone; but it is, in places, porous enough for the manufacture of filter stones, which were formerly extensively made from it.

grip. Small trench for draining a field; a narrow ditch at the side of a road.

grist. Allowance of corn to be ground at one time.

grist/grice bag. Bag for corn.

grist stave/steave. Barrel for containing a quantity of milled corn or malt; *see also* **stave**.

grobe/grubber. Large iron harrow.

groinges. Growings; land let out for arable use.

groundsell. The essential groundplate in a timber-framed structure.

ground-sill stone. Quarryman's term, for one of the beds of Portland *oolite*; used for bridges etc., where great strength was required.

9. (*Ground-sill stone*) Transporting Portland stone in 1790. Drawing by the Swiss artist Samuel Hieronymus Grimm (1734–94) showing the galleries of a Portland stone quarry and the method of transporting the unfashioned blocks across to the mainland.

grubber/grub-scuffler. Implement with broad faced curved teeth, used for cleaning drill crops. It was furnished with 'stilts' or handles, like a plough. It was an improvement upon the old wooden **scuffler** *q.v.*

grugeon. Eighteenth-century word for coarse meal or grain.

gudgeon. Metal piece let into the end of a wooden shaft.

guileing tub/vat. Vat in which the wort in brewing is put to work after the yeast has been added.

Gule of August. Lammas Day, 1 August.

gully. Large household knife.

gun/gunn. Large flagon containing ale; commonly made of pewter.

gurging trough. Trough for coarse meal or grain.

gurry butt. Dung sledge. A sort of sliding cart or barrow, usually to be drawn by one horse. The sides and ends were about 18 inches high, and were fixed, the load being discharged by over-turning the carriage.

gut. Underground drain for water in Sussex.

gympe. *See* **gimp**.

gyrking/jerkin. Close-fitting jacket, jersey or short coat, often made of leather.

gyste. *See* **geist**.

gysting. *See* **agistment**.

H

hack. 1. tool rather like a pick-axe or hoe.
2. rack to hold fodder.
3. horse let out for hire.

hacking knife. Tool used in a kitchen; meaning uncertain.

hacking the ruts. Primitive method of road repair.

hack iron. *See* **hag-iron.**

hackle. Hessian, conical straw hat to place over a bee skep to protect from rain etc.

hackman. The driver of a hack or hackney carriage; a cabman.

hackmuck/hackmuch/huckmuck. Strainer of peeled osiers for filtering new beer from the mash-tub. It was made somewhat in the shape of a quarter-sphere with a neck formed at a lower angle into which the tap of the mash-tub was fitted.

hackney. Horse of 15 hands or horse kept for hire.

hackney carriage/coach. Four-wheeled coach, drawn by horses and seating six persons, kept for hire.

hackney saddle. Saddle for use in ordinary riding.

hade. Sloping place; the slope or angle at which a fault intersects

10. *Hackney coach.*

strata. In lead mining it is applied to the slope of a vein from the perpendicular.

haggaday. Latch to a door or gate. It was frequently put upon a cottage door, on the inside, without anything projecting outwards by which it could be lifted. A little slit was made in the door, and the latch could be raised only by inserting a nail or slip of metal.

haggler. Labourer.

hag-iron/hack iron/haggon. An inverted chisel which a blacksmith put into his anvil when he wished to cut anything.

hagworm. Viper snake.

haie spaith/haye spade. Sharp, heart-shaped spade used for cutting hay.

hair cloth. Coarse fabric made from horse hair and used for drying malt over a kiln. Possibly also used for a cloth employed in cheesemaking.

halbeard/halberd. A combination of spear and battle axe consisting of a sharp edged blade ending in a point, and a spear-head, mounted on a handle, five to seven feet long.

hales/ails. Plough handles.

half-baptized. Christened privately.

half-gates. Young animals, counted as only half a gate when out to pasture; e.g. half-gate steers.

half headed bedstead. Bed with short corner-posts without canopies.

half severals. *See* **lammas lands.**

half-year lands. Lands commonable for about six months in twelve; *see also* **lammas lands.**

hall. The main living, cooking and eating room of the house.

hallyng/hawlyng. Piece of tapestry, painted or stained cloth etc., used as a hanging on the walls of a hall.

halter/haulter. Strap or rope with a noose by which a horse is led.

hamber. Hammer.

hamesucken/hamsoken. The crime of assaulting a person in his own house or dwelling place. Now only in Scottish law.

hamlet. Small settlement having neither a constable (so therefore not a township) an overseer, a parish church, or a separate rate (so therefore not a parish).

hampatts. Meaning uncertain. Perhaps a form of 'hamper' or possibly hand-pats for butter.

hamper. Large basket, with a cover, generally used as a packing case.

hamsoken. *See* **hamesucken.**

hanaborough. Coarse horse-collar, made of reed or straw.

hanap. A drinking vessel, a wine cup or goblet. Now applied, as an antiquarian term, to medieval goblets of ornate character.

hanaper. 1. case for a **hanap** *q.v.;* a plate-basket, a repository for treasure or money. 2. round wicker case or small basket in which documents were kept.

hand heck. Possibly a rack moveable by hand.

handles. Wooden devices in which teasels were set for raising nap on cloth.

handsyakes/spikes. Two pieces of wood with handles, used in country places for carrying coffins to the church, and from the church to the grave.

hand waiter. Serving tray.

hanger. Short sword.

hang fair. Public execution, sometimes treated as a holiday. The Pleasure Fair at Warminster on August 11th was known as 'Hang Fair', perhaps from the hanging of two murderers there on that day in 1813.

hanging press. Wardrobe or cupboard attached to the wall and of sufficient height to allow clothes to be at full length.

hanglesses. Hangers or **hengels**, pieces of chain on a chimney breast from which utensils were hung on pot hooks.

hanvil. Anvil.

hapence. Easter dues.

happintree/hopping tree. The stumps in front of a waggon when the shafts have been pulled out; the pole of a coup-cart.

harden. *See* **hurden.**

hard wax. Sealing wax, often made of beeswax and lac.

hardy/hardey. Fixed, shouldered chisel, placed upright in a square hole in the blacksmith's anvil, upon which he cuts hot iron.

harl. To thrust a dead rabbit's hind-foot through a slit in the other leg, so as to form a loop to hang it up, or carry it by.

harneis/harness. 1. that part of the loom which shifts the warp threads alternatively to form the **shed** *q.v.*
2. harness generally, any kind of equipment or fittings for animals.
3. the mounting or metalwork of a girdle.

harness cask. Receptacle on board ship, where the meat, after being taken out of the pickle cask, was kept ready for use. It was an upright cask with straight tapering sides narrowing to the top, which closed with a hinged lid and padlock.

harquebus. Gun supported on a stand.

harrateen/harreen. Kind of bed linen formerly used for bed-curtains.

harthstaff. Blacksmith's tool for drawing **scar** *q.v.* from the fire.

hasp. *See* **hesp.**

hastener. Semi-circular tin screen placed behind meat in roasting before the fire, to keep the cold air off and hasten the cooking by reflected heat.

hatchment. Funerary escutcheon painted on a square panel and hung, in the style of a diamond, first outside the house of a deceased person and later in church.

hauberk. Armour for neck and shoulders.

haulm. To prepare straw for thatching by combing off the leaves and cutting off the ears.

hautbois/hautboy. Wood-wind musical instrument similar in shape and tone to a clarinet, only thinner (an older form of the oboe).

hawdyng/holden. Holding; of animals, those kept for breeding.

hawker. Lopping hook.

hawlyng. *See* **hallyng.**

hawser. Large rope, used in fishing. In rope making the term 'hawser laid' means three strands, each consisting of a number of yarns, twisted together to form a rope.

hay croke. Central remnant of a haystack.

haylath. Barn for storing hay.

hayward/heyward. Communal officer responsible for the oversight of hedges. A manorial, burghal or parochial officer and, by extension, the person (officer) responsible for regulating open-field cultivation and the use of the common generally (no connection with hay).

headborough. Properly a deputy constable. In some districts the term was used as synonymous with that of constable.

headland. Space left at the head of a **selion** *q.v.* for the plough to turn on. Often the headland was commonable or belonged to a different proprietor from the long lands. The word is now used for similar land in an arable close held in severalty.

headridge. *See* **hedrudge.**

head roll. Roll of fabric used to make the complicated head-dresses fashionable in the seventeenth century.

head stakes. Head stocks at a mine.

head stall. A head collar; the halter or bridle worn by horses in the stable to tether them.

headstand. Part of a bridle which fits around a horse's head.

Head Sunday. Sunday after 6 July, known as Old Midsummer Day.

heap keeper. Miner who overlooks the cleaning of coal on the surface.

heap steed/heap stead. Platform at a pit's mouth elevated above the surface level to allow the coals to be tipped over screens into waggons. The tubs are landed on the heap steed and run to the screens.

heare. Coarse fabric made from horses' hair.

hearse/herse. Frame for holding candles. When a corpse was brought into the church this wooden framework was placed over the body, over it was placed the pall or hearse-cover, whilst at the angles and sometimes on the ridge were iron sockets for candles. Occasionally these wooden hearses were reproduced in iron or other metal and made prominent parts of the tomb of persons of distinction buried within the church, tapers being lighted at the obit and anniversary of death. Nowadays the name is used for a funeral car.

hearth tax. Tax introduced in 1662 in an effort to relieve Charles II's financial difficulties. Considerable debate took place during 1661 and 1662, and as a result a tax was proposed on hearths – or, to be more precise, chimneys. Nottinghamshire has good coverage for the two vital dates, Lady Day 1664 and Lady Day 1674.

heater. Another term for an **ironing box** *q.v.* in which hot metal or charcoal was inserted into the cavity.

11. *Hearse*, or wooden frame for holding candles. The framework was placed over a corpse when it was brought into the church and formed part of an elaborate funerary ritual of the pre-Reformation period.

heble. A plank bridge.

heck. Inner door between the entry, or lobby, and the house or kitchen. A half-heck is a door having an upper and lower half. The lower half is generally the portion closed by day.

heckell/heckle. Implement for combing flax or hemp.

heckferth/heifer. Young cow that has not had a calf.

heckling. The refuse from hemp fibre. *See* **towe.**

heder. *See* **heeder.**

hedgebill/hedge bylle. Long two-handed tool used for stopping gaps in hedges. A straight knife with a slightly curved end, set at the end of a long straight handle, it had a hook projecting from its back which was used for pushing a severed bunch of twigs into a gap in the hedge.

hedge mittens. Perhaps thick leather mittens for hedging.

hedrudge/headridge. Piece of land ploughed cross-wise at the end of other lands.

heeder/heder. Male sheep, specifically a lamb from eight to nine months until its first shearing.

heling. A coverlet of a bed, often mentioned in probate inventories.

helme/hellme. Stalks of straw used primarily for thatching.

helme racke/haulm rake. Large rake drawn over a field for gathering up cut wheat or hay stubble.

helming chaire. Either 'helmen-chair' made of **helme** *q.v.,* or else a chair used by anyone 'haulming': *see* **haulm.**

hemp/hempen. Fabric made from *Cannabis sativa,* a vigorous annual plant which it is now illegal to grow as it is the source of the drug cannabis. The male and female organs are found on separate plants and the quality of fibre produced from the two is very different. In the seventeenth century the staminate or male plant was believed to be the female because the flowers were more conspicuous and the fibres finer. The produce from this male barren plant was called fimble, and because it was ready for harvesting first, summer hemp. The coarser, female plant, was called male, carl, steel or winter hemp. The two varieties explain the variation in price found in household inventories. The residues after the fibre has been prepared included a tarry substance which burns well. The tow or very coarse fibres could be spun on a special distaff and woven into a rough cloth called **hurden** *q.v.* or used for ropes and sacking.

hempland/hemp garth. Small plot for the cultivation of hemp, in accordance with the statutes of 1533 and 1563; by extension any very small plot or **pightle** *q.v.,* especially one attached to a dwelling house.

hempstock. Wooden frame for drying hemp.

hengel. *See* **hanglesses.**

heriot. Feudal due paid to the lord of the manor on the death of a tenant; originally the return to a feudal lord of weapons on his tenant's death, the heriot had come to be the best beast. Heriots are very frequently met with in manorial records, e.g. 'a black bull, his best animal was seized to the lord's use, and two bulls in respect of two other holdings'. Most heriots were valued by the jury, in which case the lord took either the animal or cash according to valuation.

hermaphrodite. Combination of both cart and waggon, being basically a cart with an extra pair of wheels to add to the front part to make it into a four-wheeled vehicle when there were bulky loads such as hay to carry.

herse. *See* **hearse.**

hesp/hasp. 1. hank of yarn, worsted or flax; generally a definite quantity.
2. fourth part of a spindle.

heyward. *See* **hayward.**

hezzle scowb. Strong hazel wand of some three or four years' growth, used in making 'crab-creeves' (traps for crabs). A creeve has a lattice woodwork bottom, and into holes burnt along the sides the scowbs are inserted, and bent over, arch fashion, and then covered with a net.

hick. To hoist, hitch or lift with an upward jerk.

hicking barrow. Small wooden hand barrow or a frame used for lifting sacks of corn etc. on to a man's shoulders.

hide. 1. in part of England outside the Danelaw, a measure of land, varied according to region from 60 to 100 acres. Used for purpose of taxation only.
2. land holding of a peasant, the measures of which varied, as a **hide** of good arable land was smaller than a **hide** of inferior quality. Primarily, the amount considered adequate for the support of one free family with its dependants; at an early date defined as being as much land as could be tilled with one plough in a year.

Highgate, London. Has its name from a gate set up there about 400 years ago, to receive tolls for the bishop of London, when the old miry road from Gray's Inn Lane to Barnet was turned through the bishop's park.

highways, surveyor of. Parish officer appointed in accordance with the 1555 Highway Act to take charge of road repairs; a waywarden.

hilling. Bed quilt or cover.

hillock rakes. Possibly a rake for raising piles of hay in haymaking.

hind/hynde. Farm servant.

hippins. Stepping stones; large stones set in shallow water at a step's distance from each other, to pass over the water. Also called **beckstones**.

hiring fair. Fair held annually, to enable employers to find employees and *vice versa*. Mainly for domestics and farm labourers.

hitched land. Part of the common field withdrawn by common consent (especially in the fallow year) from the customary rotation, and used for some special crop, e.g. vetches or turnips.

hitch nail. Strong nail, sometimes called a **pit-hitch nail**. It was about two inches long, with a flat point, and a rose head.

hitty missy window. Window made of upright bars of wood, one half of them attached to the frame, the other half to the slide. When the window is shut no light enters; when open the bars pass behind each other, and light and air are admitted.

hoar stones. 1. stones of memorial
2. stones marking divisions between estates and parishes.

Hock Tide Days. One of the days of the year on which rent was paid. They were the second Monday and Tuesday after Easter Sunday, believed to originate in commemorating the Massacre of the Danes on St. Brice's Day 1002 — 13th November.

hogger. Receptacle at the top of a delivery pipe of a pump to receive the water before its discharge into the conduit. A spout and pipe lead away the discharged water. This arrangement was sometimes called a **collar-lander**.

hoggers. Footless stockings worn by pitmen at work. They were sometimes used for riding stockings instead of gaiters by country people; variously called **looags**, **scoggers** and **gamashers**.

hogget. 1. young sheep not yet shorn.
2. swine reared for slaughter, specifically a castrated male swine.

hogg pegge. Pig one year old.

hogshead. Large cask, with a capacity for 48 gallons of ale or 54 gallons of beer or cider. As a wine measure it contained 52½ gallons.

holden. *See* **hawdyng**.

holding. 1. **peasant holding**; a proprietary land unit held in absolute title by one who occupied the holding with his family and tilled the land with his own hands and family labour. Limits of size ranged between two and 50 acres.
2. land, farm etc. held of a superior.

holen/holegn/holm. Evergreen shrub with prickly leaves and red berries; known as this up to 1539. Now known as holly.

holey stone. Stone having a hole through it. The stone must be found already perforated, or it has no virtue. These were commonly hung behind house doors as charms. A sanctity or superstition appears to have been attached to stone implements with holes. They were supposed to have been perforated by snakes.

Holland cloth. Fine linen fabric, originally made in the Netherlands. When unbleached called brown holland. Mentioned in many inventories for bed and table linen and clearly of far better quality than other linens, and therefore extremely expensive.

Holland dish/jug. Ceramic ware from Holland, possibly Delft.

Hollardy Day. 3 May, apparently a perversion of 'Holy Rood Day'.

hollen. Wall about two and a half yards high, used in dwelling houses to secure the family from the blasts of wind rushing in when the **heck** *q.v.* was open.

holm. *See* **holen**.

holmes/homes/hames. Curved pieces of wood fastened to or forming the collar of a draught beast or a horse.

holve/wholve. 1. tree-trunk hollowed out serving as a simple drain pipe under a field-track or road, especially under a gateway.
2. hollow tree-trunk for passing the water course.

holy fire. Flame kindled by burning glass or flint on Easter Eve and from which all lamps and tapers, previously extinguished, were relighted by hallowed tapers.

holy loaf. Bread distributed before the Reformation. It was ordinary unleavened bread, commonly eaten in the parish, which was blessed by the priest after he had said Mass, cut into small pieces, and given to the congregation in the chancel. It was intended to be a symbol of brotherly love.

Holy Maid of Kent. Elizabeth Barton, who incited the Roman Catholics to resist the progress of the Reformation, and pretended to act under direct inspiration. She was hanged at Tyburn in 1534.

holy oil box. Christmatory *q.v.*

homage. Either the pledge or loyalty sworn by tenants to their lord of the manor, or the assembled body of such tenants. Acceptance of a tenant into the homage also obliged the lord to warrant him. A formal submission of tenant to lord was undertaken in return for a **fee** *q.v.* The tenant placed his hands between those of his lord and said 'I become your man, from this day forth for life'.

honour. Aggregation of manors.

hoodkin. Leather bottle formerly used by physicians.

hoop. Quart measuring cup for meal used in cake-making.

hopper. Basket in which a sower carried the seed.

hopper free. Tenant who had the privilege of grinding his or her corn at the lord of the manor's mill without payment.

hoppet. 1. yard or small close.
2. small basket, especially a small hand basket.

hopping tree. *See* **happintree**.

hops. Native plant, growing freely in the hedges; also a cultivated plant harvested in September.

horden. *See* **hurden**.

horn. Thimble used in conjunction with a knife.

hornbook. Board or a leaf of paper containing the alphabet, sometimes the digits, the Lord's Prayer, and some elements of spelling. Protected by a thin plate of translucent horn, often mounted on a tablet of wood with a handle.

horny tram. In a pit, a tram with four or more upright arms of iron used for conveying rails, props etc.

horreum. Barn or storehouse.

horse. Bench or plank on which implements or vessels, particularly beer-barrels, were placed.

horse hole. 'At a colliery, an entrance into a shaft, level with the surface, where horses were netted and put in, or landed when drawn out; timber and rails were also put in at the same place. Formerly applied to a passageway hewn out of the coal inbye at the flat for the purpose of bringing the horse round from the head of the flat to the outbye end, instead of passing by the side of the tubs as at present day' — John Rowell, Newcastle Weekly Chronicle, September 12 1891.

horse lock. A hobble or shackle for a horse's foot.

horse mill/horse mylne. Mill driven by a horse or horses walking in a circle.

horse pott. Round wooden vessel containing about a quart or peck of corn.

horse, stoned. *See* **stone colt/horse**.

horstree. A piece of wood with the chains to which the swingle-tree of a pair of harrows is attached.

hose/hussen. Long stockings, thigh length, usually of wool, worn by men.

hotter. Half circle of iron attached to the upper side of the axle tree of a cart or waggon to hinder the wheels from having too much play.

hot trod. Wisp of straw or tow mounted on the top of a spear and set on fire and carried through the Border country. Its display was the signal for every man to arm and follow the pursuit on the track of a marauder, the 'war path' of the Borderers.

hour glass. Contrivance for measuring time, consisting of a glass vessel with obconical ends connected by a constricted neck, through which a quantity of sand (or sometimes mercury) runs in exactly one hour.

house. Name given to whole residential building or the principal living room, hall etc., or may be applied to any room as a suffix, as in milk-house or kiln-house.

house duty. Fixed duty payable on all houses with fewer than ten windows. Houses with more than ten windows paid tax on them *pro rata* over and above the fixed sum.

houseling bread. Small wafers used for the communion of the parishioners in general.

houseling cloth. Cloth used at communion.

houseling people. Parishioners of an age to receive communion.

house row. Employment by a farmer of a pauper at a low rate of wages according to the value of the land the farmer held. This was in place of giving the pauper direct relief, and was the practice before the act was passed for rating Poor Law Unions as a whole.

hovell. Shed, outhouse, framework for cornstack. Sometimes without sides, but affording protection for farm produce or implements from the weather.

huckaback/huggabag. Linen fabric with the weft threads thrown up alternately to make a rough surface, as in towelling.

huckmuck. *See* **hackmuck.**

hue & cry. Loud cry made by those pursuing suspected wrongdoer. When the cry was 'raised' by the constable or injured party, it was the duty of everyone to help catch the offender. The actual cry was probably Hue! Hue!

huer. Person placed on the Cornish cliff to indicate to the boats, stationed off land, the course of the shoals of pilchards and herrings.

huggabag. *See* **huckaback.**

hully. 1. long wicker trap used for catching eels. 2. perforated box in which fishermen kept live lobsters and crabs.

hult. Cottage or small house.

hummeller. *See* **rowler/rowell.**

humstrum. Home-made fiddle. Sometimes also a large kind of Jew's harp.

hundred. Administrative subdivision of a shire.

hundred house. Workhouse serving a district larger than a mere parish, especially in East Anglia, where workhouses to serve whole hundreds were very generally established as a measure of Poor Law reform from the middle of the eighteenth century onwards.

hurden/harden/horden. Coarse linen cloth made from the hurds, pieces of flax or hemp separated by combing with a **heckell** *q.v..* Used for sheets etc.

husband. Pollarded tree.

husbandland. Generally the equivalent of a **hide** *q.v.,* but the husbandlands mentioned frequently in deeds respecting Northumberland and Scottish areas contained 20 acres, and at times 24 or 30.

husbandman. Usually tenant farmer, as distinct from **yeoman** *q.v.*

hussen. *See* **hose**.

hustlements/husselments. Odds and ends, bric-a-brac; in inventories household goods often of little value.

hutch. Large wooden box with a lid, for storage.

h-yoke. Yoke for two pairs of oxen ploughing in tandem.

Fire hook. The fear of fire was very great among the occupants of thatched cottages. These hooks were used to bring down the thatch before it could spread to the whole roof. This one was found at Lyddington Bede House, Uppingham, Rutland.

I

ice creeper. Contrivance fixed below the instep of a boot, for walking securely in slippery weather. It was made of a single piece of sheet iron, two pieces of which were turned up at the sides to form ears, whilst four points were turned down so as to touch and grip the surface of the ice below the foot.

idle. Empty or useless.

Ill May Day. A name given to 1 May 1517 when the London prentices rose up against the foreign residents in that city. Their leader was believed to be John Lincoln.

imprimis. Firstly, in the first place.

impropriate. Ecclesiastical benefice whose **tithe** *q.v.* was held in whole or in part by a layman.

impropriator. Layman having the right to receive (usually the great) **tithes** *q.v.* of the parish. *See also* **appropriator**.

inch meal. Word similar in formation and sense to piece-meal.

in chorn. Inner pocket or pouch of a fishing net.

inckle. *See* **inkle**.

inclosure. Lawyer's spelling of **enclosure** *q.v.*

increase. Profit on the church 'stock' lent by the wardens to parish gilds etc.

increment. To increase. The term was also used in some accounts for the balance of gild funds in hand at the end of the year, carried to general church funds.

incumbent. The parish priest, whether **rector** *q.v.* or **vicar** *q.v.*, but not unbeneficed clerk or curate, except perhaps a **perpetual curate** *q.v.*

indenture. A form of contract between two parties in which each kept a half-cut along an indented line; hence **indentured retainer**, one who is retained in service by means of such a contract.

India back chairs. Late seventeenth-century type of chair which had a high hooped back and a central portion carved with Indian ornamentations. The design was probably Dutch.

indifferent. Often used to describe the appraisers of inventories who were unbiased; impartial.

induction. Introduction of a clerk by the archdeacon or his deputy (except in peculiars or exempt benefices) into the temporal possession of his benefice.

information. Commonly an affidavit stating that the law relating to **burial in woollen** *q.v.* had been complied with. The affidavit, according to the law, had to be delivered within eight days from the time of burial.

ing. Meadow (usually common).

inganenthief. Jurisdiction over a thief caught in lord's manor; right to try and fine a thief so caught.

ingate. Way in; specially applied to the way into a mine at the bottom of a shaft, or at any point in a shaft where the cages are stopped to enter a seam; or the way by which the air enters the workings of a pit.

injunction. Orders issued to the clergy in pre-Reformation times by the bishops, and later especially by Cromwell as Vicegerent in 1538, by Edward VI in 1547 and by Elizabeth in 1559.

inkhorn. Portable ink holder made of horn.

inkle/inckle. Kind of linen tape, or the thread from which it was made, often a broad tape.

inmarks. *See* **outmarks.**

inniolf. Strong thread, such as shoemakers would have used.

innocent. *See* **chrisom cloth.**

innom-barley. Barley that was sown the second crop after the ground was fallowed.

inquisition. Enquiry.

inspeximus. Confirmation of a series of charters under seal.

institution. Installation of a clerk by the bishop or his deputy into the possession of the spiritualities of his benefice, i.e. to the cure of souls.

instroke rent. Rent charged by the lessor of a royalty for allowing a lessee whose pit was in another royalty to break the barrier between the two.

in stuffe. Household belongings as opposed to farm stock and equipment.

intakes. Enclosure, especially from moorland or waste.

interdict. A decree of the Roman Catholic Church to withhold services and comforts from an individual or community. Its main function was to put pressure on offenders against Canon Law or on secular powers with whom the Papacy was in dispute.

International Genealogical Index. (I.G.I.). A large number of English baptismal registers and marriage entries prepared by the commonly called Mormons. This is available on microfiche at County Archives and many Public Libraries.

interred. Often used of Quakers, Anabaptists *etc.* to mean buried without Christian rites.

Interregnum. The time a throne is vacant between the death or abdication of a king and the accession of his successor, such as the period between the execution of Charles I in 1649 and the restoration of Charles II in 1660.

intruder. Puritan minister installed in a benefice after the expulsion of the lawful incumbent during the **Interregnum** *q.v.*

inwiver/inwaver. Bar of wood put inside a **cobble** *q.v.* for the seats or thofts to rest upon. At one time no fishing boat was without a **holey stone** *q.v.* suspended from the **inwiver**.

Irish work. Embroidery done in white thread on a white cloth.

iron arm. Thin plate of iron fastened to the edges of the wooden soles of clogs to make them last longer.

ironing box/iron box. A box-iron, later term is **smoothing box** or **smoothing iron**. It was made of brass or steel and has a wooden handle. The heat was provided by inserting a piece of hot metal inside the 'box' or cavity which formed the base of the iron. Sometimes called a **heater** *q.v.*

iron rack. Rack designed to hold pipes in a fire to burn out impurities of tar, nicotine and carbon.

iron sick. Said of a wooden ship when her bolts and nails are so corroded with rust that she leaks.

isson glasse/isinglas. Whitish, semi-transparent and very pure form of gelatine, used for making jellies, clarifying liquors etc.

J

jack. 1. any labour-saving device that helps in the movement of things, specially a jack for turning a spit.
2. leather bottle for holding liquor.
3. figure outside old public clocks, made to strike the bell.
4. buff jerkin worn by soldiers or type of jacket worn by women.

jack-a-legs. Large, single bladed clasp knife, generally with a broad and square ended blade. These formidable knives were much in vogue among 18th century Tyneside keelmen.

jack's land. Scraps of land, largely unused and unusable, in a common field.

jack roll. Roller for winding the rope in a draw well.

jack straw. Straw elevator; originally a man who carried straw from the threshing machine to the stack.

jack-towel. Roller towel.

jack windlass. Windlass with two chains and wheels at top and bottom for lifting, capable of being worked by one man.

jag. Small cartload.

jagger. 1. goad used for urging on a donkey.
2. staff with an iron prong used for lifting turnips.

jagger horse. Pack horse.

japand/japanned. Treated with a black resinous varnish or lacquer which is dried and hardened by heat.

Japan glass. Lacquered glass with characteristic Japanese motifs.

jarvis. Small curved plane used for shaping spokes.

jenkin. Passage driven in a pillar of coal; or a slice taken off a pillar. A loose jenkin is a similar place driven along the side of a pillar, and open to the bord along that side. To **jenkin** means to reduce the size of a pillar. The attenuated pillar thus left is called a 'stook'.

jenny balk. Small beam near the roof of the house.

jergeare. Pieces of iron.

jerkin. *See* **gyrking**.

Jews' money. Name given to old coins, found in some parts of England.

jigger pump. Pump used in breweries to force the beer into the vats.

joggled lintel. Lintel over a fireplace in the form of a jigsaw for easy fitting.

joined/joyned. Made by a 'joiner', jointed by the use of mortice and tenon joints; used of a table, stool, chair or bedstead with legs joined to the top, not trestles. Joints were often secured by wooden pegs.

joined bed. Usually one with a canopy and tester.

joint enfeoffment. Settlement of a property on a husband and wife jointly. Such an arrangement made it possible to avoid the lord's rights of relief and wardship, if the husband predeceased his wife.

jointure. Property settled on a woman at marriage to be hers on the decease of her husband.

joisting. *See* **agistment**.

joists/joyces. Originally 'joices' or 'juicements' (from French *adjoustement*), the cross-pieces of timber that are adjusted or fitted to make the framework supporting a floor.

jonathan. Instrument used by smokers to light their pipes. It was a piece of iron the size of a short poker, fitted at one end with a handle of wood, and having at the other a protuberance or transverse bar of iron, which was kept heated in the fire for use.

jookings. Corn which fell from the sheaf while it was being thrown from the stack.

jordan. 1. pilgrim's bottle containing water from the river Jordan. 2. kind of pot or vessel formerly used by physicians and alchemists. It was very much in the form of a soda water bottle, only the neck was larger, not much smaller than the body of the vessel. 3. at a later period, the term was used for a chamber-pot, having been formerly used for a urinal.

joseph. An ancient riding habit with buttons down to the skirts.

journeyman. One hired to work by the day; a skilled mechanic or artisan who has completed his apprenticeship.

jowl. To strike two substances together, especially to strike the wall of a coal-pit by way of signal. It is used to ascertain the relative positions of one working party by another. Imprisoned pitmen, after an accident in a colliery, are heard 'jowlin' to indicate their position to the relief party.

joyces. *See* **joists.**

joyned. *See* **joined.**

Judas taper. Wooden stock painted to imitate a candle; named after Judas, the name indicates it is a sham, giving no light.

Judas torch. Large torch formerly used in ceremonial processions.

juggle pin. Pin which held the body of a cart from tipping up. When it was removed, the cart was 'slotted up' and its contents 'shot out'.

Julian Calendar. *See* **Old Style Calendar.**

juncker. Contrivance for letting off the superfluous water from a pond or moat.

junk. 'Condemned' or old rope hardened with tar and encrusted with salt, unlaid and graded. The best was used as lashings, thrums for mats, swabs and mops. The rest would be teased out to produce oakum strands. These strands would be rolled by the caulkers between the hand and knee into long threads.

jupon. Pourpoint or doublet. It was generally of silk or velvet, and was worn over the armour, frequently being emblazoned with the arms of the owner. **Jupon** later became the word for a petticoat or petty coat, which indicated a small coat.

juror. Member of a jury. A property qualification was first established in 1285. An Act of 1692 laid down that a juror should possess freehold, copyhold or life tenure land worth at least £10 per year. After 1696, lists of eligible jurors were compiled by constables and presented to Quarter Sessions. The Jury Act of 1825 limited jury service to those between 21 and 60 who possessed freehold property worth at least £10 per year, or leasehold property worth at least £20 per year, or who were householders of houses worth £30 per year.

Justaucorps. Full skirted coat worn by men.

K

kail pot. Pot for broth. The body of the pot was almost spherical, the upper portion terminating in a broad lip or collar, at the sides of which ears for suspension were cast. The pot stood on three feet, like spikes. When in use it was suspended by a bow handle over the fire. Also known as 'gipsy kettle'.

kartladder. Cart-ladder; a framework of wood erected on a cart to increase its carrying capacity. It was commonly employed to convert a farm waggon for the transporting of hay.

kavel. 1. ballot by which the working places in a pit are fixed. 2. strips of tillage lands in the common fields.

keave/keeve. Large tub for fermenting beer.

keaving table. Probably a stand for a keave.

keb hoose/house. Shelter erected for young lambs in the lambing season. The keb house was divided by small stalls or partitions called 'perricks'.

keech. Cake of consolidated animal fat from the slaughterhouse, rolled up to go to the chandler's for tallow.

keed. Bundle of brushwood used for road repair.

keeper. Person who attends to the sick and dying in place of relatives.

keeve. *See* **keave**.

kennin/kennine. A measure; half a **bushel** *q.v.*, that is, two **pecks** *q.v.*

Kent, a man of. An inhabitant of Kent, east of the river Medway. They were called 'men of Kent', from the story of their having retained their ancient privileges, particularly those of gavelkind, by meeting with William the Conqueror at Swanscombbottom. Each man, besides his arms, carried a green bough in his hand; their numbers were thus concealed under the appearance of a moving wood. The rest of the inhabitants are known as 'Kentish-men'.

kenting/ghenting. Fine linen cloth originally from Ghent.

kercher. Square scarf worn over the head, with or without a hat. French *couvre-chef* survives in handkerchief.

kerchief. *See* **kyrchiffe**.

kersey. Coarse narrow cloth, woven from long wool and usually ribbed. Contrasted with 'cloth' and 'broadcloth' since the piece was shorter and narrower. Probably took its name from the village of Kersey in Suffolk where a wool-trade was once conducted. *See also* **cawfoy.**

kettle/ketele. 1. deep vessel for cooking food, often an open pot or pan. Earlier uses of the term may be synonymous with **boyler** *q.v.*
2. in hat-making a **kettle** was part of the battery and contained water acidulated by sulphuric acid in which hats were steeped.

kettle net. Net used for taking mackerel.

kibble. 1. large bucket or small tub, used in a pit for sinking purposes, or for conveying material from one place to another, in which case it is run on a tram.
2. to bruise or grind closely.
3. to crush or mash oats or other corn. Kibbled oats are known to corn chandlers.

kid. Bunch of twigs, brushwood or gorse used for burning. To kid is to bind up in faggots.

kilderkin. Cask holding 16 gallons of ale or 18 gallons of beer, equivalent to half a barrel.

kiln. *See* **kylne.**

kiln house. Building used for baking and drying grain for brewing, and containing a malt-kiln.

kilp. *See* **pot cilp.**

kimblin/kimnel. Oval tub, often of lead, used especially for scalding and salting pigs, also for curing bacon, washing butter or keeping whey; a powdering tub.

kine. Cows; usually the milking cows in a herd.

kine-vate. Cattle trough.

king ale. Church ale, so called from the 'king' and 'queen' elected to preside over the revels.

king's evil. Scrofula, a disease of the lymphatic glands, once thought to be curable by a touch from the king's (or queen's) hand. The practice of touching for the **king's evil** continued from the time of Edward the Confessor to the death of Queen Anne in 1714. The Office for the ceremony has not been printed in the Prayer Book since 1719.

kings iron. Expression for a large piece of iron.

kip. *See* **cepe.**

kipe/kippe. *See* **cypp.**

kipskin. Leather from large calves or small breeds of cattle.

kirkmaster. Churchwarden. In some parishes the term is used of select vestrymen.

kirtell. Short gown or petticoat.

kissing-gate. *See* **cuckoo gate.**

kit/kitt. 1. any staved wooden vessel, especially a milking pail, with a cover and one or two ears; a bucket, small barrel or brewing vessel.
2. the stool on which a cobbler works, including all his tools.

kive. Large vat, also used for brewing, with a bottom drain, and sometimes used in the preparation of tobacco.

kiver dish. Dish with a cover.

kiving vat. Large wooden tub used either as a cooler in brewing for the drink to ferment in before being tunned, or else in dairying for the making of whey.

klicker. One who stands at the door of a shop, to catch and bring in customers.

knappin hammer. Small hammer, 16 to 20 ounces in weight, used in breaking stones to lay on highways.

knead cowl. Alternative name for **dough cowl** *q.v.*, a cooler used in baking.

kneading trough. Four-sided wooden vessel for kneading dough or butter.

kneestrads. Pieces of leather fastened to the knees to protect them from the ladder, worn by thatchers.

knight service. Under the feudal system, the military service which a knight was bound to render as a condition of holding his lands; hence, the tenure of land under the condition of performing military service. Could also involve duties at his lord's castle for a fixed number of days per year.

knobstick wedding. Wedding of a pregnant woman, compelled by the churchwardens and attended by them in state. So called from the staves which were their badge of office.

knock knobbler. Person who perambulates the church during divine service to keep order, often called a **dog whipper** *q.v.*

knotchel/notchel. In phrase to **cry (one) notchel**, to proclaim publicly that one will not be responsible for debts incurred by the person named.

knotter. Strainer in paper-making, for removing knots and foreign matter from paper pulp.

knowledge money. Gift from tenants to a new bishop or abbot.

known land. Unenclosed land marked out by **meer** *q.v.* stones or natural boundaries to indicate ownership.

kylne/kiln. Usually a kiln for malt, and consisting of a tall wooden frame with a hair cloth covering the top on which the malt was laid to dry. The fire beneath was usually made of burning straw, which produced less smoke than other fuels and therefore did not taint the malt.

kylpe. *See* **pot cilp**.

kymes. Part of a harrow.

kymnell. Wood trough for kneading dough before baking.

kyrchiffe/kerchief. Cloth used to cover the head.

L

labour rate. Device for employing the able-bodied poor.

lac. Deep-red resinous substance, used as a dye in the manufacture of varnish, sealing-wax etc.

lacein. Probably a leather cord on which a sword was hung.

lace/lack pepper. Inferior or black pepper.

lacleape. *See* **leap**.

ladder. Flight of shelves, particularly for storing cheese.

lade gorn/pail. Pail with a long handle to ladle out water.

ladgen. To close the seams of wooden vessels which have opened from draught, so as to make them hold water.

ladingle piggine. Utensil for transferring liquid; bailer.

lagger. Narrow strip of ground in Gloucestershire.

laine. In the south of England, open field.

lairstall/leystall. Grave inside a church.

lairstone. Stone placed over a grave inside a church.

laith(e). 1. barn for livestock, grain etc.; a granary.
2. administrative division of a shire in Kent.

lake. Kind of fine linen. Shirts were formerly made from it.

lake/liche wake. Ceremony of watching a corpse prior to burial.

lammas lands. Half-year lands *q.v.*, common land, arable or meadow, occupied in **severalty** *q.v.* for part of the year, but after the crop was taken, pasturable by the severalty owners and others; usually open to pasture on Lammas Day (1 August) or Old Lammas (12 August). Sometimes called **half severals**, 'several' being opposite to 'common'. Meadow ground was often allotted when the grass was ready to cut on a system which meant that each man's hay came from different ground each year.

lamp black. Pigment consisting of almost pure, finely divided carbon, made by collecting the soot produced by burning oil.

lanchett. *See* **landshare**.

landiron. Metal grid for supporting burning logs in the kitchen hearth.

landlouper. Person who flies from the country because of crime or debt.

landmale. Reserved rent, or annual sum of money, charged upon a piece of land by the Chief Lord of the **Fee** *q.v.*, or a subsequent mesne owner.

landry box. Box at the top of a set of pumps, into which water is delivered.

lands. *See* **selions**.

land scores. Small quantity of enclosed land allotted out for tillage. Before generalised enclosure the greatest part of the country lay in common, only some parcels about the villages and the **land scores** being enclosed.

landshare/lantchett/lynche. *See* **balk**; the word is connected with the 'lynchets' characteristic of Celtic agriculture.

land tax. Tax levied rate fashion from 1692 upon various counties, each of which had to apportion its share among its constituent parishes. It was made permanent but redeemable in 1797–8, upon a very inequitable basis and was still payable upon lands which had not been compounded for. It was assessed by local commissioners and gathered by the petty constables.

lanebegot. A bastard.

lanes/laynes. The iron rings at the end of a plough to which horses were yoked.

lang quartered. Applied to shoes made with the quarter or upper part lengthened so as to leave an unusually long open space towards the toe, with a corresponding short vamp, in order to display the stocking in front.

lang saddle. *See* **long saddle**.

lanier. Thong of leather; lash of a whip.

lanill. *See* **flannel**.

lanscot. Assessment of lands for the maintenance of the church.

lantchett. *See* **landshare**.

lanthorn. Variation of 'lantern'; a transparent case e.g. of horn, enclosing and protecting a light.

lap stone. Stone on which a shoemaker beats his leather.

laspani. A toll exacted in 1279 for pasturing on the common.

last. 1. measure, equalling 10,000, used in the sale of herrings. Also a weight estimated at 4,000 lbs, but varying according to

different commodities.
2. mould of the human foot in wood on which boots and shoes are shaped, or repaired.

latchets. Thong or lace fastening a shoe.

lath. Barn.

latten. Mixed metal of yellow colour, either identical with or closely resembling brass, often hammered into thin sheets; especially as:
1. **black latten, latten brass**, milled brass in thin plates or sheets, used by braziers and for drawing into wire.
2. **shaven latten**, a thinner kind than black.
3. **roll latten**, latten polished on both sides, ready for use.
4. **white latten**, iron tinned over, tin-plate. It was still used for spoons, but replaced for pots and pans by brass.

laund iron. Laundry iron, a smoothing iron.

laver. Vessel, basin or cistern for hand washing; in early use chiefly a metal water-jug, occasionally a pan or bowl.

lawless parson. Cleric willing to marry couples at uncannonical times and places.

lay/ley. 1. variant of levy or rate.
2. land ploughed for several years, and then put under grass for a period, then ploughed again, and so on.

laying stool. Stool of peculiar form on which sheep or pigs were laid when killed or being killed by butcher.

laynes. *See* **lanes**.

lazy keufs. Dog tongs, used for the removal of ill-behaved dogs from church during a service. The tongs had a scissor-like movement with short spikes at the end to catch the dog around the throat so it could be removed. There is a pair in the church of Clynnog Fawr, North Wales.

lea. Measure of yarn, 300 yards.

leach troughs. At the salt works in Staffordshire, troughs in which the brine was set to evaporate after the corned salt was removed from it. The resultant leach brine was preserved and reboiled as the best and strongest brine.

lead. 1. main household water container, kept indoors or outdoors. Also known as a **cistern** or **sewstern**.
2. vat or cistern used for brewing.

leading. Carting to and from the fields.

12. *Lazy keufs* or dog tongs. This photograph shows the pair that hang on the wall in the south transept of St. Bueno, an early sixteenth century church in Clynnog Fawr, Gwynedd, North Wales. The instrument is believed to date from 1815.

league. Itinerary measure of distance, varying in different countries, but usually estimated as about 3 miles, or 1½ miles in medieval period.

leap. As **bare leap**, an open basket; as **lacleape**, a woven basket.

lea sand. Whetting stone with which a scythe was sharpened.

lease/leas. 1. quantity of wheat from which impurities had been removed prior to threshing.
2. common West Country form of lease, for an unstipulated number of lives, for a period not usually exceeding 99 years provided that those named in the lease survived to the end of its term; in practice 'extra lives' could be added upon payment of an entry fine.

leasehold tenure. Tenure held for a term of years, or for life, or for up to three lives, or for a period designated by the landlord. In a **lease** *q.v.* covering three lives, the names of three persons would be recorded, possibly the reason why more than one son had the same Christian name.

leaven. Raising agent; yeast.

leawne. Levy or rate, especially in Shropshire and the neighbouring counties.

ledge. The bar of a gate, style, etc. *See also* **ledger.**

ledger. A horizontal slab of stone; a horizontal bar of a scaffold. A door made of three or four upright boards, fastened by cross pieces, was called a **ledger door.**

leech way. Path along which the dead were carried to be buried.

lees. Winter feed for cattle.

leet. *See* **court leet.**

lef silver. Composition paid in money by the tenants in the wealds of Kent to their lord for leave to plough and sow in time of **pannage** *q.v.*

leger book. Monastic cartulary.

legget. Kind of tool used by reed thatchers.

leister/lister. Trident or pronged spear for striking and taking fish, chiefly salmon. *See also* **auger.**

Lent corn. Spring wheat.

Lent grain. Spring barley, oats or peas, but not, usually, wheat.

Lent tillin. Spring planted crops.

lese/leas. To gather, to select. In Devon picking stones from the surface of the fields was called **leasing**; and throughout the Western counties the word was used for gleaning corn.

letters close. *See* **close rolls.**

letters patent. Document under the seal of the State, granting some property privilege or authority, or conferring the exclusive right to use an invention or design. The original letters were issued 'open', with the **Great Seal** *q.v.* pendant at the bottom. The royal document enabled persons to make appeal in churches for charity.

lewis. Machine to raise stones.

lewn. Tax, rate or **lay** *q.v.* for church or parish dues.

ley. *See* **lay.**

leystall. *See* **lairstall.**

leywrite. Fine due from a medieval **villein** *q.v.* to his lord if his unmarried daughter became pregnant. This was to compensate for the depreciation of her manorial value.

liberty. 1. the district in which miners search for ore. Derbyshire

had several liberties with slightly differing laws and customs.
2. a group of manors or sub-division thereof; strictly speaking a
privileged area whence the sheriff was excluded, and where the
lord has the return of writs.

liche wake. *See* **lake wake.**

lidgitt. Swing gate, set up between meadow or pasture, ploughed
land or across the highway to prevent cattle from straying.

lief coup. Sale or market of goods in the place where they stand.

lientall. A number of masses said or sung for the souls of the
departed; believed to be 50.

lie-trowe. Lye trough, a stone trough for **lye** *q.v.*

Lifting Monday. Hocktide Monday, when it was the custom for
men, in couples, to lift up and kiss each woman they met.

Lifting Tuesday. When women returned the compliment to the
men. *See above.*

light. Stipendiary endowment in the pre-Reformation church.

limbeck/alembic. Apparatus formerly used in distilling.

limber. Cart shaft.

linchet/linch. Turf between two strips of arable land in a common
field, such as a **balk** *q.v.*, a terrace.

lind/linden. One of the trees from which charcoal was made. Also
called 'lime tree'.

line man. Person who takes land for a single season for the
purpose of growing flax.

linen. Thread or cloth made from flax.

lingel. Shoemaker's wax end and sewing thread. The lingel end is
the point of the waxed thread. It is tipped with a birce (hog's
bristle) so that it can be pushed through the elshin (awl) holes
in the leather. 'Stripping the deed' is a term used by
shoemakers for the act of removing the birce from a sewn-up
thread in order to use it over again in preparing a new wax end.

linhay. Open shed attached to a farmyard. When it is attached to a
barn or house it is called a **hanging linhay.**

lining(s). 1. often a mis-spelling of **linen** *q.v.*
2. items of underwear worn one on each leg.

linsey. More correctly **linseywoollsey**: a mixed fabric of wool and
linen, or wool and flax, or inferior wool, used for furnishings
and clothing for the poorer classes.

liripipe/liripoop. 1. the point of a hood, sometimes elongated by fashion.

2. the bottom part of a graduate's academic hood.

litany stool/desk. A low movable prayer desk at which a minister kneels while reciting the litany. Also known as a **faldstool** *q.v.*

litgate. Gate with a wooden latch at the end of a path or road.

litten. Churchyard.

livery. 1. distinctive clothing bestowed by an employer on his household retinue.

2. dress peculiar to a certain group.

3. supply of food given out at stated intervals to horses etc.

livery cupboard. 1. cupboard for keeping clothes.

2. cupboard with perforated doors for the storage of food.

3. cupboard used for bread and wine in sleeping quarters.

livery table. A large side table, or one on which a **livery cupboard** *q.v.* was placed.

load. Measure of lead ore made of nine dishes and weighing about five cwt; also a measure of wood weighing about two cwt. It would vary between three and a half and four loads to a ton. Both measures were of volume rather than weight, and derived from the horse load, the amount that would commonly be carried by a single pack horse.

lode/lodd. Load; sometimes used specifically of 36 trusses of hay each weighing 56 pounds.

loeginge beade. Lodging bed, probably for the accommodation of workers living-in.

Long Parliament. A parliament which assembled in November 1640, and was dissolved by Cromwell in April 1653.

long/lang saddle. Long wooden seat with a high back and ends.

looags. *See* **hoggers**.

loom/lowm. 1. implement or tool of any kind; an open bucket.

2. machine for weaving.

3. heir-loom, chattels left to the heir under a will.

lord. 1. owner of a mineral liberty who receives the **lot** *q.v.* and usually also the **cope** *q.v.*

2. **lord of the manor**. By the time of Domesday Book (1086) the manorial system was established throughout most of the country, and can be described as a territorial unit originally held by feudal tenure — held by a landlord, not necessarily

titled, who himself was a tenant of the Crown or of a mesne lord who held land directly of the Crown. By right a **lord of the manor** could hold a court for his local tenants. This was the **court baron** *q.v.* Many manorial lords also had the right to hold a **court leet** *q.v.* There might be more than one manor within parish boundaries, and many manors overlapped from one parish into the next. If the lord was an ecclesiastic, the court was usually held in one of the episcopal or conventual buildings.

3. **lord of harvest**. A subordinate employee, chosen by the owner of the corn. He set positions, issued gloves, kept strictly the rest hours and close of work of the labourers. He also arranged the team work.

lordship. Liberty or manor.

lord's meer. Length of vein laid out by the barmaster for the lord who receives all the ore obtained from it, or makes special arrangements with the miners.

lot. 1. church rate.

2. the share of the ore belonging to the lord, usually every thirteenth dish though he may take anything from the tenth to the twenty-fifth, according to the liberty and other circumstances, measured at reckonings every six weeks or so.

lot meadow. Common meadow, the several occupation of which was determined every year or every two or three years by the casting of lots among a limited number of proprietors.

low bed. Truckle bed.

lowm. *See* **loom**.

Luddite. One of a group of factory labourers and peasants who from 1811 deliberately destroyed knitting frames and farm machinery in the Midlands and north of England. They derived their name from one Ned Ludd. The Luddite riots were severely repressed by the government, 17 men being executed in 1813.

lumber. Disused articles of furniture and the like, useless odds and ends.

lune. Rate, especially in Cheshire and the neighbouring counties.

lurched. Crowded out.

lutestring. Glossy silk fabric.

lye. Alkaline solution derived from wood ash, formerly used instead of soap (formerly a rare and expensive commodity) to wash linen. *See also* **lye dropper.**

lye dropper. Wooden box or trough with holes in its base, balanced on top of a tub with a layer of drainage — twigs or gravel — arranged at the bottom of the dropper. The drainage material was then covered with a cloth, and topped up with wood ash. Water was poured slowly over the ash and, as it trickled through to the tub beneath, it took with it the alkaline salts from the ash. The resulting liquid was **lye** *q.v.*, used for washing clothes.

lyme. Lime pit, used by tanners.

lynche. *See* **landshare.**

lyne wheel. Wheel for spinning flax.

lyn line. The fibre of flax. Hence **linen** *q.v.*

lyntelles. Lentils; like peas only smaller and yellow.

M

mace. 1. dried outer covering of nutmeg.
2. originally a club armed with iron, and used in war. Both sword and mace are signs of dignity, suited to the times when men went about in armour, and sovereigns needed champions to vindicate their rights.
3. symbol of the Speaker's authority in the House of Commons.

Mace Monday. The first Monday after St. Anne's Day, 26 July, so called in some places on account of a ceremony performed, possibly connected with Rushbearing (where garlands or rushes were carried to the church).

madder. Ground root of *Rubia Tinctorum* used for producing red dye.

madning money. Old Roman coins, sometimes found around Dunstable, and so called by the local people.

mag. Halfpenny.

Magna Carta. The Charter sealed by King John at Runnymede in June 1215 at the insistence of his barons.

maid. Clothes horse.

maiden. 1. wooden instrument consisting of a long handle with wooden feet, by means of which clothes are stirred about in a washing tub. Also called **peggy** *q.v.* or **dolly**.
2. two upright standards which supported the driving wheel of a spinning wheel. The term **maiden** was also applied to a little tripod with a fixed vertical spindle at the top. The bobbin or **pirn** *q.v.* taken from a spinning wheel ran loosely on the spindle and allowed the thread to be wound off.

mail pillion. Stuffed leather cushion used to carry luggage on horseback.

main of cocks. Match involving teams of fighting cocks.

mainpast. One for whom another is legally responsible.

mainpernors. *See* **mainprise**.

mainport. Small tribute, usually of bread loaves, paid in some parishes to the rector in lieu of certain tithes.

mainprise. Writ directed to the sheriff commanding him to take sureties called **mainpernors** for the prisoner's appearance, and to let him go at large; deliverance of a prisoner on security for his appearance on a day appointed.

malt mill. Hand-operated mill for grinding malt before brewing.

manadge man. Itinerant vendor of goods on credit for household requirements. In Newcastle sometimes called a **Scotch draper**.

managed house (public). One whose licensee is merely the wage-earning or salaried employee of the brewery company which owns or leases the premises.

Manchester ware. Goods manufactured for the Manchester markets.

manchet. Small loaf of very fine white flour.

mandamus. Order of the crown to a public officer to perform his particular duty.

mandilion/mandeville. Kind of loose garment without sleeves, or if with sleeves, having them hanging at the back.

mandrell/maundrell. Pick, sharp-pointed at each end, used for getting coal.

manger. Box or trough in a stable or cowhouse, from which horses and cattle eat.

mankeing. Rake for getting ashes out of bread oven.

manner. Manure.

manor. Land belonging to a lord; a unit of land in feudal times over which the owner had full jurisdiction.

mantle. Overcoat, cover, blanket or cloth for covering.

mantle tree. Piece of timber or stone supporting the masonry above a fireplace. Originally could have been the trunk of a tree.

mantyr/mantua. Woman's loose-fitting gown.

manuel rente. Money paid for a commuted feudal service.

manumission. The act of a feudal lord that gave a **villein** *q.v.* his freedom.

march. Border of a country, especially of Scotland and Wales with England. Can also mean a kind of boundary, such as **march dyke**.

Marcherlord. One of the petty rulers who lived in the Marches, enjoying royal liberties with exclusive jurisdiction over territory often obtained by border warfare. Abolished Act 27 Hen. VIII, c.26 (1535–6).

maritagium. Old feudal right by which a lord had the legal right to choose a husband for an heiress.

mark. Medieval unit of currency. In England, after the Conquest (1066), the ratio of 20 sterling pennies to an ounce was the basis of computation; hence the value of a mark became fixed at 160 pennies = 13s 4d. Thus half mark = 6s 8d.

marl. Kind of soil consisting principally of clay mixed with carbonate of lime, forming a loose unconsolidated mass, valuable as a fertilizer.

marling. Process of manuring with marl.

Marriage Acts. After Act 10 Anne, c.10 (1711) the marriage register books used had to contain numbered and ruled pages. Lord Hardwicke's Marriage Act 26 Geo. II, c.33 (1754) recognised as valid only those marriages contracted following the calling of banns, or a licence, which took place in the parish church of one of the parties. However marriages were accepted as legal if performed abroad.

The George Rose Act 52 Geo. III, c.146 (1812) laid down that there should be separate registers kept for births, marriages and burials.

The Marriage Act 4 Geo. IV, c.76 (1823) recognised clandestine marriages which had been performed without the calling of banns or a licence, but the minister who officiated was declared a felon.

marriage debts. It was believed if a man took his future wife out of her home by way of a window, she being naked, or only in a shift, then he would be free from her debts after the marriage.

marrow/marra. Comrade, close friend, workfellow, or pair of things; an equal.

marsh. Tract of low lying land, flooded in winter and usually more or less watery throughout the year.

Martlemass beef. Beef dried in the chimney, like bacon, so called because it was usual to kill the beast for this purpose about the feast of St. Martin, 11th November.

mashfatt/vat. Tub in which malt is mashed, i.e. mixed with hot water to form the wort in the first stages of brewing.

mashing stick. Stick used to stir the malt in the mash vat.

maslin/mashlegen. Mixed corn, usually wheat and rye; sometimes the grains were grown as a mixed crop, sometimes grown separately, and mixed after threshing.

maslin (kettle). Pan used for boiling fruit or ham and made of ordinary brass or tinned copper.

maslin ware. Utensils made from brass-like metal.

masor/mazer. 1. hard wood used as material for drinking cups.
2. bowl, cup or goblet without a foot, originally made of mazer wood (maple wood), sometimes ornamented with silver; could be wholly of metal.

master of the parish. *See* **selectman**.

mat/matt. Thick sheet, often made of rushes, laid on **cords** *q.v.* stretched across a bed frame under the mattress.

mattock. Kind of pick-axe with one end of the blade arched and flattened at right angles to the handle.

maul. Heavy hammer or club, used as a weapon.

maund. Wicker basket with handles.

maundrell. *See* **mandrell**.

mazerine/mazereen. Pie-plate.

meal house. Variant of **bolting-house** *q.v.*

meat. 1. substantial subject matter of good quality.
2. a utensil used for cooking meat.

meat stool. Stand on which meat is placed, for cutting; also on which the animal might be killed.

medale. Drinking feast after lord of the manor's meadow is mown.

medylsomes. The cords or traces extending from the first to the last of a team of oxen in a plough team.

meer/meere/mear. 1. boundary bank or hedge dividing **furlong** from **furlong** *q.v.* or field from field in open field agriculture, as distinct from **balk** *q.v.* which in some places, though not all, was used of a bank dividing **selion** *q.v.* from **selion**. In some districts **balk** *q.v.* and **meer** are used indiscriminately.
2. slide on which casks are discharged. It consists of two timbers apart like the sides of a ladder, between which the belly of the cask is held as it slides down lengthwise.
3. piece of timber that can be fixed so as to lengthen the leverage of the large **gavelock** *q.v.* used in quarry work.
4. in a lead mine, a measure of length of a vein varying in different **liberties** *q.v.*, 27, 28, 29, 30 or 32 yards.

meer, founder. **Meer** *q.v.* allocated to the discoverers of a vein in a lead mine (two **meers** were usually allocated).

meer, Lord's. Meer *q.v.* allocated to the **lord** *q.v.*, usually next to the **founder meer** *q.v.*

meer, taker. Name given to the remaining **meers** *q.v.*, allocated to any miner, after the allocation of the **founder meer** *q.v.* and **Lord's meer** *q.v.*

melder. Oatmeal when first ground, with all the dust and seeds together.

mele/meal chest. Chest for storing meal.

mell. Large mallet.

membrane. Sheet of parchment, made from the skin of an animal. The flesh side was called the 'face', and carried the main written entry. The hair side, was the 'back', or **dorse** *q.v.*

mendicant. Begging friar.

mense penny. Liberality conducted by prudence. A choice coin kept in the pocket so that the bearer was never without money.

menseful penny. The money spent at an inn in return for the use of the house as a place of resort, when the country folk come into the town.

mercery/mercenary. As applied to country trade, all kinds of linen, woollen and silk fabrics, as well as groceries.

merchet. Payment, in medieval times due from a **villein** *q.v.* to his lord when he sold a beast, gave his daughter in marriage, or sent his son outside the manor to school.

mercy. Amercement or fine.

meresman. Parish officer who attended to the roads, bridges and water courses.

merrybauks. In Derbyshire, a cold posset.

merrybegot. Illegitimate child.

mese. Another term for **messuage** *q.v.*

messel. Person afflicted with leprosy.

messor. Manorial official overseeing reapers and mowers.

messuage. Dwelling house and its appurtenances, i.e. outbuildings, garden and in some instances land.

met. 1. measure.
   2. **stroke met**, half-bushel measure.
   3. **mett poak**, a two-bushel sack.
   4. Anglo-Saxon measure equal to a **bushel** *q.v.*

mickell. Much, as in 'little and **mickell**'.

midden. *See* **mixen**.

middling. Of medium quality or size.

midgy. *See* **mistress**.

mild/milled. Pressed, rolled and fulled; used of cloth, thickened by rolling or beating.

mile. Measure of distance variable in the sixteenth century, the average length being 2140 yards. The standard mile of 1760 yards was laid down in 1593.

militia. Old constitutional force of the country, corresponding more or less to the territorial army. Counties and parishes were informed as to how many men they must provide and were fined if they did not produce their proper quota. Each parish raised its share by the method it preferred, generally by ballot, or by offering bounties for volunteers. Normally the militia arrangements in each parish were in the charge of the constable.

millhouse. Building in which milling or grinding was carried on; sometimes called a **quern house**.

mill money. French method of striking coins with a screw-press. The term **mill money** is derived from the use of water or horse-mills to supply power for the machinery, which consisted of a rolling-press for rolling out the metal to the required thickness, a cutting-punch, and a screw press for stamping with the dies. The mill coins were superior to the hammered money. First minted in England in 1561. (Also known as **milled money** which is a misnomer.)

mill peck. Kind of hammer with two chisel heads, used for deepening the grooves of the millstones.

mill staff. Flat piece of wood, rubbed with ruddle, by which the accuracy of the work done by the **mill peck** *q.v.* may be tested.

milpuff. Kind of flock used for stuffing mattresses.

mine royal. Mine containing gold or silver to a value greater than that of the associated base metals.

misericord. 1. small projection underneath a hinged seat in the choir stall giving support to the occupant when standing.
2. small dagger used by medieval knights for giving the final, fatal blow to a wounded foe.

mistress. Oblong box without a front, carried upright, for carrying a lighted candle or small lamp in a current of air; used by drivers on the main airways or ventilating passages in a coal mine. Also called a **midgy**.

mistress (Mrs). Courtesy title for women of the status corresponding to that of men addressed as 'Mr.', but throughout the seventeenth century applied both to married and unmarried women, and even through the eighteenth century to spinsters of mature age, as a mark of respect.

mixen/midden. Fold for keeping manure or compost.

mixt/mixed. Not pure.

mob. Close-fitting cap with two lappets; a woman's night-cap.

mockade/mockado. Piled cloth of silk and wool, or silk and linen, sometimes called 'mock velvet'.

mock of the church. Banns called but not followed by a wedding. Often customarily fineable by the churchwardens.

modus. Shortened form of *modus decimandi*, a customary fixed payment in lieu of tithing in kind.

moety/moity. Half share.

molasses. Syrup obtained from sugar in the process of refining; similar to a thick black treacle, and much cheaper than the cheapest sugar. Used in cooking (for things like gingerbread), and in medicine. Brimstone and treacle was a favourite country laxative into the 20th century.

monkey. *See* **prijel**.

montero. Close-fitting hood with which travellers preserved their faces and heads from frostbite and weather in winter.

monteth/monteith. Punch-bowl manufactured with notches around its edge for holding drinking vessels.

months mind. Memorial service for the dead, performed a month after the death. Legacies for the provision of candles for this ceremony were often mentioned in pre-Reformation wills.

mooter. *See* **mouter**.

mophrey. Type of cart.

moringe axe. Two-edged axe used for uprooting the stumps of trees; a pick-axe.

morther. Mortar.

mortmain. An inalienable bequest; the holding of land by a corporation or, as formerly, by a monastery, which cannot be transferred to new ownership. **Statutes of Mortmain**: acts passed as in Edward I's time, prohibiting the leaving of property to religious houses as a means of avoiding death-duties.

mortuary. Customary payment to the priest on death, usually of the second-best animal; often not made because there was no second animal.

Moseley's dole. Ancient and unusual charity which did not survive the activities of the Charity Commissioners in the early 19th century. This was the distribution on Epiphany Eve of one penny to every inhabitant of the town of Walsall and some of its adjacent hamlets, including not only permanent residents but also any visitor who was staying there. According to a long-lived tradition, Thomas Moseley, who in the 15th century was Lord of the Manor of Bascot in Warwickshire, heard a child crying for bread in a Walsall Street on the eve of Epiphany, and vowed that no person in that town should ever want for bread on that day again. It was paid until 1825.

mothergate. In a coal pit, the continuation of the **rolley-way** *q.v.* into the workings; or the place in the workings that will at a future period be converted into a rolley-way.

motte. Mound of earth, sometimes surmounted by a castle, hence 'motte and bailey' castle.

moulding plough. Hand implement. It has a small circular plough of steel at the end of a long handle, and is used to throw up earth around potatoes etc.

mould screen. Cloche or garden-frame.

mouter/mooter/mowter/multure. Toll consisting of a proportion of the grain carried, or the flour made, to the proprietor or tenant of a mill for the privilege of having corn ground at his mill. The miller would take a quart for grinding a **bushel** *q.v.*, or a bushel for grinding a **quarter** *q.v.* Two different **multures** were formerly used — the 'gowpenful', that is two handsful, and the 'handful', a term which explains itself. Each mill had its own scale of charges.

mouter dish. Round, concave, wooden dish about seven inches in diameter.

mow. Rick.

muckdrag. Muck fork with tines at right angles for dragging manure out of the cart.

mudcroom. Tool used by water workers. A large hook with three flat prongs, and a stout long wooden handle.

mudfang. 1. the earth in which a hedge grows, and about two feet on each side.
2. **right of mudfang**: right of the owner of a hedge dividing two properties to a certain portion of land, usually two feet wide, in which the roots of the hedge grow.

multure. *See* **mouter.**

muncorn. Mixed grain, often wheat and rye sown together.

murage. Tax levied for the building and upkeep of the walls in a town.

muslin. General name for the most delicately woven fabric.

mustard ball. Leaden ball used in bruising mustard seeds etc.

mynge. In phrase **in mynge and undivided** 'intermingled and unenclosed'; used in connection with arable lands in the common fields of a manor.

Misericord. A small projection underneath a hinged seat in the choir stalls which allowed the occupant to rest when standing through long services. This one was found in Beaumaris church, North Wales.

N

nackers. Lambs' testicles, which were often made into pies.

nag/nagg. Small horse.

nail. 1. measure of beef, weighing eight pounds.
2. measure of length of cloth equal to two and a quarter inches, or a sixteenth part of a yard.

naile tool. Instrument for making nails, or else gimlets, often known as nail-passers.

nail passer. Gimlet or bradawl.

naked. The note in burial register when the corpse was unshrouded and the coffin unlined. A corpse was buried **naked** because the family could not afford the expense of a woollen shroud, or the payment of a fine for using any other type of cloth.

nam. Piece of land taken into tillage when it would ordinarily have remained outside, either because it was part of the fallow field, or because it was part of the outfield.

nan's/nun's thread. Fine white sewing cotton, sometimes called ounce thread, such as was used by nuns. Also known as 'sisters' thread'. Celia Finnes at the end of the seventeenth century visited Queen Camell in Somerset and recorded that the place was famous for a 'fine ring of bells and for the fine sort of *brown* thread called Nun's thread'.

nape/nepe. Piece of wood with three feet, used to support the fore part of a loaded waggon.

nare. *See* **nave**.

native/nativi. Villein *q.v.* by birth.

nave. 1. central part or block of a wheel, into which the end of the axle-tree is inserted, and from which the spokes radiate. 2. prop to support the shaft of a cart, sometimes misspelt as **nare**.

neat/neast. Cattle, generally oxen or cows.

neck-verse. Latin verse printed in black letters (usually the beginning of the Psalm 51) formerly set before a criminal claiming **benefit of clergy** *q.v.*, by the reading of which he might save his neck and secure trial by ecclesiastical rather than secular authorities.

nepe. *See* **nape.**

nephew. This meant a grandson, descendant or kinsman, until the end of the seventeenth century.

nesp. To pick off the ends of gooseberries.

new sixpences. Coins with milled edges produced on screw-presses, following the re-coinage of 1696; contrasted with **old money** *q.v.*

New Style Calendar. The **Gregorian Calendar**, which replaced the **Julian Calendar** or **Old Style Calendar** *q.v.* It was introduced in Italy in 1582 but was not adopted in Britain until 1752, by which date Britain was 11 days behind the rest of Europe. *See also* page 249.

nick(ing). Cutting a notch in a stick; the means by which the lead miners in Derbyshire kept a reckoning. Also used in the West Riding coal fields of Yorkshire. Failure to work a mine allowed another miner to claim it, by asking the barmaster to nick the stowes. Three nickings allowed the mine to be forfeited and to be handed over to the claimant, unless excess water or lack of ventilation prevented the mine being worked.

niece. Usually a descendant, either male or female, but occasionally may refer to any younger relative.

niggard. False bottom for a grate, to reduce fuel consumption.

nine. Indefinite period between a week and a fortnight.

noble. Gold coin worth 6s 8d.

noggin. Small drinking vessel, sometimes holding a quarter of a pint.

nomansland. Variant of **jack's land** *q.v.*

nones. Ecclesiastical office said at the ninth hour — about 3 p.m. but sometimes earlier.

notary hole. Pigeon-hole.

notary (public). Commissioner for Oaths; commonly abbreviated to 'N.P.'.

notchel. *See* **knotchel.**

nothus. Bastard. Strictly the 'base' child of a gentleman by a plebeian mother, or according to other authorities, the 'base' child of a married woman. Actually in many parishes used indiscriminately of all illegitimate children.

Novel Disseisin, Assize of. One of the assizes instituted by Henry II. It provided a summary remedy when a freeholder had been unjustly dispossessed of his holding.

nuncupative. Will declared verbally.

nun's thread. *See* **nan's thread.**

nurse children. Very young children or babies, sent to the country, ostensibly for the sake of the country air. Parish registers recorded many deaths as 'nurse children', usually buried unnamed, which affords conjecture as to the real motives of the parents. The supposed care of them would now be termed 'baby farming'.

O

oakum. Loose fibre, obtained by untwisting and picking old ropes, an employment of convicts and workhouse inmates; used in caulking ship's seams and in stopping up leaks. *See* **old ropes**.

obit. Service of remembrance for one dead, usually kept annually, but sometimes monthly. Also called a **yeremind**.

ocemer/occamy. Alloy meant to resemble silver. It is very likely that the constituent metals were copper, tin and zinc as used in the manufacture of brass but that the tin was present in particularly high proportion. The word is a corruption of 'alchemy'.

october. Ale brewed in that month.

odd man. Labourer employed and paid by the day.

odd mark. One third of the arable land of a farm; thus if a farm comprised 150 acres under tillage it was divided, according to the old mode of husbandry, into three equal parts: one fallow, one under wheat, and a third under **Lent grain** *q.v.*; the **odd mark** applies to the fallow.

offal. 1. bran or mixed corn, undressed. 2. waste cuts of leather.

offold bars. Possibly offal, used in the sense of an item of very little value.

offold wood. Waste wood; small pieces of wood.

old money. Money produced before the recoinage of 1696.

old rope. Old tarry rope picked to create **oakum** *q.v.* or tow.

Old Style Calendar. The **Julian Calendar** method (before 1752) of reckoning time, the year consisting of 365 days 6 hours. Replaced by the **Gregorian** or **New Style Calendar** *q.v. See also* page 249.

oliver. Tilt hammer used in the north Derbyshire lead industry.

olive wood. Wood from the olive tree. Capable of taking a high polish, it was accordingly valued in ornamental woodwork.

on. Shortened version of 'one' wherever it precedes a named item in inventories.

on stand. Rent paid by the outgoing to the incoming tenant for such land as the former had rightfully cropped before he left the farm.

oont. *See* **want**.

open parishes. 1. those in which open fields and/or commons still remained.

2. those in which, generally because of lax administration of the poor law, or wide distribution of land and cottage ownership, settlement could readily be gained.

open tide. In early use, the time between Epiphany and Ash Wednesday, when marriages were publicly solemnised; later, in Oxfordshire and several other parts of the country, the time after harvest when cattle might be turned into the open fields.

open vestry. *See* **vestry, open**.

oppen gilt. Female pig before having a litter. Called by this name until after the second litter, when she was called a sow.

ordinary. 1. the set meal, as it were *table d'hote*, especially in the inn of a market town.

2. ecclesiastical superior of any kind: archbishop, bishop or archdeacon.

13. *Ordinary* or a meal at an inn.

osiers/withies. Shoots or rods of willow.

ouset. Few small cottages together, like a Highland clachan. The word is originally Oustead, one stead, i.e. one farm house and its appurtenances standing alone with no other near it.

out bounders. Word used in old parochial account books in Sussex for rate payers who pay rates in a parish where they do not reside.

outfangthief. Right of a lord of the manor to pursue a thief beyond his own jurisdiction, to bring him back for trial, and keep forfeited goods if he was convicted.

outmarks & inmarks. Boundaries to land, hedges, fences etc.

overlaying. Practice of allowing more animals to graze on the common than the pasture would maintain.

overseer of the highways. *See* **waywarden.**

overseer of the poor. The principal parish officer concerned with the administration of the Poor Law from 1601 until after 1834, when the duties of the **overseers** were given to the Guardians of the Poor, and the **overseers** became assessors and collectors. The office was abolished by the Rating and Valuation Act 1928 15 & 16 Geo. V, c.90 (1924/5).

owler. A smuggler.

oxen. Bulls rendered docile and fit for farm service by being castrated.

oxgang, broad. Yardland.

oxgang, narrow. Originally the area of land cultivable by one ox, half a yardland, or one-eighth of a ploughland. Later a conventional unit varying widely from parish to parish (and even within the same parish), from perhaps ten to 25 acres.

P

pace/paste board. Head dress called a 'paste' because it was fashioned from pasteboard or cardboard.

packnell. Probably a pack saddle.

Pack Rag Day. Old May Day; so called because servants being hired from Old May Day to Old May Day, pack up their rags and clothes on this day preparatory to leaving for home or fresh places of work.

pack saddle. Saddle for supporting the load to be carried by a pack animal.

packthread. Stout thread used for sewing, or tying up packs.

pack way. Narrow way by which goods could be conveyed only on pack horses.

pad. *See* **panel**.

Paddington fair. A public execution. Tyburn (where executions took place) is in the parish of Paddington.

paddle. 1. spade-like implement used for cleaning a plough.
2. **paddle-staff**, a long shaft with an iron spike at the end used for catching moles.

paid sitting. Payment made for the right to a pew in church.

painted cloths. Sheets of canvas with pictures painted on them, used to keep out the draughts and hung on walls as decoration. A cheap substitute for tapestry.

palatinate. Territory under the rule of a count palatine, usually an earl or a bishop, who enjoyed royal privileges and exclusive jurisdiction in it.

pales. Stakes for fencing, frequently in **pails and rails**.

palimpsest. 1. sheet of parchment or paper that has been written on twice, the first writing having been erased.
2. memorial brass that has been taken up and engraved on the reverse side with another figure.

pallat/pallet bed. Straw bed; a mattress, a small, poor or mean bed or couch.

palm. Steel shield with holes in it like a thimble, and straps to fasten it on, applied to the palm of the hand for pushing the needle in mending sacks, sewing leather etc.

palmer. Name used to describe a pilgrim from the custom of pilgrims returning with palms as a testimony they had made the journey to the Holy Land.

panakin. Very small pan, commonly used to warm babies' food.

pancheon. Large cask for holding liquids.

panel/panell/pannell. 1. piece of cloth placed under a saddle to protect a horse's back from being chafed. Also known as a **pad.** 2. kind of saddle, particularly a wooden saddle for asses. 3. piece of wainscot.

pannage. Payment made by tenants to their lords for the right to pasture their pigs in the lord's woods; also the right itself.

pannell chest. Chest with linenfold panels.

panneres/panyers/panniers. Light baskets set on the back of a horse for carrying produce to market.

pannier man. Servant belonging to an inn of court whose office was to announce dinner.

pankine. Earthenware.

panniyarde. Small hand-basket or trug.

pansion/panshion. Large earthenware bowl used in making bread dough.

pantables/pantofles/patten. Used for various kinds of footwear, including: mules with toe uppers only, worn as overshoes; slipper, or sort of indoor slippers or loose shoes, sometimes applied to the high-heeled cork soled chopines; out-door overshoes or goloshes, in English use from 1570–1660, consisting of a wooden sole secured to the foot by a leather loop passing over the instep, and mounted on an iron oval ring, or similar device by which the wearer is raised an inch or two from the ground.

paper-cap. White cap, a kind of wrapping paper. The use of cap in words like foolscap does not start until the fifteenth century.

papers. Term for punishment of an offender by exhibiting him, maybe in a pillory, with papers pinned to him stating his offence.

paragen. Person, office or position of the highest excellence.

paragon. Material common in the seventeenth century, possibly a strong, sometimes watered, silk.

parcel. Quantity; often a small quantity of certain things.

parcel gilt. Partly gilded, usually on the inner surface of a vessel made of silver.

parcel makers. Two officers in the Exchequer who made out the parcels of escheator's accounts, and delivered them to one of the auditors of that court.

parcenary. In common law, the holding of lands undivided by two or more tenants, otherwise called co-partners. A tenure of Norman origin.

parcener. One who has an equal share in the inheritance of an ancestor; a joint heir.

parchment. 1. skin of a sheep or goat, prepared to be written upon.
2. document written on this skin.
3. any strong superior paper resembling the above.

parchment lace. Lace, braid or cord with a parchment core.

pargeting. Ornamental plasterwork especially on a timber-framed house.

paring spade. Pointed spade used for clearing stubble from land after harvest. It had one edge turned up, and a handle about eight feet long, fitted into a cross bar. This cross bar was supported by a leather thong put round the neck of the man who used the spade. He wore a pad and pushed the spade before him.

parish, civil. District for which a separate rate was, or may have been, levied.

parish clerk. Lay officer discharging minor duties connected with the church, and often wrongly entrusted with the entering up of the registers.

parish, ecclesiastical. Area of ground committed to the charge of one minister, including a church with full rights of sepulture etc.

parish priest. Properly, an unbeneficed clerk to whom the cure of souls is deputed by the parson; curate.

parish registers. Until 1752 the year began in March. **New Style Dating** *q.v.* In consequence parish registers took March as the first month of the year, and so some entries prior to 1752 are shown as 7ber for September; 8ber for October; 9ber for November; and 10ber for December.

parlour. 1. in the cottages of poor people, a ground-floor room. If there were two rooms on the ground floor the best room they lived in was called the **house** *q.v.*; the other was called the parlour, though often used as a bedroom.

2. in earlier times, a room for private conversation, or retirement. The common room in religious houses into which after dinner the religious withdrew for discourse or conversation.

3. the room for entertaining; where there were enough rooms the parlour had the function of the hall or dining room or the master's bedchamber, but never that of the kitchen.

parson. Properly, a rector; a vicar is not strictly speaking a parson, nor is an unbeneficed curate.

parterres. 1. ornamental arrangement of flower beds and paths in a garden, generally on level ground.

2. pit of a theatre.

partlett. Woman's neckerchief, collar or ruff.

paschal money. Levy originally for the cost of the paschal taper kept lighted from Easter to Holy Thursday, and lighted again at Whitsuntide. The levy was collected when the parishioners 'took their rights' — *see* **rights**.

pashe. Poker.

paste board. *See* **pace**.

patronage. Right of appointment to an ecclesiastical living.

patten. *See* **pantables**.

paulls. In Sussex etc., **selions** *q.v.*

pavement. Stone flagged indoor floor, or outdoor path.

pax bread. Small tablet with a representation of the crucifixion upon it, presented in the ceremony of the mass to be kissed by the faithful.

peace keeper. Minor official of the church.

peale/peel. Long-handled implement with a broad, flat end to draw bread from the oven. Sometimes a corruption of pail.

peasant. Countryman of relatively humble status, but often having some stake, great or small, in the land.

peck. 1. quarter of a **bushel** *q.v.*; two gallons.

2. raw skin of a sheep.

peculiar. Ecclesiastical district exempt from the jurisdiction of the bishop of the diocese.

ped. Obsolete word for a wicker pannier.

14. *Pedlar* and ballad-monger.

pedlar or petty chapman. Man or woman who travelled from place to place, selling small articles, such as lace, garters, pins, needles, bodkins, cottons and sometimes cloth. He also knew the latest gossip. The name comes from the **ped** or hamper he carried on his back.

peel. 1. cushion used in lace making.
2. square fortified tower, built for defence.
3. baker's stave made either of wood or iron, and anything up to eight feet in length with a paddle-shaped blade at one end. It was used for placing dough in baking ovens, and for removing the baked loaves.

peggy. 1. slender poker, with a small portion of the end bent at right angles for raking a fire together.
2. night light. Often made of sheep's fat, surrounding a wick formed from a stalk of lavender wrapped in cotton.
3. washing stick or ponce.

pelf. Property stolen or pilfered.

pell wool. Inferior wool, cut off after a sheep's death.

pennant/penent. Densely-compacted sandstone of Coal Measure age, much used as a building material in the south Gloucestershire area.

penny. Standard unit of currency from c. 775/780 A.D. The coinage of silver pennies for general circulation ceased with the reign of Charles II; a small number have since been regularly coined as Maundy money. Copper pennies began to be coined in 1797; copper halfpence and farthings were used from the time of Charles II.

pentecostals. Tax levied originally as **Peter's pence** *q.v.*, later paid by each parish church to the cathedral church of the diocese. Also known as **Romescot**.

peppercorn rent. Nominal rent, as the berry or fruit of the pepper-plant is of no value; something insignificant.

perambulation. Beating the bounds of the parish at Rogation tide. Also called **possessioning**.

perch. Measuring rod between 15 and 24 feet in length. The statute **perch** = 16½ feet, but there were many local variations, e.g. eight yards of hedging work in Leicestershire. Also known as **pole**, **roll** or **rod** *q.v.*

percher. Large wax candle, generally used for the altar.

perpent stone. 1. in the North of England, a thin wall constructed from stones set on edge.
2. large stone reaching through a wall so as to appear on both sides.

perpetual curate. Clerk holding cure of souls, though formerly not strictly speaking beneficed, in a parish or chapelry where there was no regularly endowed vicarage. Unlike a mere stipendiary curate, he was not removable at the caprice of his employer — in this case the impropriator; incumbent of a parochial chapelry, i.e. one having some rights of burial etc.

perpetuana. Kind of glossy cloth, generally called everlasting.

perse. Very fine deep blue/grey cloth, dyed only with woad, one of the more expensive dyes.

Persian silk. Thin, soft silk, used for linings.

Persian wheel. Large wheel with buckets fixed to the rim, for raising water sufficient for overflowing lands that border the banks of rivers, where the river lies too low to do this effectively.

peson. Instrument in the form of a staff, with balls or crockets, used for weighing before scales were employed.

pess. *See* **doss.**

pestall/pessell. Pestle, the instrument with which substances are pounded in a mortar.

peter boat. Boat built sharp at each end, and able to be moved either way.

Peter's pence. Old tribute of silver penny per household to support St Peter's, Rome; *see* **pentecostals.**

petrified kidneys. Kidney-shaped stones formerly used to pave the footpaths, and even now occasionally found in remote villages and small towns.

petty constable. *See* **constable.**

petty sessions. *See* **sessions, petty.**

pewter, garnish of. Full set of pewter platters, dishes, saucers and chargers, comprising 12 each of the first three items.

piccage/pickage. Payment to allow ground to be broken for a booth or stall.

pickadils. Armhole joins of a doublet hidden by padded rolls of material, or by tabs, and later by projections like epaulettes.

piddling. Process of sprinkling with drops of water; also, of a job: small and fidgety; of a thing: insignificant.

pie. Heap of potatoes covered with earth to preserve them from frost.

pie powder court. Court able to dispense instant justice at fairs and markets; often held in a building called a tolbooth or tolsey.

pier glass. Looking glass; designed so as to be placed on the wall space between windows, known architecturally as a 'pier'.

pig. 1. oblong block of cast lead with rounded ends produced by the ore hearth. Derbyshire **pigs** weighed between 300 and 315 lbs and were called **great pigs**; **half pigs** or **little pigs** were also cast at some mills. Lead produced by the ore hearth was called **pig lead**. Commonly eight **pigs** made one fother.
2. block of cast lead metal in the smelter's works.

piggin. Small wooden vessel or pail with one stave longer than the rest to serve as a handle.

pig, holding. Pig being kept for breeding.

pightle. Gore *q.v.*, or triangular piece of land, after enclosure; any small scrap of land, sometimes called **pigtail** or **pyke.**

pigtail. *See* **pightle.**

pike. *See* **fold bar.**

pike-evell. Pitchfork.

pike-wall. Gable wall converging to a point at the top.

pile mow. Wooden hammer used in fencing.

pillion. Saddle, especially a light one for a woman, or a special cushion attached to the rear of an ordinary saddle to enable a second person to ride a horse.

pillow. Slightly dish-shaped wooden block on which stone was placed for carving.

pillow beer. Pillow case or slip.

pin. Cask holding 4½ gallons of ale or beer. This is the smallest of the casks. Two **pins** = a **firkin** *q.v.* or nine gallons. Two firkins = a **kilderkin** *q.v.* or 18 gallons.

pin basket. Youngest child of a family, often the weakest and smallest.

pin block. Tool used by a currier.

pine house. Place where cattle for slaughter were confined for a period of time without food before they were killed.

pinfold. In the Midland counties, a pound for stray animals.

pining stool. Stool of punishment; a 'cucking stool' or **ducking chair** *q.v.*

pin-money. Sum of money settled on a wife for her private expenses.

pinner. 1. constable with special duty of impounding stray animals. 2. narrow piece of cloth which went round a woman's gown at the top near the neck, or the upper parts of a lady's head-dress when lappets were in fashion.

pintado/pintatho. Chintz, coloured cotton fabric generally used for hangings.

pipe. 1. large round cell in a beehive used by the queen bee. 2. charge of powder or shot, which was formerly measured in the bowl of a pipe. 3. large barrel holding 126 gallons of wine or ale; a butt. 4. in lead mining, a long narrow body of ore lying more or less horizontally. Grades into a flat by broadening. Many pipe-veins are in fact ancient caverns filled with ore and **gangue** *q.v.* Pipes may branch out of **rakes** *q.v.*

pipe rolls. The record of the annual audit of the Accounts of Sheriffs and of other debtors to the Crown. Properly known as 'The Great Roll of the Exchequer'.

pippin/pipkin. Small earthenware pot or pan.

pirn. Bobbin on a spinning wheel etc.

pise. Stiff clay or earth kneaded, or mixed with gravel, and used for building. It was rammed between boards, which were then removed as it hardened.

pitch. Thick resinous substance obtained from boiling tar.

pitched market. One in which corn is bought and sold by the sack, not by the sample.

pitch-hitch nail. Hitch nail *q.v.*

pitch skillet. Pan for boiling tar to make pitch for branding sheep.

pit grate. Grating over a kitchen ash-pit.

pit money. Customary fee for burial within the church. It was an easy way of adding to church funds. Eventually this practice was carried to excess, and was thought to be among the primary causes of the constant outbreaks of the plague, as the churches were packed with dead bodies gradually decomposing in shallow graves constantly disturbed by new burials.

pittance. Extra allowance of food; allied to 'pity'.

plain, plains. Cloth similar to flannel, mainly from Wales.

plaite/plate cote. Corselet of leather on which were sewn a number of small plates of iron or steel.

planchers. Planks for flooring.

planks. Workman's bench surrounding a hatter's **kettle** *q.v.*

plashing. The bending down and intertwining of twigs and branches so that separate bushes form a stout hedge.

pleysher/pleacher. Tool for cutting and trimming hedges; the stems were cut halfway through so as to allow them to be bent down in order to thicken the bottom of the hedge. The cut stems sent up numbers of vertical branches and so renewed the hedge.

plocks. Blocks of sawn wood, but sometimes roots or stumps, cumulatively measured in **cords** *q.v.*

plocloutes. Clouts or washers for the plough.

15. Double-wheeled *plough*.

plod/plaid. Woollen cloth with a chequered pattern.

plonkett. Blue woollen cloth of narrow weave.

plough. Implement for turning up the soil in ridges and furrows. Ploughs varied according to the type of soil to be turned; for example the **double-wheeled plough** was used on flinty or gravelly soil and drawn by two horses or oxen.

plough-alms. Penny paid by each plough team to the parish priest. It was collected within a fortnight of Easter.

plough beam. Central longitudinal beam in a plough, to which the other principal parts are attached.

plough duty. (Highway) statute duty assessed per ploughland.

ploughjags. Labourers begging on the first Monday after 'twelfth day', generally called **Plough Monday** *q.v.*

ploughland. Originally, an area of land cultivable by one eight ox-plough; later, a conventional amount containing anything from perhaps eighty to two hundred statute acres, but always containing four yardlands or eight oxgangs.

Plough Monday. First Monday after Epiphany (6 January), notable for rustic jollifications with monetary collections, often for church funds.

ploughrey. Plough gear.

plough stots. Procession of ploughs without **shares** *q.v.* drawn along the streets preceded by a number of rustics decorated with ribands and blowing a cow's horn. This continued until the end of the nineteenth century in Yorkshire, and took place on the second Monday of the year. The rustics often required small sums of money not to damage gardens with the ploughs.

ploughstringes. Reins by which the ploughman controlled his horse.

pluralism. Simultaneous holding of more than one ecclesiastical office or benefice, which continued despite a Papal Bull of 1317, and strenuous efforts to prevent it at the Council of Trent in 1561–62.

poatestone. Sharpening stone for tools; possibly composed of **pennant** *q.v.* which might have been sufficiently hard for the purpose.

pocket borough. Borough whose parliamentary representation was in the hands of an individual or family.

pockett/poskett. 1¼ cwt measure of hops. In south-east England the dimensions were 5¾ feet in circumference and 7½ feet long, four pounds being allowed for the weight of the canvas.

podder. 1. beans, peas, tares, vetches or other vegetables having pods.
2. gatherer or seller of these.

poke. Long narrow bag, often of leather.

poke cloth. Sack cloth.

Poke Day. Day on which an allowance of corn is made to labourers who in some places received a part of their wages in kind.

poker. Single barrel gun.

poking stick. Instrument for putting the plaits of a ruff in a proper form. It was originally made of wood or bone; afterwards of steel, in order that it might be used hot.

pole. *See* **perch**.

pole axe. 1. long handled military axe, a halbert. 2. butcher's axe, with a hammer on the side opposite to the blade.

pole puller. Worker who held a key position in the hop fields. He cut the hop-bines and lifted the supporting poles out of the ground in order to bring them low enough to be stripped by the pickers. It was necessary that he should stand out in the hop-gardens and therefore he wore a brightly coloured neck-cloth, called a **pole puller's neck-cloth**.

polldavy. Coarse cloth or canvas.

polraike. Probably the head of a rake, or the 'poll' or head of an axe or pick.

pomice/pomace. Residue of apples after the juice has been extracted.

pontage. Local tax or toll levied for the maintenance of a bridge.

pook. Cock of hay or barley.

poole. Measure of work in slating, or covering houses with slate, where every **poole** of work is either 6 feet broad and 14 feet upon both sides, or 168 feet in length and one in breadth.

porket. Small or young pig or hog.

portcullis. 1. strong grating of cross timbers pointed with iron hung over a gateway of a castle etc., to be lowered as an aid to defence. 2. coin struck in Elizabeth's reign with a portcullis stamped on the reverse.

poskett. *See* **pockett**.

posnet. 1. small iron pot for use inside larger vessel, e.g. for cooking porridge. 2. small metal cooking pot with a handle and three feet, often funnel shaped.

possessioning. *See* **perambulation**.

possett/possit. Drink composed of hot milk curdled with ale, wine or other liquor, often with sugar, spices etc.

post and pan. Building without bricks or stones, with posts and wattles or laths daubed over with road-mud, commonly called **stud and mud walling** *q.v.*

post mill. Type of windmill, the body of which is supported on a massive wooden post, upon which it may be rotated to face the wind; the post rests upon two wooden cross-trees with four supporting struts or quarter bars.

16. *Post mill.* The sails attached to the arms are to offer a resistance to the wind. In this early type a wooden lattice-work was covered with sails, laced to the arms, and they could be furled when not in use. The outer ends of the sails are all in the same plane, but the outside tips of sails next to the axle are deflected. Called a post-mill, because it turns on one central post.

post obit. Bond to secure to a lender a sum of money on the death of a specified individual from whom the borrower has expectations.

potato bodger. Cross-handled implement of wood, pointed and shod with iron, for making holes in the earth into which seed potatoes are set; also known as a **dibber** or **dibble**; *see also* **setting pin**.

pot cilp/kilp/kylpe. 'Pot-clip'; i.e., an iron hook in the chimney on which the pots were hung; also a detachable handle used to suspend a pot from the gallows.

pot-hook/link. Hook for suspending a pot over the fire, variable in length.

pot kylpe. *See* **pot cilp**.

potle pot. Drinking vessel holding a pottle or two quarts.

potwalloper. Prior to 1832, a man entitled to vote by virtue of having a fireplace of his own, and therefore classed as a householder.

pouling room. 1. room lined with wainscot from Poland (Fr. *polaine*). 2. probably a child's room; from 'pullen' (young) or 'puling' (a weak child).

poulter/pewter. Alloy of tin and lead.

pounce. 1. fine powder used to prevent ink from spreading on unsized paper. 2. powder used for dusting over perforations in order to trace a pattern.

pouncet-box. Small perfume box with a perforated lid.

pound. Small fenced inclosure for keeping animals found straying.

pound house. In cider manufactory, a building or room where apples were pounded. The apples being thrown into a large trough or vat, five or six persons stood round the vessel and pounded them with large club shaped wooden pestles, whose ends were guarded and made rough with the heads of nails.

powder horn. Container used for carrying gunpowder, normally made from an ox or cow horn, with a wooden or metal bottom at the larger end.

powdering tub. Tub for salting or pickling meat.

poy. Probably a dipping hook, a variation of the traditional shepherds' crook used to push sheep down in the water when dipping.

praysinge. Estimating the value of items.

precisian. Strict observer of rules, forms etc., especially in religious matters.

predial tithes. Tenth part of the main produce of the land (corn, oats, wood etc.). *See also* **tithe**.

presentation. Nomination of a clerk by the patron to the ordinary.

presented. Accepted in church after 'half-baptism'. *See also* **presentment**.

presentment. Statement of fact made on oath, e.g.:
1. churchwarden's in the bishop's or archdeacon's correctional court.
2. that made by **petty constable** *q.v.* at **quarter sessions** *q.v.* or assizes.
3. report of a jury concerning an offence brought to its notice.
4. report of the homage at a manor court concerning alienations.

press. Cupboard, usually a large one with shelves. A hanging press is one in which clothes could be hung, i.e. a wardrobe.

presser stool. Stand on which an object may be placed.

prews/prows. Lips, spouts or pointed projections.

pricket. Candlestick.

prijel. Iron tool for forcing nails out of wood, otherwise called a **monkey**.

primer. Textbook.

principal. 1. heirloom; sometimes the **mortuary** *q.v.*, the principal or best horse led before the corpse of the deceased.
2. corner post of a house, tenoned into the ground plates below, and into the beams of the roof.

pringle. Little silver Scotch coin, about the value of a penny, from the northern parts of England.

prior. 1. superior of a priory; one next in dignity to an abbot.
2. cross bar to which the doors of a barn are fastened and which prevents them from being blown open.

pritchel. Iron share fixed on a thick staff for making holes in the ground.

privy coat. Light coat of defence of mail, concealed under an ordinary habit.

processioning. *See* **perambulation**.

proctor. 1. lawyer in ecclesiastical (including probate) courts. 2. one who collected alms for lepers and other persons unable to do it for themselves.

progress. The travelling of the sovereign and court to various parts of the kingdom.

proker. Poker for a fire.

protestation oath returns. Lists of all who signed the Protestation Oath. In 1641–42 members of the House of Commons swore an oath 'to live and die for the true Protestant religion, the liberties and rights of subjects and the privilege of Parliament'; later that year all Englishmen aged 18 and over were encouraged to sign a similar oath, and those who refused were said to be unfit to hold office in church or state. Lists were made of all who signed, and these lists are now in the House of Lords Record Office; some have been printed.

provant master. Person who provided apparel for soldiers.

provost. Constable.

prows. *See* **prews**.

prunella. Strong material, originally silk, later worsted, formerly used for graduates', clergymens' and barristers' gowns, later for the uppers of women's shoes.

psalter. Book of Psalms.

puddle dock. Ancient pool in the river Thames used for the disposal of sewage. An affected woman was sometimes termed 'Duchess of Puddle Dock'.

pug. An upper servant.

pug's parlour. Steward's or housekeeper's room in a large establishment.

Pulver Wednesday. Ash Wednesday.

pulvering day. Any day when the community assembled to let to farm the town lands; but the contract was always confirmed on a particular day.

pumpet ball. Ball with which a printer lays ink on the forms.

pumping-tool. Pump-drill used for drilling stone and metal. It operated with a pump-like action.

puoy. Long pole with spikes at the end, used for propelling barges or keels.

purgatory. Receptacle for ashes beneath or in front of a fire.

purlieu. Land on the borders of a royal forest originally claimed to be part of the forest, but later given back to the owner.

purn. Instrument for holding a vicious horse by the nose whilst the blacksmith is shoeing it.

purprestre. Encroachment on land, especially on deer pasture under forest law, or in other royal lands. The offence could mean forfeiture of the encroacher's land, but often the offence was merely noted, and a rent or fine paid to the sheriff.

purveyance. Royal right of buying provisions etc. for the household at prices below market rates, exemption from which was often bought by the villagers through the constable.

put/putt. 1. two-wheeled farm cart so constructed as to be turned up at the axle to discharge the load.
2. in coal mines, similar cart used to bring the coals from the workings to the crane or shaft.
3. a basket for catching fish.

putchkin. Wicker bottle.

putrid fever. Old name for a group of diseases that included typhus and smallpox.

putter. Man or boy employed in putting or propelling the trams or barrows of coal from the workings. Originally one who pushed the tram or barrow from behind.

puttock candle. Smallest candle in a pound, put in to make up weight.

pyke. Gore *q.v.*; a leg of mutton or triangular shaped plot of land in a corner of the ploughlands. *See* **pightle**.

Q

quadrell. A piece of peat or turf cut from the ground in a square block.

quadripartite, division of tithe. *See* **tithe**.

quant. Pole used by the bargemen on the Waveney between Yarmouth and Bungay, for pushing on their craft in adverse or scanty winds. It had a round cap or cot at the immersed end to prevent its sticking in the mud. Some of the quants were nearly 30 feet long.

quar. Quarry.

quarentene. A linear measure, a furlong.

quarier/quarion. Wax candle, consisting of a square lump of wax with a wick in the centre. It is frequently mentioned in old inventories.

quarrell. Pane of glass often of rhombus shape.

quarter. 1. division of a parish for poor law purposes, especially in large parishes. Often used as equivalent to township or **constablewick** *q.v.*
2. approximately **8 bushels** *q.v.* of grain.
3. container holding 28 lb.

quarterage. County rates paid quarterly through the parish officers.

Quarter Days. These are 25 March — Lady Day; 24 June — Midsummer; 29 September — Michaelmas; 25 December — Christmas.

quartering. Turning a church bell through at an angle of 90° so that the clapper may strike a fresh place.

quarterne. Quartern; a quarter-peck measure.

quarter sessions. *See* **sessions**, **quarter**.

Queen Anne's Bounty. Fund established in 1704 by Queen Anne for the augmentation of the maintenance of poor clergy from her revenues from first fruits and tithes.

quern. 1. hand mill.
2. two circular stones, one rotated on top of the other, for grinding corn.

quern house. *See* **millhouse**.

quest house. Chief watch house of a parish, generally adjoining a church, where sometimes quests concerning misdemeanours and annoyances were held.

questman. Sidesman or assistant to the churchwarden. The Canons seem to use the term as synonymous with that of churchwarden.

queystirk. Heifer, one to two years old.

quicksilver. Mercury.

quill. Reed on which yarn was wound.

quillets. Surviving **selions** *q.v.*, still in separate ownership, but situated entirely within the boundaries of a close belonging to another owner.

quill turn. Machine or instrument in which a weaver's quill was turned.

quill/twill wheel. Spool of a spinning wheel, on which the weft was wound for placing in the shuttle.

quishan. *See* **cushion**.

quit claim. Release and disclaimer of all rights, interest and potential legal actions from a grantor to a grantee.

quoin. Dressed stone used decoratively to finish external corner of a building.

Quern. Two circular stones, with a handle to rotate. The corn is ground by trickling it through the hole in the top stone. From Heage Windmill, Derbyshire.

R

racks/reackes. Pair of iron racks in which spits were kept when not in use.

rafter ridging. Particular kind of ploughing used in Hampshire, so called from each ridge being separated by a farrow; balk ploughing.

ragged robbin. Keeper's follower in the New Forest.

ragman. 1. charter by which the Scots acknowledged their dependence on the English crown under Edward I, popularly called a **Ragman Roll**; hence the term, with or without the last word, came to be applied to several kinds of written rolls and documents, especially if of any length.
2. ancient game.
3. sometimes applied to the devil.

ragout. Patchwork; an item of variegated pattern and design. Also (in eighteenth century) in forms of **ragot**, **ragoust**.

rail. Garment, a dress or cloak; also a neckerchief worn by a woman.

rails. Horizontal section of fencing.

raine/reine. Balk or **meer** *q.v.*

rains. *See* **reeans**.

raisin. Piece of timber placed under the end of a beam in a wall to support it.

rake. 1. rack for storing bacon.
2. main type of mineral vein in the Peak District, a body of ore and gangue minerals disposed vertically between two walls of rock and thus having a straight course across country. Rakes may be up to several miles long, but grade in size down into **scrims**, which are, broadly speaking, small rakes.

ralhe. Weaver's reel.

Ramper, The. Nickname for the Great North Road. Generally applied to any turn pike road, but more particularly to highways on the site of old Roman roads.

randing knife. Knife for cutting meat into strips.

rantan. Riot or drinking bout.

rap. Selions *q.v.*; often used in Somerset.

rape. 1. crop grown for the seeds from which oil is extracted.
2. administrative division of a shire in Sussex.

rapire/rapier. Originally a long, pointed two-edged sword adapted either for cutting or thrusting, but chiefly used for the latter. Later, a light, sharp-pointed sword designed only for thrusting, a small sword.

rate pitt/rateing dike. Pit or dyke for rotting hemp or flax by soaking it in water to disengage the fibres.

rathe. Rail on a cart.

rattan/ratton. 1. rat.
2. to take away a w rkman's tools, or to destroy his tools so that he will be unable to work.

rattle. In weaving, a comb-like article used to arrange the warp threads evenly.

ratt stock. Rat-trap.

ravel. Of fabric: to fray, unravel.

ravelling. Process of fraying fabric.

raves. Two frames of wood laid on the top of a waggon in such a way as to meet in the middle and projecting on all sides beyond the body of the vehicle, thus enabling it to carry a larger load of hay or straw. Side boards are fitted in order to carry higher loads.

raying/rying sieve. Fine sieve of brass or iron wire used for riddling and cleansing corn.

reackes. *See* **racks**.

readeption. Literally the re-attainment (of the throne by Henry VI in 1470).

rean. Meer *q.v. See also* **reeans**.

rearing feast. Meal and ale usually given to the workmen when the roof was 'reared' or put on a house. Sometimes called the **topping out** ceremony.

receptaculum. Part of a house which on the death of the owner or tenant, was to be retained by any elderly members of the family residing there. Supposed to be one third of the house, but it usually consisted of two rooms.

recke. Open cupboard or dresser.

reckenteam. Ratcheted hook supporting the pans etc. over the fire from the gallows or chimney irons.

reckon crook. Iron hook in a chimney for suspending a pot over an open fire.

recognisance. Sum of money pledged as security by a bond for the future performance of an act or the avoidance of an offence, which was forfeited if the act was not performed or the offence was committed.

recto. Right hand page of an open book; the opposite of **verso** *q.v.*

rector, clerical. Incumbent having both great and small tithe, or lands or moduses in lieu of these.

rector, lay. Layman owning the great tithe of a rectory impropriate. The rector, whether clerical or lay, was liable to repair the chancel of the parish church.

recusants. Nonconformists, especially Roman Catholics, declining to attend their parish church.

redger. Chain fixed on the rods of a waggon which passed over the horse's back.

reeans/r'yans/rains. 1. grassy terraces or flat strips rising like steps one above the other on a hillside, resembling sheep tracks, but wider. 2. (in singular) raised bank.

reed. *See* **slay**.

reed billy. Bundle of reeds.

reed holder. Thatcher's bow fastened to the roof to hold the straw.

reeke. *See* **rick**.

reel(e). 1. reel on which thread is wound from the distaff.
2. plumb-line or measuring string.
3. device used for spinning without a wheel.

reeve. Manorial/communal officer of almost any kind, especially one concerned with the management of open fields and commons, and often elected from customary tenants.

regrate. To buy corn or other commodity and sell it again in the same market or fair, or another within 4 miles.

regress. Act of going or coming back; a return or withdrawal; re-entry to or into the place of issue or origin.

regulations of commons. Stinting *q.v.* Under the General Enclosure Acts, regulation included also such measures as fencing, draining etc., thought necessary in order to maintain the utility of the common to the commoners and to the community at large.

reine. Balk or **meer** *q.v.*

relict. Widow or widower.

relief. Payment due from every freehold tenant, if he was of full age, or had reached his majority, on his taking possession of land at the death of his father or other 'ancestor'; the sum was 'certain', that is, fixed. The actual amount depended on custom and might be half, one, or two years' rent (quitrent), but was usually one year. Corresponded to 'fine' paid by a copyholder.

removal. Transfer of a pauper or potential pauper to his place of legal settlement.

removal order. Justice's warrant for effecting a removal.

rennet. An infusion of the inner membrane of the fourth stomach of an unweaned calf, or any preparation from animal intestines used for curdling milk and in the preparation of cheese.

rennin. *See* **rining**.

repille stock. Kind of rod or staff used for beating flax.

replevin. Action which may be undertaken by a tenant to recover goods removed under any illegal distress.

rest wimble. Type of **wimble** *q.v.*, possibly for making part of a plough.

retainer. One who was attached in the service of a lord by annuity or indenture.

retting. Preparation of flax by steeping or watering to season the fibres. **Retting ponds** were the ponds where this was carried out.

rialle/rial. Gold coin, first issued by Edward IV in 1465.

rick. Stack of grain or hay in a field.

rick barton. Enclosure for **ricks** *q.v.*; farm-yard.

rickheay/rick hey. Roof supported by four posts; a wall-less barn common in the West Country.

rickle. Little **rick** *q.v.*; a pile of stone, peat.

rickstavel/staddle. Frame of wood set on stones of mushroom shape, or oak posts, on which a corn-rick was built.

riddle. *See* **ryddle**.

rides. Iron hinges fixed on a gate, by means of which the gate was hung on the hooks in the post, and which enabled it to swing or ride.

17. *Ridge-and-furrow*, Watford, December 1968. This photograph shows the effect of different agricultural treatments on the survival of *ridge-and-furrow* in these fields, which lie to the east of the Watford Gap service area on the M1 motorway.

ridge-and-furrow. Raised or rounded strip of arable, usually one of a series with inter furrows and often still seen in present permanent grassland, the mark of former open-field cultivation.

riggilt. Ram with one testicle.

rights, taking one's. Communicating in one's parish church; it was the legal right of every parishioner 'devoutly and humbly desiring the same', unless there was lawful cause to the contrary. In pre-Reformation times this also included confession and the receiving of absolution. *See also* **paschal money**.

rind. Inner section of oak bark, the part of value in tanning.

ring. A cider or cheese-press.

ring house. Building which contained a cider or cheese-press.

ringing and tanging. Process of retrieving a swarm of bees by following it beating a tin pan.

ring of the town. *See* **vicar's ring**.

rining/rennin. A casein-digesting enzyme or ferment in the gastric juice which curdles milk; the active principle of **rennet** *q.v.*

ripp/reap hook. Scythe with a curved steel blade about 18 inches long and having a serrated edge.

ripple. 1. set of rails added to a cart or waggon to increase its carrying capacity when loaded with hay.
2. iron rim on a cart wheel.

roasting iron. Utensil used for roasting eggs, similar to a **gridiron** *q.v.*

Robin Redbreast. Nickname for a soldier wearing a red uniform jacket. Also a slang name for Bow Street runners, who wore blue dress coat, brass buttons and a bright red waistcoat.

Rochester earth. Name for saltpetre, potassium nitrate. Saltpetre is a white crystalline substance having a saline taste; it was the chief constituent of gunpowder and was used medicinally.

rocker. 1. long handle of the bellows in a smith's forge, which was drawn down to raise the moving board of the bellows.
2. long wicker sieve used in dressing beans.

rockstaff. Part of the apparatus of a blacksmith, possibly the staff upon which the handle of the bellows was fastened, or the handle itself.

rod. Also known as a **pole** or **perch**, equal to five and a half yards or 16½ feet. A standard measure for brickwork.

rode land. Land which has been cleared or grubbed up; as land recently reclaimed and brought into cultivation.

rodney. Helper on canal banks, the one that opens the locks.

Rogation Week. Three weeks before Ascension Thursday.

rogue money. Annual payment by the constable of each parish to the high constable of the county for the maintenance of prisoners in the county gaol.

roll. *See* **perch**.

rolley. Coal truck.

rolley-way. Passage or way for coal trucks.

Romescot. *See* **pentecostals** and **Peter's Pence**.

rood. 1. one quarter of an acre; 660 feet long or 40 square perches in area. 2. eight yards linear measure, in draining, hedging and ditching. 3. Cross of Christ or crucifix, especially one placed in a church over the entrance to the Choir or Chancel.

rood loft. Gallery or platform, over the screen, at the entrance of the chancel, upon which was the rood or cross.

rood-screen. Screen of open woodwork or stone dividing chancel from nave in a church. The **rood** *q.v.* was fixed on top.

roots. Any root vegetables, e.g. turnips, swedes and mangold-wurzels.

Rope Monday. The second Monday after Easter Day.

rosin. Solid residue after the distillation of oil turpentine from crude turpentine. Often confused with gum.

rota men. Name given to certain politicians during the Commonwealth (1649–1660) who suggested that a third part of parliament should be re-elected by rotation.

rotation meadow. Variant of **lot meadow** *q.v. See also* **shifting severalties**.

rotten stone. Light stone found in the Peak district; in its powdered state much used in the polishing of iron by the manufacturers of Sheffield.

rotulet. Small roll of parchment, or a small membrane bound up in a roll.

roundabout chair. Lavishly ornamented chair with canework seat, semi-circular back and cabriole legs; also known as Burgomaster Chair. It was made in the East Indies and exported to England via Holland.

roundel. Iron ring for holding candles, a **trendal** *q.v.*

roundhead. Puritan, so called because their hair was cut in a close circular fashion.

roundsman system. Device for employing the able-bodied poor; it took several different forms, as:
1. the ordinary system, under which the parish paid the difference between the labourer's wages and an agreed scale;
2. the special system, whereby the parish contracted with individuals to perform certain work, the work being done by pauper labour and the parish paying the paupers;
3. the pauper auction, whereby each pauper labourer was auctioned off separately each week or month to the highest bidder.
See also **labour rate** and **house row**.

rowler/rowell. Roller, possibly a barley roller or **hummeller**.

rowling stone. Stone roller.

Royal Oak Day. 29 May, the anniversary of the Restoration (1660) once commemorated by the wearing of oak-leaves, recalling the Boscobel Oak, near Worcester, as the hiding place of Charles II.

R.R. *regni Regis*, meaning in the —th year of King —.

rubber file. Tool used to take the scale off red hot iron.

rudder beast/cattell. Horned cattle, usually oxen.

rudge wash. Kersey cloth made of fleece wool, worked as it came from the sheep's back, and not cleansed after being shorn.

ruffell/ruffle. Strip of lace or other fine material gathered on one edge and used as an ornamental frill, especially at wrist, breast or neck.

runagate. Vagabond.

runlet/rundlett/rundle tub. 1. cask of varying capacity, particularly for wine, or for holding wort when brewing.
2. circular wooden trencher.

running cowle. Rennet-cooler.

running pig. Piglet being suckled by a sow but not part of her own litter.

Rushbearing. Often either (a) St. Bartholomew's day, 24 August, or (b) the feast of the dedication of a particular church. It was the ceremony of carrying garlands or rushes to decorate the church.

russell. Kind of woollen fabric, probably of Flanders origin.

russet. Coarse home-spun woollen cloth of a reddish brown, grey or neutral colour, formerly used for the dress of peasants and country folk.

r'yans. *See* **reeans**.

ryddle/riddle. Coarse meshed oblong sieve used to separate seed from corn.

rying sieve. *See* **raying sieve**.

S

sac (or **sake**) **and soke.** Phrase used in charters from the reign of Cnut (commonly known as Canute, 1016–1035) onward to denote certain rights of jurisdiction, as the right to hold a court, which by custom belonged to the lord of the manor, and which were specified (along with others) as included in the grant of a manor by the crown.

sack. 1. measure, particularly of hops, varying according to locality.

2. when listed indoors, especially in bedchambers or parlour, probably a sack used for window covering. Glass was the wealthy man's luxury.

saddle tree. Framework of a saddle.

safe. Ventilated cupboard for meat.

saffron. Flowers (purple not yellow as popularly supposed), which about the end of September were gathered before dawn, the stigmas first being removed and then dried in little kilns over a gentle fire, pressed into cakes, and finally bagged. It is estimated that it takes about 4,000 flowers to produce one ounce of saffron.

sagathy. Woollen stuff, sometimes mixed with a little silk. Associated with **drugget** *q.v.* and **camlet** *q.v.*

sage cheese. Kind of cheese flavoured and mottled by mixing the liquid pressed from sage leaves with the cheese curd.

sailorboy. Horse-drawn reaping machine.

St. Anthony's Fire. Erysipelas; so-called from the tradition that those who sought the intercession of St. Anthony recovered from the pestilential erysipelas called the sacred fire, which was known to be fatal in 1089. One form of the disease could have been due to Ergot poisoning caused by eating bread made from infected grain.

St. Thomas Leet. 21 December, the Archbishop's Court at Southwell.

sake and soke. *See* **sac and soke.**

salle. Salt container; often of silver.

sallemander/salymander. Square or circular plate attached to a long handle; the plate was warmed in the fire until red hot and then used to 'brown' pastry.

sallet. Head piece or helmet of a suit of armour.

salting cowle. Kymnell *q.v.*, tub or trough for salting meat; a brine tub.

salting plank/stone. Trestle used for salting meat or bacon.

sarcinett/sarsenett. Fine, soft, silken fabric, used for quilts and bed-hangings, also for linings and dresses.

sarser. *See* **saucer.**

sasafras/sasufrax/saxifrage. Dried bark of the tree *Saxifraga granulata*, from North America, used as a medicine.

sash line/cord. Two sash frames containing glass, moved by a line or cord counterbalanced by a weight. Sash windows gradually came into fashion from the end of the 17th century.

sate/set rod. Pliant stick of hazel or willow used to hold the stamp mark or engraved piece of steel by which a die was struck. One man twisted the sate rod round the mark and held it whilst another struck it on the top with a hammer.

satin. Silk fabric with a glossy surface on one side produced by a method of weaving by which the threads of the warp are caught and looped by the weft only at intervals.

saucer/sarser. Any small shallow dish or deep plate of circular shape, in which salt and sauces were placed on the table; not a saucepan nor a saucer to go under a cup.

saunce/sanctus bell. Small silver bell rung to mark the progress of the office of the Mass.

saveguard/safeguard. Outer skirt or petticoat worn by women to protect their dress when riding.

sax. Slate dresser's knife; it had a spike to make the hole for fixing the nails to a roof.

saxifrage. *See* **sasafras**.

say. Fine cloth like serge, made of twilled worsted.

scadding of peas. Custom in the North of boiling the common grey peas in the pod, and eating them with butter and salt. According to tradition, one pea pod would have a bean placed in it, and whoever got this pod was supposed to be the first to get married.

scaile/scale balk. Bar of a balance.

scalding tub. Early form of sterilizer for cleansing vessels used to contain liquids, especially milk.

scapebegotten. Bastard.

scar. Rough burnt out cinder left in a furnace.

scarlet. Finest of all woollens, not necessarily red. It was most used by the royal court.

scavel. Small spade.

sconce. *See* **skonce.**

sconce glass. Looking glass fitted with sockets to contain candles.

scoot. *See* **skutt.**

Scotch draper. *See* **manadge man.**

scotch hands. Pair of wooden tools used to make butter pats.

scowstone. Scouring stone.

screen. *See* **skreen.**

screwplate. Plate with threads on it of various diameters, used by smiths etc. for cutting the threads of screws.

scrim. Small **rake** *q.v.*

scriptorium. Room in a monastery for reading and writing or copying manuscripts, often in the north walk of the cloisters.

scoggers. *See* **hoggers.**

scrutore/scretoir. Escritoire, a writing desk.

scuffler. Sort of plough with a pointed share, used for removing weeds from a turnip field.

scull. Armoured head-piece to go with a cap.

scummer/skummer or **skimmer/skimer.** Utensil with a long handle and a spoonlike bowl with perforations. It took two forms:
1. an iron utensil, used for taking the ash out of the hearth.
2. a brass utensil, used as a ladle to remove scum from the cooking pot.

scutage. Annual payment of money to a feudal lord to provide a military force in support of the crown. Also called **shield money**.

scuttell/scuttle. Large shallow open basket or wickerwork bowl used for carrying corn, earth, vegetables etc.

sea coal. Coal known as such because it was shipped down the coast by boats.

sealing. Wainscotting or panelling.

seam/seame. 1. eight bushels of grain or malt.
   2. horse load of wood.
   3. British glass weight equivalent to 120 lbs.

seaman's needle. Compass.

seam set. Shoemaker's instrument for smoothing the seams of boots and shoes.

searce/search. Sieve or cloth made of bristles, used in the dairy; also a tool used for nicking wrought iron or steel.

season. Two or more open fields or parts of such fields simultaneously under the same crop or fallow.

seat/set. Pieces of leather pegged or sewn to the boot as a foundation for the heel.

second poor. Poor not in receipt of relief.

secular services. Worldly services owed to a lord, as opposed to spiritual or ecclesiastical services; often took the form of money payments or the provision of labour.

seedleap/seedlip. Seed-basket shaped so as to fit to the waist of the sower.

seething of sous. Part of the process of pickling meat by plunging into brine and leaving to steep.

seg cart. Tub on wheels in which urine was collected from house to house for the use of cloth mills.

segg chair. One made of, or with, a seat of basketwork.

seild chair. Panelled chair.

seisin. Lawful possession; the right to hold.

selectman. Vestryman (of a select vestry).

select vestry. *See* **vestry, select.**

selions. (Originally probably acre) parallel strips of arable land in an open field, not uniform in size, and often very far removed in area from either statute or local acre.

senior of the parish. Select vestryman; *see* **vestry, select.**

serecloth. Cloth impregnated with wax, used as a water-proof covering or winding sheet.

serf. Unfree labourer, a bondman. Of lower status than a villein, in that even his body belonged to his lord. A serf who wanted to reside away from his **vill** *q.v.* could obtain an albenarta, or licence, but he remained a serf. A serf who was freed was given a **chirograph** *q.v.*, a duplicate of his charter of manumission.

serge. Very durable, twilled cloth of worsted or a warp of worsted and weft of wool, mainly used for clothing, but could also be used for bed curtains.

serges. Large corpse candles.

sessions money. County rate, paid quarterly by the constable at the quarter sessions.

sessions, petty. (Until 1830) meetings of two or three justices for minor local business.

sessions, quarter. General sessions of the peace for the county, held quarterly for both criminal and administrative business.

sessions, special. Monthly and somewhat informal meetings of the justices in each division of the county.

sesterne. Cistern, pond.

seton. Thread or tape drawn through a fold of skin in order to maintain an opening for discharges.

set pot. Iron cauldron fixed in brickwork and used for boiling clothes.

set rod. *See* **sate.**

setting pin. An implement, approximately four feet eight inches in height, resembling a gardener's dibble. It had a cross-pin or half crutch near the top to rest the palm upon and a groove on each side of the handle for the forefinger and thumb. The length of the dibble was about eight inches, and was two inches square in the middle, tapering to a sharp point at the bottom. This implement enabled the setter to drop the beans into the ground without bending. *See also* **tucking.**

settle/settlas. 1. box-type seat with straight back. 2. raised shelf or frame of brick or wood for supporting barrels or milk cans.

settlement certificate. *See* **certificate of settlement.**

settlement examination. *See* **examination.**

set-work(e). Kind of embroidery used in working tapestry.

seur. Kind of net or apparatus for catching fish.

severalty, land held in. Enclosed consolidated area of land entirely held by one person, as opposed to scattered strips in the open field system or **champaigne** *q.v.*

sewstern. *See* **cistern.**

sextary. Measure of wine; seems to have comprised four English gallons.

shack. Right of grazing upon open fields after the crop has been lifted, e.g. in **lammas lands** *q.v.*

shackle. Chain, rope, or twisted band of straw used for securing cows.

shag/shagged. Rough hairy cloth, or made from such cloth.

shagreen. Kind of leather from the hides of horses or asses which was dyed green and used as covering for small boxes and cases.

shalloon. Closely-woven material chiefly used for linings.

shalm/shawm. Ancient double reed instrument; form of pipe or trumpet, somewhat resembling the later clarionet or oboe; a religious instrument of the Jews.

shamy skins. Kind of soft, pliable leather, or wash leather. Originally 'chamois skins'.

share/shere. Iron blade in a plough which cuts the ground at the bottom of the furrow; a ploughshare.

sharevill/sherwill. Shovel.

shaul/shawle. Wooden shovel without a handle, used for putting corn into a winnowing machine.

shawm. *See* **shalm**.

sheaf. *See* **shyfe**.

shean. *See* **skain**.

shearing frame. Cloth-dressing machine that trimmed away the superfluous nap.

shed. The space formed between the upper and lower warp of a loom traversed by the shuttle carrying the weft.

sheeder/shedar. Female sheep, specifically a lamb from eight or nine months to its first shearing.

sheep(e) barr/sheep-bar. Kind of hurdle on which sheep were laid when clipped; also, a hurdle used in fields to fold sheep in.

sheep brand. Branding iron for sheep.

sheers/shears. Type of large scissors, especially ones used for cutting nap on cloth.

shelbreade. Shieldboard, the mouldboard of a plough.

sheluyges/shelvings. Framework to put on a cart for carrying hay.

shepe hog. Sheep before its first shearing.

shepen/sheippinge. Shippon; a cow-house or shed.

shere. *See* **share**.

sheriff. Originally the governor of a shire or a shire-reeve in England; later, the chief officer of the Crown in every county, appointed annually and nominally entrusted with the execution of the laws and the maintenance of peace and order.

Sheriff's Tourn. Special session of the Hundred Court, presided over by the sheriff and held twice a year, after Easter and Michaelmas. It was officially abolished in 1887.

sherwill. *See* **sharevill.**

sheyd/shide. Small plank.

shield money. *See* **scutage.**

shifting severalties. Lands such as lot or rotation meadow, held in **severalty** *q.v.* for part of the year only, and the several ownership of which varies from year to year or through a prescribed period, being determined by lot, rotation or some similar method.

shingles. Wooden tiles made of oak, used for roofs, steeples etc.

shoat. *See* **shott.**

shocks. Sheaves propped against each other.

shodd wayne. Wain *q.v.* with iron hoops on the wheels.

shoddy. Inferior textile material made up from woollen waste or discarded woollen cloths and rags which have been pulled to shreds by a **shoddy-machine.**

shoit. *See* **swyne.**

shoppe/shop. Place of work of a craftsman.

shott/shoat. 1. part in an open field, usually about 30 acres, with all strips or lands going the same way, and with a headland at each end.

2. young pig, or one castrated.

3. idle, worthless person.

shovelboard. Also **shuffleboard**, **slidethrift**. Early names for shove-ha'penny.

shrovetide. The period comprising Quinquagesima Sunday (the last Sunday before Lent) and the two following days, Shrove Monday and Tuesday. The word 'shrove' is connected with 'shrive', and refers to the custom of being shriven: making confession, and receiving absolution and penance, before Lent begins on Ash Wednesday.

shuffleboard. *See* **shovelboard.**

shuttle. Instrument used in weaving, for passing the thread of the weft to and from one edge of the cloth to the other between the threads of the warp.

shyfe/sheaf. Sheaf of arrows.

sidbedstead. Bed with only two posts, one at the head and one at the foot, which was placed against a wall.

sideboard/sidbord/sidbreid/sidecupboard. Not the modern object but a long table without a lower cupboard incorporated in it, placed against a wall and used primarily for the display of household plate.

side press. Alternative name for a **sideboard** *q.v.* This was probably the closed variety, nearer in form to the modern sideboard.

side saddle. Woman's saddle so made that both the rider's legs are on the same side of the horse.

sidesman. Originally, and still properly, synodsman or questman. Actually a deputy churchwarden: the derivation of the word from 'synodsmen' is not accepted by all ecclesiastical historians.

sie bole. Bowl for use with a **searce** *q.v.* for straining liquids, especially milk.

sike. Gully, dip, hollow; also, a stretch of meadow.

sile. Strainer or sieve, especially for milk.

simony. Offence of offering or accepting money or other reward for nomination or appointment to an ecclesiastical office.

singing bread. Large wafers used in the celebration of the mass.

sinker/synker. Circular board which presses the curds down into the cheese vat under the press.

sirpcloth. Surplice worn by a minister of the church.

skain/shean. 1. crooked sword or scimitar.
2. highland dagger or dirk; a long knife.

skarne/squirm. Part of the warping complex on which the yarn was placed as it came from spinning. It was then wound from the squirm on to the warping-bar.

skeal/skeel/skeil. Wooden bucket, pail or tub, or any similar vessel, used for holding water or milk.

skelboose. Front boards of a cow stall.

skellet/skillett/skivett. Small iron cooking pot with handle and legs. Alternative name for a **posnet** *q.v.*

skep. 1. straw bee hive; also known as a **bee-pot**.
2. basket for grain or coals. *See also* **strike**.

skimmer/skimer. *See* **scummer**.

skimmington. 1. burlesque procession in which a henpecked husband was compelled either to ride with his face towards the horse's tail or walk backwards, or astride a pole, while women beat him with a ladle, hence to **ride the skimmington**.
2. a row or commotion.

skine/skin wool. Wool taken from the skin of a dead sheep.

skivett. *See* **skellet**.

skonce/sconce. Flat candlestick with a handle for carrying.

skreen/screen. Wire instrument on a frame used for separating corn from dust or other impurities.

skummer. *See* **scummer**.

skutt/scoot. Small irregular plot of ground; a part or division of a larger area.

slab. Stone part of the **bason** *q.v.* on which the first part of the felting process in hatting was performed.

slaiff. Shallow dish, almost a **trencher** *q.v.*

slane. Tool used in cutting out peat.

slath. Rod used in the central structure of a round or oval bottom when making a basket.

slaughter cradle. Pen for impounding an animal prior to killing it.

slay. Instrument used in weaving, sometimes termed **reed**, which separates the threads of the warp and beats up the weft. These are among the loom's chief accessories.

sleck trough. Trough in which a blacksmith quenches his iron.

sled/slid. Sledge, for drawing heavy loads; a small flat-bottomed truck which slid over the ground. It was used to move a plough or any other unwieldy equipment.

sledge/sledg. Sledge-hammer, a smith's large hammer used for beating out iron on an anvil.

sleepe/slip. Pig eight weeks old.

slice/sliece/slis. Fire shovel used particularly for getting the ashes out of a baking oven. The end was shaped like a spade or paddle.

slidethrift. *See* **shovelboard.**

sling. Chain made with either rings or hooks attached to it used for hoisting sacks of malt etc.

slink piece. Probably skin from aborted calf or from weak, sickly beast.

slip. *See* **sleepe.**

sluggard waker. 1. dog-whipper.
2. minor official of the church.

smart. The second swarm of bees from a hive. *See also* **chit.**

smock windmill. Windmill boarded down to the ground, as opposed to a **post mill** *q.v.*

smoke farthings. Pentecostals.

smoothing box/iron. *See* **ironing box.**

snaffle bridle. Bridle and snaffle without a curb.

snaithe/snate. Crooked handle or shaft of a scythe.

snapper. Handgun.

snead/sneede. Curved handle of a scythe.

sneck. Part of the iron fastening of a door which is raised by moving the latch.

snip. White or pink patch on a horse's nostril or lip.

snocksnarl. Knot or twist in a thread which is over twisted and runs into kinks.

snuffer. Instrument used to snuff out candles.

soak dyke. Ditch beside a large drain or canal for the purpose of receiving water which percolates through banks.

socage. Tenure of land by certain fixed services other than knight service, but not servile. Often, in fact, rent paid.

soe. Large tub.

soil. Human faeces used as manure.

sokeman/socman. Under Danelaw, a free peasant.

solar. *See* **soller.**

soller. Originally **solar**, a room where a lady could be alone. Later, simply an upstairs room.

sorrell/sorall. Red roan horse with red, white and yellow hairs.

sorry. Decrepit.

sough. 1. also called an **adit**, a passage like a vault, cut out under the earth to drain water from a mine.

2. the mouth of a drain, guarded by a barred or pierced cover called a **suff-grate**.

soul scot. Ecclesiastical **heriot** *q.v.* In some parishes after the lord has taken his heriot, usually the best **chattel** *q.v.*, the parish church was entitled to take the second best chattel.

souse. 1. to steep in brine; to pickle.

2. various parts of a pig, especially the feet and ears, pickled.

spancel. Rope to tie a cow's hind legs.

spaning. Weaning of a calf or pig.

spare/spar. Pole or piece of timber of some length and moderate thickness.

spaved/spayed. Of a female animal: castrated.

spavin/spavined. Of a colt: having a distended hock-joint.

speake. Spoke; part of a wheel.

speciality/speshalty. Legal term meaning 'deed under seal', 'sealed contract'.

special sessions. *See* **sessions, special.**

specie. Cash.

Speenhamland system. System of poor relief developed by magistrates in Berkshire and followed by southern counties under which allowances of bread were to be given on a sliding scale, regulated by the price of bread, thus enabling farmers to pay less than an average wage.

spelk. Basket that is woven with a warp and weft, of thin slats usually of oak.

spence. Generally a larder or store-room equated with a dairy.

sperate/speriality. Debt of which there is hope of recovery.

spere. 1. young oak after it has passed beyond the sapling stage.

2. spear.

speshalty. *See* **specialty.**

spete basket. Basket for weeds.

spigot. *See* **spygott.**

spindle chair. Arm-chair with long slender spindles forming the back, arms and legs.

spinning. Art or process of drawing out and twisting wool, cotton, silk etc. into threads using a hand spindle or spinning wheel. On the latter, the large wheel was turned by hand or a treadle. Prior to spinning, the fibres were first separated by an instrument similar to a wire brush, a **card** *q.v.*

spit. Iron contraption to hold meat, game, poultry etc. in front of fire for roasting; turned by hand, or by a dog in a wheel-cage, or mechanically.

spital houses. A charitable institution; also called 'Bede' house or alms house. Also, a hospital.

spitting tubb. Spittoon.

splenting. Thin strips of wood nailed across upright beams to form base on which plaster or daubing could be spread.

splints. Armour for the elbows.

splott. Piece or patch of land.

sprigged. Of cloth, often muslin: adorned with a pattern in the form of a spray of flowers. Very common form of fabric decoration from the middle of the eighteenth century.

spring corn. Barley and/or oats, or (by extension) vetches or peas and beans.

spruzzing. *See* **brian**.

spud. Small narrow spade for cutting the roots of weeds.

spurget. Tagge, or piece of wood to hang anything on.

spurre way. Horse-way through a man's ground, on which one may ride by right of custom.

spygott/spigot. Small wooden peg, or pin used to stop the vent-hole of a barrel or cask; a vent-peg.

square quarters. Probably containers for hundredweights of cheese cut into four quarters of 28 lbs each.

squab. *See* **squob**.

squatter. Person enclosing a scrap of common and building a dwelling on it without the leave of quarter sessions and the lord of the manor.

squire. Technically, a man of blood and coat-armour two degrees above the commonalty (the grades being gentleman, esquire, knight). In fact, the principal landowner in any rural village provided that he or his family have been there long enough to establish customary right to the title. Often the ultimate successor to the medieval lord of the manor.

squirm. *See* **skarne**.

squob/squab. Originally a cushion, but later extended to mean sofa or couch.

stack/staik. 1. pile of grain in the sheaf, of hay, straw, fodder etc. gathered into a circular or rectangular form, usually with a sloping thatched top to protect it from the weather.
2. measure, particularly of coal, usually four cubic yards.

stackstone. Stone for the base of a **rickstavel** *q.v.*

stacktimber. Timber for the construction of a **rickstavel** *q.v.*

staddles. Wooden uprights of a **rickstavel** *q.v.*

stag. Male of cow, sheep, pig, or a young horse, especially an unbroken one.

stail engine. Tool used to smooth the haft or long handle of a rake.

staithe. Small landing stage or quay.

stallage. Right of erecting stalls or booths in a market, fair etc. and the rent paid for this.

stamp. Probably an instrument for making holes in horse shoes.

stamper. 1. copper mallet used for beating felt placed on a **block** *q.v.* into the shape of a hat.
2. person, especially a boy, whose occupation it was to beat the ore from a lead mine small and fit for the washers.

stampt paper/stamped paper. Paper having a government revenue stamp impressed on or affixed to it.

stand bed. Bed with posts.

stander/stande. Frame or horse for supporting pails or barrels.

stand heck. Rack for fodder or straw standing on four posts, and for use in a farm-yard.

standish/stadysche/standige. Stand containing ink, pens and other writing materials and accessories; an ink stand, inkpot.

standle. Sapling.

stang/stong. Rood of land.

stanhope. Light two or four-wheeled open carriage, called after the inventor.

statute. A unit of measurement or weight fixed by parliamentary statute.

Statute of Mortmain. Act 7 Edw. I, St. 2, forbidding alienations in **mortmain** *q.v.*, as being against the interests of the crown and the mesne lords.

staule. Cattle-stall.

stave. Section making up the sides of a barrel; also (in plural) the whole container.

stayes. Laced under-bodice, stiffened by the insertion of strips of whalebone, wood or metal, worn by women, to give shape and support to the figure. The use of the plural is due to the fact that **stayes** were originally made in two pieces and laced together.

stayrs. Bed-steps; set of two or three steps for getting into a bed.

stay tape. Used for lacing a woman's stays/**stayes** *q.v.*, but also used by tailors for binding the edge of a fabric.

stean. Earthenware vessel with two handles or ears, used for storing liquids or butter.

steapfat. Vat in which barley was placed to steep, for malting.

steel/steell. 1. implement for sharpening cutting tools or utensils. 2. mason's cold-chisel.

steel mill. Device for producing a spark by rotating a steel disc against a flint.

steel yard/stilliard. Balance with unequal arms. The item to be weighed was attached to the shorter arm, and the counter-weight was slid along the longer one until equilibrium was reached, the position indicating the weight of the object. Used particularly for weighing meat.

steer/steyre. Bull or ox which has reached maturity in its third year of life.

steille bonet/cap. Steel cap, armour for the head.

stemple. 1. one of a series of transverse pieces of wood at the side of a shaft of a mine used by miners as rungs allowing them to climb without ropes.
2. piece of wood wedged across a working or vein, or as part of a platform or lodgement for stacking **deads** *q.v.*, or part of a roof support. Stemples of dressed stone occur in a few mines.

sterk/stirk. Young bullock or heifer, one or two years old.

sterling. Standard of silver coin current in the realm.

stetch. Ridge of land, the ploughed land between two furrows.

stew. Hatter's drying room.

steward. Presiding officer of the **barmote** *q.v.* court; the lord's executive.

sticking the church. *See* **garnishing the church** *q.v.*

Stemples   Ladders   Footholes

18. Shaft climbing. Men entered the mine either by a level or a series of short climbing shafts. The climbing shafts were generally about 50 feet deep with a short level at the bottom, at the end of which would be another short shaft, so leading in stages to the deepest part of the mine. These shafts had pieces of wood called *stemples* let into the walls at both sides of the shaft, and the miners descended and ascended on these crude ladders. More rarely stone footholes were used, and a good example of this latter arrangement can be seen at the rear of the cottage at the Magpie Mine, near Sheldon, Derbyshire.

sticks. Willows of two or more years, used for making square work and handles in basket-making.

still. 1. stand for barrel or tub. 2. apparatus for distilling. 3. alternative name for a cooler.

stilliard. *See* **steel yard**.

stint. 1. to regulate the number of cattle allowed to graze on a common. Hence **commons** *q.v.* were classified into **stinted** and **unstinted pasture**. The practice was known as **stinting**.

2. last two or three yards of a **selion** *q.v.* meeting another **selion** end to end, which the owner of the neighbouring **selion** had the right to use for access to his own land, and which therefore was not cultivable until after the sowing of the neighbouring selion had been completed.

stirk. *See* **sterk.**

stirrup. Kind of footless stocking with a strap under the foot, also the strap itself.

stitch. Strip of ploughed land between two furrows.

stithy. Anvil.

stobe/stub. Horse-shoe nail.

stoce. *See* **stowce.**

stock(s). 1. swarm; bees in a hive or skep.
2. block or table on which a butcher cut meat.
3. animal kept for breeding.
4. hub of a wheel.

stockes and blockes. Odds and ends.

stock, parish. 1. before the Reformation, the church capital in cash or cattle, lent out on bond by the wardens to suitable parishioners, in the former case for the whole profit, in the latter for an annual rent payable to church funds.
2. after the Reformation, the stock of wool, flax, hemp, wood, thread, iron and other necessary ware to provide work for the poor, supplied by the overseers and churchwardens at the parish expense.

stoes. *See* **stowce.**

stomacher. Kind of waistcoat worn by men, or an ornamental covering for the chest worn by women.

stone. Measure of weight, particularly of wool or yarn, usually 14 lbs, but in Herefordshire 12 lbs.

stone blue. Mixture of indigo with starch or whiting, used in laundrywork.

stone colt/horse. Uncastrated colt, male horse or stallion.

stong. *See* **stang.**

stoneman. Waywarden.

stool. Chair without a back, used especially with a table: *see* **buffet stool, throne stool, close stool**. Also a stand on which an object may be placed: *see* **presser stool**, **meat stool**.

stool of easement. Close-stool, a commode.

stooper. Wedge used for tilting a barrel.

stopt. Stuffed, filled.

store pig. Animal acquired for fattening.

stoupe. Pail or bucket.

stowes/stowce/stoes/stoce. Wooden windlass over a shaft for raising ore. The **stowes** had to be made to a definite pattern, and the existence of a stowes (i.e. one windlass) was a symbol of ownership of a mine.

stowpes. Wooden fencing.

strawen. Made of straw.

straw, lady in. Woman in child-bed. For centuries, as a woman was about to give birth, she would be placed on a straw bed, which could afterwards be removed and burnt.

streking/striking. Old term for casting or moulding wax in taper form.

strickle. 1. specially rounded knife used to scrape skin to a smooth even thickness prior to making parchment.
2. instrument used for levelling the top of a measure of grain.

strike/skep. 1. dry measure, usually half a **bushel** *q.v.*, but varying locally.
2. cylindrical wooden measuring vessel containing this quantity.

string. Ploughstring; the rein by which a ploughman controlled his horse.

string course. Continuous horizontal band projecting from surface of facade or exterior wall.

stroke met. *See* **met**.

stropper. Dry cow.

strum. Wickerwork basket used in brewing to put before the bung-hole of a mash tub when the liquor was drawn off to hinder the hops from coming through.

stryner. Strainer; a flat ladle with fine holes in it, for removing scum from beer.

stub. *See* **stobe**.

stud and mud walling. Building without bricks or stones. The walls were of wooden posts interlaced with twigs or with laths nailed upon them, and covered with mud or plaster.

stump. Remains of a round haystack left after the rest has been cut away. Stump of hay is frequently mentioned in farm inventories in West Sussex.

stund/stound. Earthenware jar.

substitute. Person provided either by the parish or by an individual inhabitant to replace a parishioner drawn for service in the militia.

suck. Part of a plough which cuts through the slice of earth cut out by the colter from below.

sucken/sucturne. Compulsory resort of a tenant to a mill for the grinding of his corn.

sucking pig. New born or very young pig.

suff-grate. *See* **sough**.

sugar loaf. Conical loaf of sugar weighing between 3 and 14 lbs, made by pouring sugar liquid into moulds at the end of the refining process. For domestic use pieces of the loaf were chipped off and pounded.

suit of mill. Tenant's obligation to resort to special mill for grinding of corn.

suling. In south eastern England, the fiscal unit of land corresponding to the hide and carucate of other counties.

sumack. Preparations of the *rhus* species for a black dye, or for use in tanning.

surcharging the common. Overstocking the common; i.e., turning on to it more stock than it can feed properly, or more than the equivalent of the number of **gates** *q.v.* one holds; *see* **regulating** *q.v.*, **stint** *q.v.*

surcingle. Girth for a horse.

sureties. 1. godparents.

2. those giving security for the performance of a bond of any sort, e.g marriage, indemnification for maintenance of bastards etc.

surrogate. Clergyman authorised to issue marriage licences.

surtout. 1. man's long, close-fitting overcoat.

2. knee-length sleeveless over-tunic.

surveyor of the highways. Waywarden *q.v.*

sute. 1. suit of clothes;

2. chute or skid for removing barrels from one place to another.

3. device designed to slide up and down the side of a fermenting vessel, from which yeast was skimmed to receptacles beneath.

swade. Leather strap of a spinning wheel.

swage. Tool used by workers in metals for shaping their work; a die or mould used in shaping wrought iron by hammering or pressure.

swape. Lever carrying bucket for raising water from a well.

swape well. Well from which water was raised by aid of a loaded lever.

sway knife. Knife with a long handle, the handle being used as a lever, and the end of the knife being fixed upon a pivot.

sway pole. Crane over a fire.

sweath/swaithe rake. Wooden rake with wooden teeth and a long head, pulled by both hands and used in haymaking.

sweating sickness. Common epidemic disease, swift and fatal.

sweddle belt. Probably a swaddling band, long binder wrapped round infants.

swile. Either swill, pig-food, or else a variant of soil.

swill. 1. pig-food.
2. basket made from oak that had been split, boiled and torn by hand into thin strips of spale.

swinestock. Swine yoke or collar, i.e. a wooden frame placed around a pig's neck, to hinder the animal from going through hedges.

swingle/swinglehand. Flail, often one used for treating flax.

swingletree. On a plough, a cross bar, pivoted at the middle, to which the traces were fastened, giving freedom of movement to the shoulders of the horse or other draught animal.

swyne/shoit/shott. Young pig.

syke. Area of common meadow, often damp.

synker. *See* **sinker**.

syth (cog). One of the short handles on the pole of a scythe.

sythe stone. Whetstone for sharpening scythes.

T

tabby. General term for silk taffeta, apparently originally striped but afterwards applied also to silks of uniform colour, waved or watered.

tabern. Cellar under a building.

table. Flat board supported on trestles or on a frame, the latter being known as a **fraymed table** *q.v.* It could also be hinged to the wall, as a folding table.

table form. Trestle for a table.

tack. 1. clasp or metal band securing container for cheese. 2. hanging shelf.

tackling. Generally, equipment, the word 'tackle' being so used in the Bristol area today; also, harness for horses.

tackman. Manorial officer whose duty it was to collect rents and fines due to the lord.

taffeta. Name applied at different times to different fabrics. In the seventeenth century it seems to have referred to silks, often ribbons.

tagge. *See* **spurget**.

tale. Shortening of the word **talent** *q.v.* in accounting of money according to the nominal valuation of money excluding clipping and wear.

talent. A weight and denomination of money.

tallage. Arbitrary tax levied by Norman and early Angevin kings upon the towns and the demesne lands of the crown; hence, a tax levied upon feudal dependants by their superiors; a municipal rate; a toll or customs duty; a grant, levy, imposition, aid.

talle/tallow. Substance used for making candles, soap, dressing leather etc.

tallet. Hay-loft.

tallet poles. Poles supporting a hay-loft.

tallet stuffe. Farm materials usually stored in the **tallet** or hayloft, and then dispersed in other buildings; fodder put out for animals.

tallow cake. Fat of animals rolled up in the form of a cake ready for the chandler.

tally. Stick notched to act as a record of an amount of money. It was then split in two, from top to bottom, payer and payee each receiving half. In the case of any dispute, the two halves had to **tally**.

tammy. Fine worsted cloth of good quality, often with a glazed finish. Much mentioned in the seventeenth and eighteenth centuries, but obsolete by 1850.

tang. Large girth used to fasten the load or panniers on a pack-saddle; a metal spike fastened into a handle.

tangarth. Tan yard.

tantrell. Idle, unsettled person.

taper. Rush or string dipped in wax, to give light in houses and used in churches as part of ritual.

targe. Small round shield.

taster. Small shallow cup of silver, for tasting wines etc.

tatched end. Cord made of hemp, having a hog's bristle at the end and stiffened with shoemakers wax, used for stitching leather.

taw. Whip.

teagles. Three posts used as a crane for lifting stones and other articles.

team. Set or group of anything according to context.

teaster/tester. Ceiling or canopy over a bed, made with wood or cloth.

ted. To scatter hay to dry.

tedder. Machine for scattering hay.

teinse. Possibly a sieve.

temple wire. Ornament of jewellery or needlework formerly worn by ladies on the side of the forehead, but apparently only prior to 1650. **Temple wires** could also be used to decorate the fashionable French Hoods.

temser/temse. Small fine-meshed sieve used particularly for the sifting of flour, but also in the brewing and woollen trades.

tenanted public house. One whose 'landlord' (properly 'licensee') had a degree of independence in the management of his business, so long as he observed the conditions of his 'tie' to the brewery company.

tenant in chief. One who holds land directly from the king as distinct from a lesser lord.

tenant sawe/tenisar. Tenon-saw.

tenebrae. Name given to the office of matins and lauds usually sung on the afternoon or evening of Wednesday, Thursday and Friday of Holy Week, at which the candles lit at the beginning of the service are extinguished one by one after each psalm, in memory of the darkness at the time of the crucifixion.

tenement. Holding consisting of house and land.

tenter. Wooden framework on which cloth was hung with weights to be stretched after milling so it might dry evenly and without shrinking.

terrier. 1. inventory of possessions, especially of landed property. 2. church inventory.

tester. *See* **teaster.**

testes. Witnesses, i.e. godparents.

testimonial. 1. parish certificate of almost any kind, but usually that given to labourers in husbandry wishing to leave the parish under an Act relating to servants leaving employment 5 Elizabeth, c.4 (1562–3).
2. licence to beg given to poor persons.

tew iron. Tube of iron put on the nose of a bellows to prevent the nose being destroyed in the fire.

tewtaw. Implement for breaking hemp or flax.

thacking gear. Thatching gear.

thegn. Anglo-Saxon noble.

thirdborough. Tithingman *q.v.* or deputy constable.

thirdendale. Pot which holds three pints.

thixle. Carpenter or cooper's tool used for chipping, having a thin arching blade set at right angles to the handle. Sometimes known as an adze.

thoft. Rower's bench in a boat; also called a **thwait.**

thoole, in thole. Altogether (in the whole).

thorn drains. Trench filled with sticks, often with thorns in them, dug by farmers to drain land before draining tiles became common.

thrave. Measure of straw etc., usually either 12 or 24 bundles.

three-field system. Arrangement of open arable lands in three great open fields, corresponding to the three-course rotation of winter corn, spring corn, and fallow.

thripple/thrillbell. Chain tug leading from the collar of a horse to the shaft of a cart or waggon.

throne stool. A commode, with a pan.

thruff. Table tomb in the north of England.

thrum. 1. small utensil of wicker-work affixed to the pole in a mash tub in brewing, to hinder the malt from escaping when the wort was run off.
2. *see* **thrumb**.
3. coarse or waste yarn which would be used for mats or swabs etc.

thrumb. Also as **thrum**. In weaving: each of the ends of the warp-threads left unwoven and remaining attached to the loom when the web is cut off. Also, a cloth with tassels, or a fringe left at the side.

thrum coverlet. Covering with a fringe of threads or tassels.

thwait. *See* **thoft**.

thwart saw. Cross-cut saw.

tick. Case in which flock, feathers, chaff etc. were put to make a bolster or mattress.

tickney/ticknall. Coarse earthenware, especially that made at Ticknall in Derbyshire.

tied cottage. One occupied by a farm worker in connection with, and conditional upon, his employment. The advantage of the **tied cottage** was that its rent was (often fantastically) below the economic level. The disadvantage was that on leaving or being dismissed from his employment, the worker might well find himself homeless.

tile land. Tilled land, i.e. that which has been cultivated or ploughed, probably referring in inventory usage to the work put into the land. *See also* **arders**, **clod**.

tilth. Land which had been ploughed in previous autumn and was ready for sowing in early spring.

tilt hammer. Heavy hammer used in iron works which was lifted and tilted by a wheel.

timothy. *See* **dimity**.

tinetor. Variation of **tenter** *q.v.*

tinnen. Made of tin.

tippet. Garment for neck and shoulders.

tithe. Ancient obligation of all parishioners to maintain their parish priest from the fruits of the earth in his parish. **Great tithe** (of corn, hay and wood) was payable to a rector. A vicar, perhaps in addition to a modest cash stipend, received **small tithe** on everything else (especially wool, and the annual increase of farm stock, fruit, eggs, etc). **Tithes** were commuted to monetary payments in the mid 19th century.

tithe, great. That of corn, hay and wood.

tithe, mixed. That arising from beasts and fowls fed on the earth's produce.

tithe of garbs. That of sheaves (i.e. of white corn); part of the **great tithe** *q.v.*

tithe, predial. That arising from the produce of the earth.

tithe, quadripartite. Supposed former division into four parts, for the bishop, the church fabric, the poor and the maintenance of the priest respectively.

tithe, small. Tithe *q.v.*, whether **predial** *q.v.* or **mixed** *q.v.*, upon everything save corn, hay and wood.

tithe, tripartite division of. Alleged former division of the total **tithe** *q.v.* received into three portions (after the diocesan bishop had been provided for in other ways), the equal shares being respectively for the church fabric, the maintenance of the priest, and the relief of the poor.

tithing. Group of householders in the frank-pledge system – originally ten but numbers later varied. Mutually responsible for the good behaviour of the group.

tithingman. Before the Conquest, the chief man of a **tithing** *q.v.*, a **headborough** *q.v.*; in later use, a parish peace-officer or **petty constable** *q.v.*

tobacco tongs. Pair of tongs with a spring between the arms, sometimes pocket-sized, used to pick up embers to light tobacco.

tod. 1. weight of wool, about 28 lbs.
2. fox.
3. clump of bushes.
4. ivy bush.

to-fall/tuffold. Lean-to outbuilding, a hovel.

toftstead. House or the site of a former house, especially one having common right which attached to the site even if the house had disappeared.

token, communion. Stamped piece of lead or other metal given usually after confession as a voucher of fitness to take holy communion.

toll dish. Dish or bowl of stated dimensions for measuring the toll of grain at a mill; a multure dish.

Tolpuddle Martyrs. Six agricultural workers from Tolpuddle in Dorset who formed a Union branch in 1834, were found guilty of taking a seditious oath, and were given the maximum sentences of transportation to Australia for seven years. A widespread public outcry led to their pardon in 1836.

tommy. Provisions given to workmen in manufacturing districts, instead of money.

topping out. *See* **rearing feast.**

torches. Skeins of rope dipped in pitch etc., carried at funerals as part of ritual. The dead person made provision in his will for the torches at his own funeral.

torn/torne/toren/tourn/turn. 1. spinning wheel.
2. churn. **Sheriff's tourn** *q.v.*

touchbox. Primer for a gun or musket.

touffa. Small shed at the end of a farm house to house implements of agriculture and gardening.

towe. Hemp fibre, much coarser than flax, used for making canvas, rope and sheets. Also, the refuse left by **heckling** *q.v.*

towed yarn. Flaxen or hempen yarn from which the tow has been removed.

township. Ultimate unit into which the country was divided for purposes of civil government before the development of the parish as a civil unit in Tudor times.

towser. In Devon, coarse apron worn by maid servants.

traces. Pair of ropes, chains or leather straps by which the collar of a draught animal was connected with the splinter bar or swingletree attached to a cart or implement.

trailrake. Horse-drawn rake.

train. *See* **trayne.**

trammel. Iron instrument suspended in the chimney from which pots or kettles were hung over the fire.

transcripts of parish registers. Duplicate copies of entries in parish registers transmitted annually or triennially to the archdeacon or bishop.

traverse. To appear in court to plead 'not guilty'.

travis. Open shed or lean-to commonly attached to a smithy.

tray. Wooden hurdle commonly used when putting sheep in a pen.

trayne/train. Oil or fat from whale blubber or various fishes, similar to tallow.

T.R.E. *Tempore regis Edwardi*: in the days of King Edward (used in Domesday to mean before 1066).

treasure trove. Money or coin, gold, silver, plate or bullion found hidden in the earth. If the owner is unknown, it belongs to the Crown.

treen/trenen/trine. Wooden ware; small domestic articles such as bowls and platters.

trenchard chair. Probably, a chair with wide arms incorporating holes or depressions to contain trenchers; possibly also a chair with a flat circular seat.

trencher. Flat piece of wood, square or circular, on which meat was served and cut up; a plate or platter. The name derives from the earliest type of plate, which was a thick slice of bread known in France as a 'tranche'.

trencher salt. Large salt cellar.

trenching tools. Tools used in meadow or pasture ground to cut out the sides of trenches or drains.

trendal. Ring circle or hoop on which candles were fixed. It was suspended in front of the **rood** *q.v.* It corresponded with the **roundel** *q.v.* which was the more usual term in the Midlands.

trenen. *See* **treen**.

trental. Roman Catholic office for the dead consisting of 30 masses for 30 successive days.

trindle bed. *See* **truckle**.

trine. *See* **treen**.

trinklements. Odds and ends; miscellaneous small belongings.

trinoda necessitas. Collective term for the three great obligations upon land holders in Anglo-Saxon times of military defence,

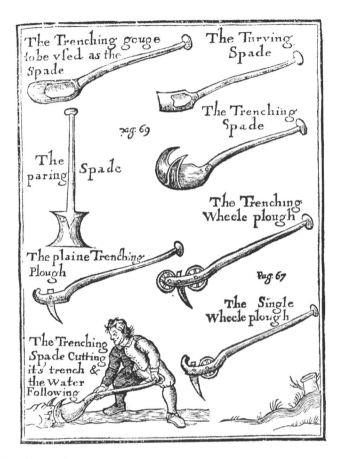

19. *Trenching tools.*

the maintenance of roads and bridges, and the upkeep of fortresses.

trippet/trivett. Iron grid for supporting pans placed adjacent to a fire. *See also* **crow.**

trolubber. Husbandman, a day labourer in Exmoor.

trophy money. Militia rate.

truckle. Wheel or possibly roller, which could be large or small.

truckle/trindle/trundle bed. Low bed, usually on wheels, often kept out of use beneath a standing bed.

trumperie/trumpery. (Term used to describe) something of no value; trash, a trifle.

trus/trushinge bed. Travelling bed; one whose frame and hangings could be taken apart and packed into trusses or bundles.

truss. 1. bundle, as of hay or straw.
2. measure of weight for hay and straw, 56 lbs old hay, 60 lbs new hay and 36 lbs straw.
3. to bind or pack close; to tie very firmly.

trussband. Bundled hay etc.

trusser. Strong heavy bench or table.

tucking. Satchel used in setting beans. Each setter was furnished with a **setting-pin** *q.v.* and a **tucking** hung by a string round his waist in which to carry the beans.

tuffold. *See* **to-fall**.

tugwithe. Band used to attach the swingletree to the head of the plough, or to the cart or harrow.

tumble-down gate. Gate on a towing path, so constructed that horses might pass over it while one end is pressed down. It recovered its position through being weighted at the opposite point.

tumbrel/tumbril. 1. cart so constructed that the body tilted backwards in order to empty out the load, especially a dung cart. Often with two wheels.
2. open rack for hay for cattle in the field or crew-yard.

tun. Vessel holding 252 gallons, usually of wine.

tundish/tuning dish. Shallow wooden vessel with a hole in the bottom used as a funnel in brewing or in a dairy.

tup. 1. ram. 2. head of hammer.

tup-hog. One-year-old ram.

Turkey work. Woollen material woven in the same way as a Turkish carpet.

turn. *See* **torn**.

turn barrell. Winding apparatus at a mine.

turn churn. Revolving churn, replacing the earlier type of churn which was a conical shaped vessel, fitted with a perforated plunger which was worked with an up and down motion.

turnell. 1. large oval tub, especially one used for salting meat, kneading bread, or putting under a cheese press.
2. **turnell with a rene**, the windlass over a well with a 'rein' or check to the windlass.

turnpike trustee. Local person empowered, especially in the eighteenth century, to supplement the work of the parish waywardens by charging tolls for the use of the roads, and expending the proceeds on their maintenance and improvement. Also known as turnpike commissioners.

turn wrist plough. Plough on which the mould board could be shifted from one side to the other at the end of each furrow, so that the furrow-slice was always thrown the same way.

turves. Peat cut for fuel.

twill wheel. *See* **quill wheel.**

twinter. Two year old beast, usually a cow.

twinter gate. The right to pasture a **twinter** *q.v.*

twist. Fine silk thread used by tailors, hatters etc., but also thread generally made of two or more filaments wound round one another.

twy-crooks. Little crooks bent in contrary directions in order to lengthen out the rings or links on which pot hooks were hung.

tyburn ticket. Certificate of exemption from parish office in reward for capture and successful prosecution of a felon.

tyning. Small area of enclosed ground.

tynnen/tynkyn. Made of tin or tin plate.

tything barne. Tithing barn; a barn in which tithe corn was stored.

U

unbraked hemp. Uncombed hemp.

upholder. Undertaker.

Uppingham trencher. The trencher kept at Uppingham used as the standard measure for the weights and measures of the county by a statute of Henry VIII. This town was probably famous for the art of **trencher** *q.v.* making. Having the standard measure in this town helped to induce turners and other makers of measures to settle here.

uterine. Born of the same mother but by a different father.

uxoratus. Married man.

V

vagrancy. Condition of being without regular employment or settled home. From the fourteenth century vagrancy was strictly controlled. If vagrants were capable of working they were subjected to very severe penalties, ranging from whipping or loss of ears to hanging. Vagrants incapable of working had to obtain a licence from the magistrate to beg within a specified area.

20. *Vagrancy.* Beggars, vagrants, lunatics, witches and miscreants figure prominently in descriptions of Tudor society. The development of the Poor Law recognized different categories of poor, from the infirm to the dangerous. After 1598 beggars were to be whipped by statute.

vail. Tip to a servant when visiting; frequently in plural form. The servants lined up in rows when a guest departed from a house to receive the gratuity appropriate to their calling. In some houses there was a fixed scale of charges for all the various services provided for guests.

vallence/vallans/vallians. Curtain round a bed, completely enclosing it; later simply a curtain round the bottom of the bed.

Valor Ecclesiasticus. Tax book in which all the ecclesiastical property in England was valued by the Commissioners appointed by Thomas Cromwell as a prelude to the Dissolution of the Monasteries in 1535.

vantage. Profits arising.

vassal. One who holds land directly from the king as distinct from a lesser lord.

vault. Arched roof or ceiling.

vellies. Joined pieces of wood making up the rim of a cartwheel. *See also* **felloe**.

verdigriss/verninice. Greenish substance used in dyeing, formed by the action of acetic acid on copper.

vergee. Land measure, about four-ninths of an acre.

verjuice. Acid juice of crab-apples or other sour fruit, used in cooking. Also known as **crab vinegar** *q.v.*

verso. Left hand page of an open book; opposite of **recto** *q.v.*

vestry, open. (Meeting of) the ancient customary governing body of a parish which all ratepayers might attend, in order to deal with matters, civil or ecclesiastical, of local concern. It still exists as the Parochial Church Council, but now it has lost nearly all its civil powers and duties.

vestry, select. 'Close' governing body of a parish, the members generally having a property qualification, and being recruited more or less by co-option.

vetch. *See* **fetch**.

viaticus. Wayfarer, tramp.

vicar. Originally the mere deputy of the parson (rector), later usually the incumbent of a benefice appropriate or impropriate, i.e. receiving small tithes or their equivalent, but generally not receiving great tithes. Exceptionally there were benefices neither appropriate nor impropriate, but having a clerical (sinecurist) rector as well as a resident **vicar**.

vicar's ring. Ancient enclosure of a township, often tithable to the vicar for both **great** *q.v.* and **small tithe** *q.v.*, although in the rest of the township the great tithe belonged to the rector.

vill. Village or town, the Norman French equivalent of the Old English term **township** *q.v.*

villanus. One of the class of serfs in the feudal system; specifically a peasant occupier or cultivator entirely subject to a lord or attached to a manor. Sometimes called **villager**, **villein**.

villein. Unfree but land-holding countryman of early feudal times.

vipse. *See* **gipsey.**

virgate. Measure of land, a quarter of a **hide** *q.v.* The actual size was variable, depending on the soil quality, it could be from 15 to 60 acres. Also known as **yardland**, **wista** or **yoke.**

virgater. Tenant of a **virgate** *q.v.*

virginals. Keyed musical instrument, a kind of spinet with one string to a note set in a legless case. Common in England in the sixteenth and seventeenth centuries.

virgintall. Twenty masses said or sung for the soul of a dead person.

visitation. Official inspection of the parish by or on behalf of the bishop or his representative, the archdeacon. *See* **apparitor.**

voice/vise. Vice; probably one which could be clamped to a table.

voussoir. One of a series of wedged shaped stones forming an arch.

voyder/voider. Basket or tray used to clear the table of dirty dishes and broken food, also known as a butler's tray.

vyall. Viol, a musical instrument with five, six or seven strings, played with a bow.

Waggon, Suffolk type, circa 1880. The Suffolk waggon is generally larger and carries heavier loads than a cart. At Rutland County Museum, Oakham.

W

wachet. Bright blue colour, used for cloth.

wadmol/wadmal. Coarse woollen cloth, used for lining saddles and horse collars.

wafering/waffring iron. 1. leather tie or rope used particularly for binding a load to the back of a cart.
2. baking iron used for making crisp cakes or wafers.

wager of law. Formal oath of innocence sworn in court by accused person and supported by the oaths of compurators. To **wage one's law** was to defend an accusation in this way.

waggon. Strong open four-wheeled vehicle, built for carrying corn, hay etc.

waif. Any property which was found ownerless; **waifs** included 'wreck of the sea'. By law **waifs** and estrays had to be publicly proclaimed in the nearest markets, and in the parish church. If not claimed by the owner within a year and a day, they were valued and fell to the lord. The early sense of 'waive' implied abandoning goods, especially stolen goods, and most **waif** had been cast aside by fugitive thieves when pursued in hue and cry.

wain/waine/wane/wayne. 1. large cart, usually with four wheels, and usually an ox-cart, with an open body and furnished with shelvings, formerly used for carrying corn and hay.
2. *see* **wainscot.**

wain(e) blades. Shafts.

waine clout. Plate of iron, fixed on an axle-tree to prevent wear.

wainscot. Oak imported from northern Europe and used for panelling walls prior to the introduction of wall-paper. Particular items of furniture before which the word **wainscot** appears were made of oak and the general term wainscot furniture should be understood in the present day sense of furnishings incorporated in a chair or screen.

wallett. Bag with a receptacle at each end used for carrying provisions when travelling either on foot or on horseback.

wanded chair. 1. wickerwork chair made from wand, the young shoot of a willow.
2. chair with woven rush seat and back.

want/oont. Dialect word for a mole.

wanting brush. Very obscure term; perhaps a brush for cleaning mole-skins, or 'moling brush'; *see* **want/oont**.

wanty. Rope or band to fasten a pack.

wapentake. Territorial division in certain English counties, corresponding to the **hundred** *q.v.* of southern counties. By the tenth century England was divided into shires, units of unequal size later to be called counties; each of these had a court which met twice a year and was presided over by the king's representative, the shire reeve or **sheriff** *q.v.* The shires in their turn were divided into **hundreds** *q.v.*, or in the Dane's lands **wapentakes**, unequal in size and each with their own court; this was the court most used by the rural population.

ward. *See* **watch and ward**.

wardbrace. Guard, presumably of leather, strapped to the left forearm to protect it from the friction of the bowstring on discharge. Also known as **garde-bras** or **bracer**.

wardpenny. Payment in lieu of keeping watch.

wardship. Control and use of the lands of a tenant who is a minor; guardianship of an infant heir (including the right to arrange marriage) until that heir has attained his or her majority.

warming-pan. Pan of brass or copper, with lid and long handle, for inserting between the sheets to warm a bed. It was removed when the occupant got in.

warping bar. Bar which was part of the frame for preparing the warp or lengthwise threads in weaving.

warping fatt/vat. Container in which the warp was sized before weaving.

wash ball. Ball of soap, sometimes perfumed or medicated, used for washing the hands and face, and for shaving.

waste. Inferior land used commonally.

wastel. Superior form of white flour.

watch. 1. heifer; a young cow before producing its first calf. A dialect term. 2. clockwork contrivance for operating a jack. 3. *see* **watch and ward**.

watch and ward. Patrolling of a town both by night (**watch**) and by day (**ward**), a duty to which citizens of the town were liable. Initially introduced under Statute of Winchester 13 Edw. I, St. II, c.6 (1285).

watch bill. Kind of concave axe with a spike at the back and having a shaft ending in a spearhead; a halbert. A weapon often carried by **watchmen**: *see* **watch and ward**.

water candlestick. Vertical tube filled with water, to hold a floating piece of wax candle.

Waterloo teeth. Teeth taken from the bodies of dead soldiers on battlefields, and shipped to England in thousands after the end of the Napoleonic Wars to use instead of artificial teeth. Similarly, in the 1860s certain dentists no longer troubled to make artificial teeth, relying on teeth sent across the Atlantic in barrels by tooth-drawers from the battlefields of the American Civil War.

wax silver. Easter offering.

waywarden. Parochial official having, from the time of Philip and Mary to that of Queen Victoria (c. 1550 to 1900), responsibility for the maintenance of the highways in the parish, and the supervision of the labour of his fellow parishioners in their statutory duty of maintaining and repairing these. Also called **surveyor of the highways** or **boonmaster**.

weather/wether. Male sheep, usually castrated and in its second season.

weather glass. Barometer.

web. Whole piece of cloth in the process of being woven, or after it comes from the loom.

webster. Weaver.

weear hoock. Weir hook; a tool for cleansing weir-sluices.

weed hook/wedhocke. Hook for cutting away weeds.

week work. Work done for the lord so many days per week by his tenants.

weighbeame/weighing beam. Transverse bar of a set of scales; sometimes known simply as a beam or **beame** *q.v.*

weighte/wey. Measure of wool; thirteen to fourteen stone.

welcroobe. Probably the framework over a well.

welldrag/weldrage. Three pronged drag for retrieving the bucket or things dropped in a well.

wether. *See* **weather**.

whafer iron. Apparatus for baking wafers. It consisted of two iron blades between which the paste was laid.

whelm. Half a hollow tree, laid under a gateway, to form a passage for water. A kind of substitute for an arch.

whetstone. Shaped stone used to give a smooth edge to cutting tools when ground.

whim. Winding engine worked by horses or steam.

whimsey. Steam-driven winding engine.

whin. Common furze or gorse.

whings. *See* **wings**.

whipcord. Thin tough kind of hempen cord.

whipp whang. Long thin strip of leather, used for the lash of a whip.

whipping post. Used for public whipping. There were three shackles each side to secure the hands of the offender.

whirlicote. Open carriage.

whirrer. Spindle.

whiskett. Osier basket used in the garden or for feeding cattle.

whitch/which. Meal-bin made of planks of split oak wedged and pegged together.

white coal. Fuel used in the ore hearth in Derbyshire made from wood which was debarked, chopped small and dried in a woodland kiln. Large hollows, the remains of **white coal kilns**, can sometimes be found in the woods near the former smelting mill sites. Also used for the smelting of silver.

whitemeat. Dairy produce.

whiteware. Earthenware, probably of good quality and white in appearance.

Whitsun farthings. *See* **pentecostals**.

whittle. 1. double blanket worn by West country women over their shoulders, like a cloak.
2. common or ordinary labourer's knife, in some counties called a 'dull knife', often used to whittle wood.
3. to cut off thin slices or shavings of wood with a knife.

wholehose. Breeches worn with stockings sewn to them.

whole year lands/every year lands. Lands in the open fields cropped every year, having no fallow in their rotation.

wholve. *See* **holve**.

whymble. *See* **wimble**.

21. *Whipping post.* The Whipping Irons at Stow, near Cotes, Lincolnshire. The left-hand irons are dated 1769. There are three clasps of varying size on each side of the post to fit the size of the hands. Made by William Hill, Blacksmith.

wick. 1. bay or small port on the side of a river.
   2. village so situated.

wick/witch. Shed in which cheese from ewes milk was made.

wide awake. In the nineteenth century, a soft wide-brimmed hat.

widow's bench. Share of a husband's estate which the widow had the right to claim for life or until her remarriage. This portion was usually one-third, and sometimes one-half.

wife-sale. Form of divorce by an ancient custom in which the wife, with her consent, was taken to market with a halter round her neck, and sold to the highest bidder, usually a purchaser who had already agreed to buy her. This was a custom which, both illegal and constantly condemned as immoral, continued until at least 1887.

willow garth/withybed. Bed of willows for basket making.

wimble/whymble. 1. gimlet or auger drill, particularly used in mining.
2. hay-trusser's tool.
3. as **rest wimble**, possibly a tool for making part of a plough.

winding blade. Spindle for winding yarn.

winding cloth. 1. large cloth on which corn was winnowed.
2. shroud.

windle. *See* **wyndell**.

window cloth. Cloth used instead of glass for filling a window. *See also* **sack**.

windowleams/windowleaves. Removable windows, including both glass and frame.

windrow. Sheaves of corn set up in a row one against the other; so the wind could blow between them; or a row of grass in hay making.

wings/whings. Iron side pieces of a grate.

winnow/winnore. Winnowing-fan used to separate grain from chaff.

winsor/windsor. Chair with a solid seat and the back and legs made of spindles.

winze. Small underground shaft sunk from one part of a mine to another.

wista. *See* **yardland**.

withybed. *See* **willow garth**.

withies. *See* **osiers**.

witnesses. Godparents.

wong. 1. furlong in the open fields, especially in the counties of Danish and Scandinavian settlement. 2. enclosed meadow. 3. low lying land, often marshy.

woodward. Manorial official concerned with protection of woodland.

woole card/combe. Toothed instrument with iron teeth used to part and comb out fibres of wool and hemp, to straighten them before spinning.

woollen, burial in. Burial in woollen *q.v. See also* **information.**

wool sack. Sack suspended from a beam in a barn so that it hung down to floor level and two wool packers stood inside it and as the fleeces were thrown up to them, they packed them down, footing them into the corners and treading down the layers tightly. As the layers rose, the packers would be treading the top of a high wall of wool. When the last layer was thrown up, they stepped out along the top, sewing up the sack as they went. The **wool sack** would then be lowered to the ground, eight holds tied at the corners to make it easier to handle.

woort/wort. Infusion of malt or other grain, which after fermentation becomes beer.

workhouse test. Offer made to applicants for outdoor relief of either admission to the workhouse or no relief at all.

worm tub. Tub used in distilling.

worsted. Type of woollen cloth, but also the yarn from which it was made. This was a well twisted yarn made from longstaple wool, combed to lay the fibres parallel.

wring. Press for making cheese or cider.

wrought. Of towels, napkins etc.: decorated or ornamented with needlework.

wych. Salt works. The house in which the salt was boiled was called a **wych-house**. This is why towns ending with **wych** are associated with salt and salt mines, e.g. Namptwych, Middle-wych, (now Nantwich, Middlewich), etc.

wyndell/windle. Basket, especially a basket used in winnowing corn.

Y

yardland. Measure of land, originally no doubt, as much as would serve to occupy a yoke of oxen. Later a conventional unit, varying very widely in area, perhaps 20 to 50 statute acres, but always containing two oxgangs, and forming a quarter of a carucate, hide or ploughland, a variable land measure dependent on soil quality. Also called a **virgate** *q.v.*, **wista**, or **yoke**.

yarr. To plough, i.e. one ploughing of the land during the fallow season.

yarre. Fallow plough.

yarwingle/yarwind. Appliance for winding a skein of yarn into a ball.

yathouse. High carriage gateway through a building.

yealing house. Place where beer wort, the liquid portion of the mash of malted grain, was left to ferment.

yearne ware. Earthenware.

yellow belly. Person born in the Fens of Lincolnshire.

yeoman. Freeholder cultivating his own land; an occupying owner. Also used much more loosely to mean small or medium farmer generally.

yeremind. *See* **obit**.

yetling. Small iron pan with a bow handle and three feet.

yeveshep. Customary service of hogget given at Whitsuntide.

yevewerke. Boonwork *q.v.*

yielding tub. Wooden or lead trough for brewing beer.

yoke. 1. wooden frame fastened over the necks of two oxen to hold them together, and to which a plough is attached.
2. frame fitted to a person's shoulders for carrying a couple of buckets with equally weighed loads, e.g. of milk or water, suspended from each end.
3. bar used with a double harness to connect the collar of each horse to the tongue of a waggon, coach or other trailer.
4. collar fastened round the necks of hogs or swine to restrain them from breaking through hedges.
5. a Kent term for a **virgate** *q.v.*; *see also* **yardland**.

22. Milk delivery in the eighteenth century. Drawn from a contemporary picture. The illustration shows the *yoke* and covered pails, although many were just open buckets. The measures hang around the bucket.

yokings. Pieces of wood joined together to mark out a claim in mining.

yorne. Yarn.

yronware. Iron ware.

Regnal Years 1066–1952

This section is reproduced from *A Handbook of Dates for Students of British History*, C. R. Cheney (ed). New edition revised by Michael Jones (Royal Historical Society Guides and Handbooks No. 4).

William I

25 December – 24 December		10	1096–97
1	1066–67	11	1097–98
2	1067–68	12	1098–99
3	1068–69	13	1099–2 August 1100
4	1069–70		
5	1070–71		

Henry I

6	1071–72	5 August–4 August	
7	1072–73	1	1100–01
8	1073–74	2	1101–02
9	1074–75	3	1102–03
10	1075–76	4	1103–04
11	1076–77	5	1104–05
12	1077–78	6	1105–06
13	1078–79	7	1106–07
14	1079–80	8	1107–08
15	1080–81	9	1108–09
16	1081–82	10	1109–10
17	1082–83	11	1110–11
18	1083–84	12	1111–12
19	1084–85	13	1112–13
20	1085–86	14	1113–14
21	1086–9 September 1087	15	1114–15
		16	1115–16

William II

26 September–25 September		17	1116–17
1	1087–88	18	1117–18
2	1088–89	19	1118–19
3	1089–90	20	1119–20
4	1090–91	21	1120–21
5	1091–92	22	1121–22
6	1092–93	23	1122–23
7	1093–94	24	1123–24
8	1094–95	25	1124–25
9	1095–96	26	1125–26
		27	1126–27

28	1127–28
29	1128–29
30	1129–30
31	1130–31
32	1131–32
33	1132–33
34	1133–34
35	1134–35
36	1135–1 December 1135

Stephen
26 December–25 December

1	1135–36
2	1136–37
3	1137–38
4	1138–39
5	1139–40
6	1140–41
7	1141–42
8	1142–43
9	1143–44
10	1144–45
11	1145–46
12	1146–47
13	1147–48
14	1148–49
15	1149–50
16	1150–51
17	1151–52
18	1152–53
19	1153–25 October 1154

Henry II
19 December–18 December

1	1154–55
2	1155–56
3	1156–57
4	1157–58
5	1158–59
6	1159–60
7	1160–61
8	1161–62
9	1162–63
10	1163–64
11	1164–65
12	1165–66
13	1166–67
14	1167–68
15	1168–69
16	1169–70
17	1170–71
18	1171–72
19	1172–73
20	1173–74
21	1174–75
22	1175–76
23	1176–77
24	1177–78
25	1178–79
26	1179–80
27	1180–81
28	1181–82
29	1182–83
30	1183–84
31	1184–85
32	1185–86
33	1186–87
34	1187–88
35	1188–6 July 1189

Richard I
3 September–2 September

1	1189–90
2	1190–91
3	1191–92
4	1192–93
5	1193–94
6	1194–95
7	1195–96
8	1196–97
9	1197–98
10	1198–6 April 1199

John

John was crowned on Ascension Day 1199 and this movable feast became the date at which his regnal years began. They are thus of unequal length.

1	27 May 1199–17 May 1200
2	18 May 1200–2 May 1201
3	3 May 1201–22 May 1202
4	23 May 1202–14 May 1203
5	15 May 1203–2 June 1204
6	3 June 1204–18 May 1205
7	19 May 1205–10 May 1206
8	11 May 1206–30 May 1207
9	31 May 1207–14 May 1208
10	15 May 1208–6 May 1209
11	7 May 1209–26 May 1210
12	27 May 1210–11 May 1211
13	12 May 1211–2 May 1212
14	3 May 1212–22 May 1213
15	23 May 1213–7 May 1214
16	8 May 1214–27 May 1215
17	28 May 1215–18 May 1216
18	19 May 1216–19 October 1216

Henry III

28 October–27 October

1	1216–17
2	1217–18
3	1218–19
4	1219–20
5	1220–21
6	1221–22
7	1222–23
8	1223–24
9	1224–25
10	1225–26
11	1226–27
12	1227–28
13	1228–29
14	1229–30
15	1230–31
16	1231–32
17	1232–33
18	1233–34
19	1234–35
20	1235–36
21	1236–37
22	1237–38
23	1238–39
24	1239–40
25	1240–41
26	1241–42
27	1242–43
28	1243–44
29	1244–45
30	1245–46
31	1246–47
32	1247–48
33	1248–49
34	1249–50
35	1250–51
36	1251–52
37	1252–53
38	1253–54
39	1254–55
40	1255–56
41	1256–57
42	1257–58
43	1258–59
44	1259–60
45	1260–61
46	1261–62
47	1262–63
48	1263–64
49	1264–65
50	1265–66
51	1266–67
52	1267–68

53	1268–69
54	1269–70
55	1270–71
56	1271–72
57	1272–16 November 1272

Edward I
20 November–19 November

1	1272–73
2	1273–74
3	1274–75
4	1275–76
5	1276–77
6	1277–78
7	1278–79
8	1279–80
9	1280–81
10	1281–82
11	1282–83
12	1283–84
13	1284–85
14	1285–86
15	1286–87
16	1287–88
17	1288–89
18	1289–90
19	1290–91
20	1291–92
21	1292–93
22	1293–94
23	1294–95
24	1295–96
25	1296–97
26	1297–98
27	1298–99
28	1299–1300
29	1300–01
30	1301–02
31	1302–03
32	1303–04
33	1304–05

34	1305–06
35	1306–7 July 1307

Edward II
8 July–7 July

1	1307–08
2	1308–09
3	1309–10
4	1310–11
5	1311–12
6	1312–13
7	1313–14
8	1314–15
9	1315–16
10	1316–17
11	1317–18
12	1318–19
13	1319–20
14	1320–21
15	1321–22
16	1322–23
17	1323–24
18	1324–25
19	1325–26
20	1326–20 January 1327

Edward III
25 January–24 January

1	1327–28
2	1328–29
3	1329–30
4	1330–31
5	1331–32
6	1332–33
7	1333–34
8	1334–35
9	1335–36
10	1336–37
11	1337–38
12	1338–39
13	1339–40

14	1340–41
15	1341–42
16	1342–43
17	1343–44
18	1344–45
19	1345–46
20	1346–47
21	1347–48
22	1348–49
23	1349–50
24	1350–51
25	1351–52
26	1352–53
27	1353–54
28	1354–55
29	1355–56
30	1356–57
31	1357–58
32	1358–59
33	1359–60
34	1360–61
35	1361–62
36	1362–63
37	1363–64
38	1364–65
39	1365–66
40	1366–67
41	1367–68
42	1368–69
43	1369–70
44	1370–71
45	1371–72
46	1372–73
47	1373–74
48	1374–75
49	1375–76
50	1376–77
51	1377–21 June 1377

Richard II
22 June–21 June

1	1377–78
2	1378–79
3	1379–80
4	1380–81
5	1381–82
6	1382–83
7	1383–84
8	1384–85
9	1385–86
10	1386–87
11	1387–88
12	1388–89
13	1389–90
14	1390–91
15	1391–92
16	1392–93
17	1393–94
18	1394–95
19	1395–96
20	1396–97
21	1397–98
22	1398–99
23	1399–29 September 1399

Henry IV
30 September–29 September

1	1399-1400
2	1400–01
3	1401–02
4	1402–03
5	1403–04
6	1404–05
7	1405–06
8	1406–07
9	1407–08
10	1408–09
11	1409–10
12	1410–11
13	1411–12
14	1412–20 March 1413

Henry V
21 March–20 March
1   1413–14
2   1414–15
3   1415–16
4   1416–17
5   1417–18
6   1418–19
7   1419–20
8   1420–21
9   1421–22
10 1422–31 August 1422

Henry VI
1 September–31 August
1   1422–23
2   1423–24
3   1424–25
4   1425–26
5   1426–27
6   1427–28
7   1428–29
8   1429–30
9   1430–31
10 1431–32
11 1432–33
12 1433–34
13 1434–35
14 1435–36
15 1436–37
16 1437–38
17 1438–39
18 1439–40
19 1440–41
20 1441–42
21 1442–43
22 1443–44
23 1444–45
24 1445–46
25 1446–47
26 1447–48

27 1448–49
28 1449–50
29 1450–51
30 1451–52
31 1452–53
32 1453–54
33 1454–55
34 1455–56
35 1456–57
36 1457–58
37 1458–59
38 1459–60
39 1460–4 March 1461
    and
49 September–October
    1470 to 11 April 1471
Edward IV fled the country
on 29 September 1470; Henry
VI was released on 3 October
and re-crowned on 13
October. His restoration
ended with his capture by
Edward IV on 11 April 1471.

Edward IV
4 March–3 March
1   1461–62
2   1462–63
3   1463–64
4   1464–65
5   1465–66
6   1466–67
7   1467–68
8   1468–69
9   1469–70
10 1470–71
11 1471–72
12 1472–73
13 1473–74
14 1474–75
15 1475–76

16	1476–77		21	1505–06
17	1477–78		22	1506–07
18	1478–79		23	1507–08
19	1479–80		24	1508–21 April 1509
20	1480–81			
21	1481–82		***Henry VIII***	
22	1482–83		22 April–21 April	
23	1483–9 April 1483		1	1509–10
			2	1510–11
Edward V			3	1511–12
1	9 April 1483–25 June		4	1512–13
	1483		5	1513–14
			6	1514–15
Richard III			7	1515–16
26 June–25 June			8	1516–17
1	1483–84		9	1517–18
2	1484–85		10	1518–19
3	1485–22 August 1485		11	1519–20
			12	1520–21
Henry VII			13	1521–22
22 August–21 August			14	1522–23
1	1485–86		15	1523–24
2	1486–87		16	1524–25
3	1487–88		17	1525–26
4	1488–89		18	1526–27
5	1489–90		19	1527–28
6	1490–91		20	1528–29
7	1491–92		21	1529–30
8	1492–93		22	1530–31
9	1493–94		23	1531–32
10	1494–95		24	1532–33
11	1495–96		25	1533–34
12	1496–97		26	1534–35
13	1497–98		27	1535–36
14	1498–99		28	1536–37
15	1499–1500		29	1537–38
16	1500–01		30	1538–39
17	1501–02		31	1539–40
18	1502–03		32	1540–41
19	1503–04		33	1541–42
20	1504–05		34	1542–43

35 1543–44
36 1544–45
37 1545–46
38 1546–28 January 1547

Edward VI
28 January–27 January
1 1547–48
2 1548–49
3 1549–50
4 1550–51
5 1551–52
6 1552–53
7 1553–6 July 1553

Jane
1 6 July 1553–19 July 1553

Mary
1 19 July 1553–5 July 1554
2 6 July 1554–24 July 1554
Mary dated her second year from 6 July, ignoring Jane's intrusion.

Philip and Mary
1&2 25 July 1554–5 July 1555
1&3 6 July 1555–24 July 1555
2&3 25 July 1555–5 July 1556
2&4 6 July 1556–24 July 1556
3&4 25 July 1556–5 July 1557
3&5 6 July 1557-24 July 1557
4&5 25 July 1557–5 July 1558
4&6 6 July 1558–24 July 1558
5&6 25 July 1558–17 November 1558

Elizabeth I
17 November–16 November
1 1558–59
2 1559–60

3 1560–61
4 1561–62
5 1562–63
6 1563–64
7 1564–65
8 1565–66
9 1566–67
10 1567–68
11 1568–69
12 1569–70
13 1570–71
14 1571–72
15 1572–73
16 1573–74
17 1574–75
18 1575–76
19 1576–77
20 1577–78
21 1578–79
22 1579–80
23 1580–81
24 1581–82
25 1582–83
26 1583–84
27 1584–85
28 1585–86
29 1586–87
30 1587–88
31 1588–89
32 1589–90
33 1590–91
34 1591–92
35 1592–93
36 1593–94
37 1594–95
38 1595–96
39 1596–97
40 1597–98
41 1598–99
42 1599–1600
43 1600–01

44   1601–02
45   1602–24 March 1603

James I
24 March–23 March
1   1603–04
2   1604–05
3   1605–06
4   1606–07
5   1607–08
6   1608–09
7   1609–10
8   1610–11
9   1611–12
10   1612–13
11   1613–14
12   1614–15
13   1615–16
14   1616–17
15   1617–18
16   1618–19
17   1619–20
18   1620–21
19   1621–22
20   1622–23
21   1623–24
22   1624–25
23   1625–27 March 1625

Charles I
27 March–26 March
1   1625–26
2   1626–27
3   1627–28
4   1628–29
5   1629–30
6   1630–31
7   1631–32
8   1632–33
9   1633–34
10   1634–35

11   1635–36
12   1636–37
13   1637–38
14   1638–39
15   1639–40
16   1640–41
17   1641–42
18   1642–43
19   1643–44
20   1644–45
21   1645–46
22   1646–47
23   1647–48
24   1648–30 January 1649

The Commonwealth
After the execution of Charles I on 30 January 1649, the kingship was abolished (17 March 1649) and government by a Council of State was set up on 14 February 1649. Oliver Cromwell took the office of Lord Protector on 16 December 1653 and held it till his death on 3 September 1658. His son, Richard succeeded to the same office on the day of his father's death and abdicated on 24 May 1659. After a year of parliamentary government Charles II was proclaimed king on 5 May 1660 and returned to England on 29 May 1660.

Charles II
His regnal years were calculated from the death of his father.
29 May–29 January
12 1660–61
30 January–29 January
13 1661–62
14 1662–63
15 1663–64
16 1664–65
17 1665–66
18 1666–67
19 1667–68
20 1668–69
21 1669–70
22 1670–71
23 1671–72
24 1672–73
25 1673–74
26 1674–75
27 1675–76
28 1676–77
29 1677–78
30 1678–79
31 1679–80
32 1680–81
33 1681–82
34 1682–83
35 1683–84
36 1684–85
37 1685–6 February 1685

James II
6 February–5 February
1 1685–86
2 1686–87
3 1687–88
4 1688–11 Dec 1688

Interregnum
12 December 1688–12 February 1689

William and Mary
13 February–12 February
1 1689–90
2 1690–91
3 1691–92
4 1692–93
5 1693–94
6 1694–27 December 1694

William III
6 28 December–12 February 1695
13 February–12 February
7 1695–96
8 1696–97
9 1697–98
10 1698–99
11 1699–1700
12 1700–01
13 1701–02
14 1702–8 March 1702

Anne
8 March–7 March
1 1702–03
2 1703–04
3 1704–05
4 1705–06
5 1706–07
6 1707–08
7 1708–09
8 1709–10
9 1710–11
10 1711–12
11 1712–13
12 1713–14
13 1714–1 August 1714

George I
1 August–31 July
1   1714–15
2   1715–16
3   1716–17
4   1717–18
5   1718–19
6   1719–20
7   1720–21
8   1721–22
9   1722–23
10 1723–24
11 1724–25
12 1725–26
13 1726–11 June 1727

George II
11 June–10 June
1   1727–28
2   1728–29
3   1729–30
4   1730–31
5   1731–32
6   1732–33
7   1733–34
8   1734–35
9   1735–36
10 1736–37
11 1737–38
12 1738–39
13 1739–40
14 1740–41
15 1741–42
16 1742–43
17 1743–44
18 1744–45
19 1745–46
20 1746–47
21 1747–48
22 1748–49
23 1749–50

24 1750–51
25 1751–52
26 1752–53
27 1753–54
28 1754–55
29 1755–56
30 1756–57
31 1757–58
32 1758–59
33 1759–60
34 1760–25 October 1760

The regnal year of 1753 was extended to 21 June so that it should consist of 365 days despite the omission of eleven days in September 1752, when the New Style was adopted. The Regnal Year of 1753–54 therefore covers 22 June–21 June, and this continues to be the operative period for the rest of his reign.

George III
25 October–24 October.
1   1760–61
2   1761–62
3   1762–63
4   1763–64
5   1764–65
6   1765–66
7   1766–67
8   1767–68
9   1768–69
10 1769–70
11 1770–71
12 1771–72
13 1772–73
14 1773–74

15	1774–75		53	1812–13
16	1775–76		54	1813–14
17	1776–77		55	1814–15
18	1777–78		56	1815–16
19	1778–79		57	1816–17
20	1779–80		58	1817–18
21	1780–81		59	1818–19
22	1781–82		60	1819–29 January 1820
23	1782–83			

George IV
29 January–28 January

24	1783–84
25	1784–85
26	1785–86
27	1786–87
28	1787–88
29	1788–89
30	1789–90
31	1790–91
32	1791–92
33	1792–93
34	1793–94
35	1794–95
36	1795–96
37	1796–97
38	1797–98
39	1798–99
40	1799–1800
41	1800–01
42	1801–02
43	1802–03
44	1803–04
45	1804–05
46	1805–06
47	1806–07
48	1807–08
49	1808–09
50	1809–10
51	1810–11

George IV	
1	1820–21
2	1821–22
3	1822–23
4	1823–24
5	1824–25
6	1825–26
7	1826–27
8	1827–28
9	1828–29
10	1829–30
11	1830–26 June 1830

William IV
26 June–25 June

1	1830–31
2	1831–32
3	1832–33
4	1833–34
5	1834–35
6	1835–36
7	1836–20 June 1837

Victoria
20 June–19 June

1	1837–38
2	1838–39
3	1839–40
4	1840–41
5	1841–42
6	1842–43

Regency began
6 February 1811

52	1811–12

7	1843–44
8	1844–45
9	1845–46
10	1846–47
11	1847–48
12	1848–49
13	1849–50
14	1850–51
15	1851–52
16	1852–53
17	1853–54
18	1854–55
19	1855–56
20	1856–57
21	1857–58
22	1858–59
23	1859–60
24	1860–61
25	1861–62
26	1862–63
27	1863–64
28	1864–65
29	1865–66
30	1866–67
31	1867–68
32	1868–69
33	1869–70
34	1870–71
35	1871–72
36	1872–73
37	1873–74
38	1874–75
39	1875–76
40	1876–77
41	1877–78
42	1878–79
43	1879–80
44	1880–81
45	1881–82
46	1882–83
47	1883–84

48	1884–85
49	1885–86
50	1886–87
51	1887–88
52	1888–89
53	1889–90
54	1890–91
55	1891–92
56	1892–93
57	1893–94
58	1894–95
59	1895–96
60	1896–97
61	1897–98
62	1898–99
63	1899–1900
64	1900–22 January 1901

Edward VII
22 January–21 January

1	1901–02
2	1902–03
3	1903–04
4	1904–05
5	1905–06
6	1906–07
7	1907–08
8	1908–09
9	1909–10
10	1910–6 May 1910

George V
6 May–5 May

1	1910–11
2	1911–12
3	1912–13
4	1913–14
5	1914–15
6	1915–16
7	1916–17
8	1917–18

9	1918–19
10	1919–20
11	1920–21
12	1921–22
13	1922–23
14	1923–24
15	1924–25
16	1925–26
17	1926–27
18	1927–28
19	1928–29
20	1929–30
21	1930–31
22	1931–32
23	1932–33
24	1933–34
25	1934–35
26	1935–20 January 1936

Edward VIII
1 20 January 1936–11 December 1936

George VI
11 December–10 December

1	1936–37
2	1937–38
3	1938–39
4	1939–40
5	1940–41
6	1941–42
7	1942–43
8	1943–44
9	1944–45
10	1945–46
11	1946–47
12	1947–48
13	1948–49
14	1949–50
15	1950–51
16	1951–6 February 1952

English Currency

Currency Before Decimalisation

Prior to decimalisation on 15 February 1971 English currency was shown as £.s.d. These abbreviations came from the Roman words *libra, solidus* and *denarius*.
Libra was the amount of silver weighing one pound and shown as '£' or 'l'. *Solidus* and *denarius* — *see below*.
This section is printed by permission of Spink & Son Ltd., the publishers of (Spink) *Standard Catalogue of Coins of England*, edited by Stephen Mitchell and Brian Reeds.

Coin Denominations

Gold

Angel. Eighty pence (6s 8d) from 1464; later seven shillings and six pence, ten shillings and 11 shillings.

Britain Crown. Five shillings, 1604–12; five shillings and six pence (66d), 1612–19.

Broad. Twenty shillings, Cromwell, 1656.

Crown. Five shillings, from 1544 (*see below* and Britain Crown *above*).

Crown of the Rose. Four shillings and 6 pence, 1526.

Crown of the Double Rose. Five shillings, 1526–44.

Florin (Double Leopard). Six shillings, Edward III.

George Noble. Eighty pence (6s 8d), 1526.

Gold 'Penny'. Twenty to twenty-four pence, Henry III.

Guinea. Pound (20s) in 1663, then rising to thirty shillings in 1694 before falling to twenty-one shillings and six pence, 1698–1717; twenty-one shillings, 1717–1813.

Halfcrown. Thirty pence, 1526 intermittently to 1612; two shillings and nine pence (33d), 1612–19.

Helm (Quarter Florin). Eighteen pence, Edward III.

Laurel. Twenty shillings, 1619–25.

Leopard (Half Florin). Three shillings, Edward III.

Noble. Eighty pence (6s 8d, or half mark), 1344–1464.

Pound. Twenty shillings, 1592–1600 (*see also* Unite, Laurel, Broad, Guinea and Sovereign).

Quarter Angel. One shilling and ten and a halfpence, 1544–7 and 1558–1600.

Rose-Nobel or Ryal. Ten shillings, 1464–70.

Rose-Ryal. Thirty shillings, 1604–24.

Ryal. Ten shillings, Edward IV and Henry VII; fifteen shillings under Mary and Elizabeth I (*see also* Spur Ryal).

Solidus. Roman currency unit (1/72nd lb) from A.D. 312; the 's' of the £.s.d.

Sovereign. Twenty shillings or pound, 1489–1526 (22s 6d, 1526–44), 1544–53, 1603–04 and from 1817 (*see also* Pound, Unite, Laurel, Broad and Guinea and Fine Sovereign).

'Fine' Sovereign. Thirty shillings, 1550–96 (*see also* Rose Ryal).

Spur-Ryal. Fifteen shillings, 1605–12; sixteen shillings and six pence, 1612–25.

Stater. Name commonly given to the standard Celtic gold coin.

Third Guinea. Seven shillings, 1797–1813.

Thistle Crown. Four shillings, 1604–12; four shillings and five pence, 1612–19.

Triple Unite. Three pounds, Charles I (Shrewsbury and Oxford only, 1642–4).

Unite. Twenty shillings, 1604–12 and 1625–62; twenty-two shillings, 1612–19.

Silver (and Cupro-Nickel)

Crown. Five shillings, 1551–1965.

Denarius. Roman, originally 10 then 16 asses (25 to the aureus), later debased; the 'd' of the £.s.d.

Farthing. Quarter penny, 1279–1553.

Florin. Two shillings, 1849–1967.

Groat. Four pence, 1279-c.1305 and 1351–1662 (halfgroat from 1351). 'Britannia' groat, 1836–55 (and 1888 for Colonial use only) (*see also* **Maundy Money** page 220).

Halfcrown. Thirty pence (2s 6d), 1551–1967.

Halfpenny. Intermittently, c.890–c.970, c.1108 and, more generally, 1279–1660.

Maundy Money. Four, three, two and one penny from 1660.

New Pence. Decimal coinage: 50p from 1969, 25p (crown) 1972 and 1977, 1980, 1981, 10p and 5p from 1968. 'New' removed in 1982.

Penny (pl. pence). Standard unit of currency from c. 775/780 A.D.

Sceat. Early Anglo-Saxon, small thick penny.

Shilling. Twelve pence, 1548–1966.

Sixpence. From 1551–1967.

Testoon. Shilling, Henry VII and VIII.

Threefarthings. Elizabeth I, 1561–82.

Threehalfpence. Elizabeth I, 1561–82, and for Colonial use, 1834–62.

Threepence. From 1551–1944 (*see also* **Maundy Money** page 220).

Twenty pence. Decimal coinage from 1982.

Copper, Bronze, Tin, Nickel-Brass, etc.

As. Roman, an early unit of currency, reduced in size and equal to 1/16th *denarius* in Imperial times.

Dupondius. Roman, brass two asses or one-eighth of a *denarius*.

Farthing. Quarter penny: Harrington, Lennox, Richmond, Maltravers and 'rose' farthings, 1613–49; regal issues, 1672–1956 (tin, 1684–92).

Half Farthing. Victoria, 1839–56 (and for Colonial use 1828–37).

Halfpenny. From 1672 to 1967 (tin, 1685–92).

New Pence. Decimal coinage: 2p, 1p and ½p from 1971. 'New' removed in 1982.

Penny. From 1797 to 1967 (previously a silver coin).

Pound. Decimal coin from 1983.

Threepence. Nickelbrass, 1937–67.

Twopence. George III, 'Cartwheel' issue, 1797 only.

Rulers and Coins

Henry III (1216–1272). The Short Cross coins were replaced by the Long Cross coins in 1247. This was to prevent the coin being clipped dishonestly as part of the cross would disappear, and this could be seen at a glance. Moneyers were in trouble if they minted coins that were below the required weight; 20 pennies should weigh one ounce, and the weight of 240 pennies was the same as a pound of silver.

Edward I (1272–1307). The practice of cutting up coins in order to obtain the metal for small transactions was ended in 1280. In order to restrict this activity Edward I issued the smaller denomination coins. These were the groat (valued at fourpence), pence, halfpence and farthings. The design of these coins influenced later issues as well as coins issued abroad for many years.

Edward III (1327–1377). The Noble was issued in 1344. It was a gold coin depicting the King in a sailing boat holding weapons.

Henry VII (1485–1509). In 1489 the first gold sovereign was minted. It was the largest English coin produced up to that time.

Henry VIII (1509–1547). The amount of valuable metal in coins was reduced by Henry during his reign, the gold as well as silver coinage being debased on several occasions. Debasement was a risky process as the metal content of the coins at that time was regarded as equal to the face value. These were the 'standard' coins, but by the substitution of base metal during Henry VIII's reign, the coins only had about one-seventh of the silver that the coins had contained at the beginning of his reign.

Elizabeth I (1558–1603). Sovereigns, ryals, angels, pounds and crowns were struck during her reign. They were also produced in half and quarter values. The smaller denomination silver coins included shillings, sixpences, groats, three halfpennies, pence and halfpence.

George I (1714–1727). During this reign a gold quarter-guinea was produced in addition to the usual guinea, and the silver coins included crowns, halfcrowns, shillings, sixpences, fourpences, twopences and pence. The copper coins were the halfpence and farthings which were commonly nicknamed 'dumps' on account of being small and fat.

George III (1760–1820). Currency was put on the gold standard in 1816, and silver became a token coinage. Old silver coins were called in and new silver coins of reduced weight were minted. The values were the halfcrown, shilling and sixpence. Prior to the 1971 decimal changeover, British silver coins dating back to 1816 were legal tender, though it was unusual that coins earlier than ones issued during Victoria's reign were in circulation. Bronze coins dating from 1860 were also legal tender.

George IV (1820–1830). This reign saw the issue of gold two-pound coins, sovereigns and the usual silver coins. Copper pence, halfpence and farthings were issued. Cheques, as known today, were first introduced in 1825.

William IV (1830–1837). Full sets of all denominations were not issued owing to the short period of his reign. Gold sovereigns and half-sovereigns were issued as well as the groat (fourpenny silver coins) showing Britannia on the reverse. Groats had not been issued since the seventeenth century, and they were nicknamed 'Joeys' after the promoter, Joseph Hume.

Victoria (1837–1901). During this reign there were many issues of coins, in particular the different heads. The first was the 'Young Head' coins; the second was known as the 'Jubilee' issue and this dated from 1887; from 1893 the third and final coinage was minted and became known as the 'Old Head'. Unusual coins in the Jubilee issue were the five-pound and the two-pound coins in gold, and also the double-florin which was the four shilling coin. The threepence coin was revived in 1845 and it did not differ from the Maundy threepence until 1928. It was last minted in 1944.

Edward VIII (1936). Only one new coin was produced in this reign: the nickel-brass twelve-sided threepence, which was supposed to replace the small silver coin. Most of these nickel-brass coins were melted down, but a few still survived and these are extremely valuable; they are dated 1937.

George VI (1936–1952). This reign saw the introduction of the new nickel-brass twelve-sided threepence coin. In 1947 British 'silver' coins ceased to contain any silver; instead they were made of cupro-nickel, the content being 75 percent copper and 25 percent nickel. Pre-1920 and pre-1947 silver coins can still be found. In 1951 the five shilling (25p) crown with St. George and the dragon on the reverse was minted. Many were sold as souvenirs of the Festival of Britain and the coin proved so popular that more than two million were minted.

Elizabeth II (1952–). The Coronation crown shows the Queen on horseback on the obverse — the first time a monarch on horseback had appeared on coinage since the time of Charles I. Farthings were withdrawn from the 1 January 1961, and the old halfpenny, penny, the threepence and the halfcrown disappeared in the decimalisation of the coinage on 15 February 1971. A unique issue was the 1965 Winston Churchill commemorative crown which depicts the head of a commoner on one side and the head of the sovereign on the other.

Maundy Money

Silver coins of one, two, three and fourpence are minted for this service and a number of men and women are selected (the number of those selected is the same as the sovereign's age) to receive them. Each person receives Maundy Money in an amount equivalent in pence to the age of the monarch. The coins are presented in a white purse.

Coinage prior to decimalisation and its equivalent decimal coinage (if applicable)

	shown as	*value*
Farthing	¼d	one quarter of a penny.
Halfpenny	½d	half of a penny, 480 in a pound.
Penny	1d	twelve to a shilling.
Shilling	1/-	twenty to a pound; now 5p.
Florin	2/-	two shilling piece, ten to a pound; now 10p.
Halfcrown	2/6d	two shillings and six pence, eight to a pound.
Ten Shillings	10/-	a bank note equalling 120 pence; now 50p.
One Pound	£1.0.0d	a bank note equalling 240 pence.

Decimal Currency Converter, 1971

Old	New	Old	New	Old	New	Old	New	Old	New
		2/0	10	4/0	20	6/0	30	8/0	40
1d.	½	2/1	10½	4/1	20½	6/1	30½	8/1	40½
2d.	1	2/2	11	4/2	21	6/2	31	8/2	41
3d.	1	2/3	11	4/3	21	6/3	31	8/3	41
4d.	1½	2/4	11½	4/4	21½	6/4	31½	8/4	41½
5d.	2	2/5	12	4/5	22½	6/5	32	8/5	42
6d.	2½	2/6	12½	4/6	22½	6/6	32½	8/6	42½
7d.	3	2/7	13	4/7	23	6/7	33	8/7	43
8d.	3½	2/8	13½	4/8	23½	6/8	33½	8/8	43½
9d.	4	2/9	14	4/9	24	6/9	34	8/9	44
10d.	4	2/10	14	4/10	24	6/10	34	8/10	44
11d.	4½	2/11	14½	4/11	24½	6/11	34½	8/11	44½
1/0	5	3/0	15	5/0	25	7/0	35	9/0	45
1/1	5½	3/1	15½	5/1	25½	7/1	35½	9/1	45½
1/2	6	3/2	16	5/2	26	7/2	36	9/2	46
1/3	6	3/3	16	5/3	26	7/3	36	9/3	46½
1/4	6½	3/4	16½	5/4	26½	7/4	36½	9/4	46½
1/5	7	3/5	17	5/5	27	7/5	37	9/5	47
1/6	7½	3/6	17½	5/6	27½	7/6	37½	9/6	47½
1/7	8	3/7	18	5/7	28	7/7	38	9/7	48
1/8	8½	3/8	18½	5/8	28½	7/8	38½	9/8	48½
1/9	9	3/9	19	5/9	29	7/9	39	9/9	49
1/10	9	3/10	19	5/10	29	7/10	39	9/10	49
1/11	9½	3/11	19½	5/11	29½	7/11	39½	9/11	49½

Old	New	Old	New	Old	New	Old	New	Old	New
0/0	50	12/0	60	14/0	70	16/0	80	18/0	90
0/1	50½	12/1	60½	14/1	70½	16/1	80½	18/1	90½
0/2	51	12/2	61	14/2	71	16/2	81	18/2	91
0/3	51	12/3	61	14/3	71	16/3	81	18/3	91
0/4	51½	12/4	61½	14/4	71½	16/4	81½	18/4	91½
0/5	52	12/5	62	14/5	72	16/5	82	18/5	92
0/6	52½	12/6	62½	14/6	72½	16/6	82½	18/6	92½
0/7	53	12/7	63	14/7	73	16/7	83	18/7	93
0/8	53½	12/8	63½	14/8	73½	16/8	83½	18/8	93½
0/9	54	12/9	64	14/9	74	16/9	84	18/9	94
0/10	54	12/10	64	14/10	74	16/10	84	18/10	94
0/11	54½	12/11	64½	14/11	74½	16/11	84½	18/11	94½
1/0	55	13/0	65	15/0	75	17/0	85	19/0	95
1/1	55½	13/1	65½	15/1	75½	17/1	85½	19/1	95½
1/2	56	13/2	66	15/2	76	17/2	86	19/2	96
1/3	56	13/3	66	15/3	76	17/3	86	19/3	96
1/4	56½	13/4	66½	15/4	76½	17/4	86½	19/4	96½
1/5	57	13/5	67	15/5	77	17/5	87	19/5	97
1/6	57½	13/6	67½	15/6	77½	17/6	87½	19/6	97½
/7	58	13/7	68	15/7	78	17/7	88	19/7	98
/8	58½	13/8	68½	15/8	78½	17/8	88½	19/8	98½
/9	59	13/9	69	15/9	79	17/9	89	19/9	99
/10	59	13/10	69	15/10	79	17/10	89	19/10	99
/11	59½	13/11	69½	15/11	79½	17/11	89½	19/11	99½

23. Some English silver coins showing the obverse (above) and the reverse (below). Top: 'Long Cross' penny of Henry III (1216–72). Centre left: groat of Henry VII (1485–1509). Centre: shilling of James I (1603–25): the Prince of Wales' feathers above the shield signifies that this coin was struck in Welsh silver. Centre right: shilling of George II (1727–60), dated 1758. Bottom: threepence of Elizabeth I (1558–1603), dated 1581.

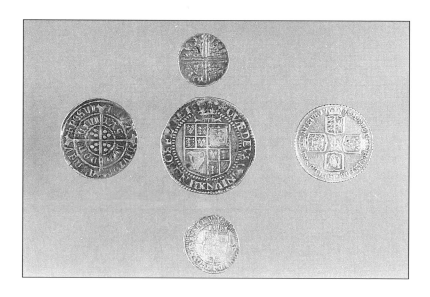

Cost of Living Over Two Hundred Years

Money is not, and has never been, worth the same over the whole country, wages and goods were always higher in the south. Therefore, absolute accuracy is impossible. The price of food varied with the changing of the seasons and the weather.

Bread was the staple food in any household, and the price of a quarter of grain was 3s 4d (16½p) in 1245; 6s 5d (32p) in 1250, while famine conditions could raise it to 13s 8d (68½p) as in 1315. Between 1760 and 1792, a quarter of wheat varied between 43s (£2.15p) and 126s (£6.30p), due to the rapidly rising population, the Industrial Revolution and foreign wars. The 1815 Corn Law introduced a sliding scale. Finally in 1828 there was a duty of 1s (5p) a quarter when the price was 73s (£3.65p). Between 1828 and 1831, the harvests were bad and corn was imported. The Repeal of the Corn Laws in 1846 allowed foreign corn into Great Britain free of duty.

During the 17th century the general wage for an agricultural labourer was 8d (3½p) a day, his wife might get 6d (2½p) and children 3d (1p) a day. In 1795 the Speenhamland system was adopted by the overseers of the poor as a method of supplementing low wages with an allowance paid out of the rates. This allowance varied according to the cost of bread: 'When the gallon loaf (8½lb) shall cost 1s 4d (6½p) then every poor man shall have 4s (20p) weekly for his own and 1s 10d (9p) for the support of other members of his family'. The system was discredited in the Poor Law Amendment Act, 1834.

In 1852 a clerk received 10s 9d (54p) for an 11 hour, 6 day week, and was expected to wear clothes of a 'sober nature', (though neck scarves and headgear could be worn in inclement weather). He was also expected to bring 4 lb of coal with him each day in the winter to use in his workroom.

Certain commodities such as coal varied greatly in the price charged not only at the pithead, but also in all parts of the country owing to differing costs of transport. In one area per ton was:

1915–20	1921–30	1931–40	1941–44	1945–50	1951–60	1961–70
£1.35p	£1.50p	£1.35p	£1.70p	£3.60p	£7.66p	£15.00

Coal was the main means of cooking and heating in most of the poorer homes for many years.

The 20th century saw more changes than any other in the amount of goods which can be bought. At one time, a working class family could live comfortably on a wage of less than £2 a week, his rent would be five to six shillings (25 to 30 new pence), and a joint of beef could be bought for 10d (4p).

Comparative prices for a standard loaf of bread weighing 4lb 5½oz

The price would vary according to district and quality of flour.

1700	1757	1801	1812	1841	1887	1914
6½d	10d	15½d	17d	8½d	6d	5¾d

1919–20	1950	1960	1961	1964	1969
12¼d	5d	8½d	9½d	10¾d	13½d

During 1946–49 a 1¾lb loaf cost 4½d and the 14oz cost 2¾d.

After decimalisation in 1971 the 1¾lb loaf of white bread, not sliced or wrapped cost:

1972	1973	1974	1975	1976	1977	1978
10p	11½p	14p	15p	21p	28p	30p

Contemporary Values of the Pound

The following shows the amount of money required as at October 2000 to equal £1 at the date shown. This does not take into consideration the cost of real property, or the level of wages. The figures are derived from the Retail Prices Index, based at January 1987 = 100.

The RPI is based on the combined cost of a number of specific goods and does not take into account other factors relevant to a comparison of values.

Thus, £74.61 would have been required in October 2000 in order to have the same purchasing power as £1 in 1700.

£1	In 1500	In 1550	In 1600	In 1650	In 1700
=	£429.00	£286.00	£122.57	£71.50	£74.61

£1	In 1750	In 1800	In 1850	In 1900	In 1950
=	£81.71	£30.11	£49.03	£55.35	£20.43

£1	In 1960	In 1970	In 1980	In 1990	In 1999
=	£13.84	£9.28	£2.57	£1.36	£1.04

	1971	1972	1973	1974	1975	1976	1977	1978
Gas Cooker	£55	£65	£75	£80	£90	£100	£110	£130
Sewing Machine	£45	£45	£55	£55	£70	£75	£85	£90
Refrigerator	£60	£70	£75	£80	£85	£90	£90	£100
Electric Fire	£25	£28	£35	£38	£45	£53	£59	£70

The Tax Year

Why April 5 as the end of the tax year? In the Middle Ages the English Calendar ran from Lady Day, March 25, chosen by the Church as the beginning of its year. All official years ran from the same New Year's Day. The financial year remained at that date, but by the eighteenth century, January 1 had become generally regarded as the beginning of the year. Time was measured by the Julian calendar which, since its inception in 46 BC, had 'lost' a number of days, when the country adopted the Gregorian Calendar in 1752, 11 lost days had to found. So 2 September 1752, was followed by 14 September. The authorities then thought that 11 days' revenue could be lost if nothing was done about the missing days. So 11 days were tacked on to the end of the financial year – the date was moved from March 25 to April 5. In 1854, the financial year was changed to 31 March, but for some reason the tax year (or fiscal year) continued to run from 6 April to 5 April.

Civil Registration of Births, Marriages and Deaths

This began on 1 July, 1837.

Bibles

Bible means, simply, a book, but is now exclusively confined to the 'Book of Books' (Greek, *biblos*, a book).

The headings of the chapters were prefixed by Miles Smith, Bishop of Gloucester, one of the translators.

This section is reproduced by permission of Cassell plc, the publishers of *Brewer, The Dictionary of Phrase and Fable.*

Bibles named from errors of type or from archaic words

The Breeches Bible 1579. So called because Genesis iii.7 was rendered "The eyes of them bothe were opened ... and they sowed figge-tree leaves together, and made themselves breeches". By Whittingham, Gilby and Sampson, 1579.

The Idle Bible 1809. In which the words "idole shepherd" Zechariah xi. 17 is printed "the idle shepherd".

The Bug Bible 1551. So called because Psalm xci. 5 is translated "Thou shalt not be afraid of bugges (bogies) by nighte".

The Great Bible. The same as **Matthew Parker's Bible** *q.v.*

The Placemaker's Bible. So called from a printer's error in Matthew v. 9, "Blessed are the placemakers (peacemakers), for they shall be called the children of God".

The Printer's Bible makes David complain that "the printers (princes) have persecuted me without a cause". Psalm cxix.161).

The Treacle Bible 1549 (Beck's Bible), in which the word 'balm' is rendered 'treacle'. **The Bishop's Bible** *q.v.* has 'tryacle' in Jeremiah iii. 28; xlvi. and in Ezekiel xxvii. 17.

The Unrighteous Bible 1652 (Cambridge Press). So called from the printer's error "Know ye not that the unrighteous shall inherit the Kingdom of God?" 1 Corinthians vi. 9.

The Vinegar Bible 1717. So called because the heading to Luke xx. is given as the "parable of the Vinegar" instead of Vineyard. Printed at the Clarendon Press in 1717.

The Wicked Bible. So called because the word 'not' is omitted from the seventh commandment, thus making it "Thou shalt commit adultery". Printed by Barker & Lucas, 1632.

Bibles named from proper names or dignities

Bishop's Bible. The revised edition of Archbishop Parker's version. Published 1568.

Coverdale's Bible 1535. Translated by Miles Coverdale, afterwards Bishop of Exeter. This was the first Bible sanctioned by royal authority.

Cranmer's Bible 1539. This is **Coverdale's Bible** *q.v.* corrected by Archbishop Cranmer. It was printed in 1540, and in 1549 every parish was enjoined to have a copy under penalty of forty shillings a month.

The Douay Bible 1581. A translation made by the professors of the Douay College for the use of English boys designed for the Catholic priesthood.

The Geneva Bible. The Bible translated by the English exiles at Geneva. The same as the **Breeches Bible** *q.v.*

King James Bible. The Authorised Version; so called because it was undertaken by command of James I. Published 1611.

Matthew Parker's Bible. Or **The Great Bible** published in the reign of Henry VIII under the care of Archbishop Parker and his staff (1539–1541). In 1572 several prolegomena were added.

Matthews' Bible is Tindal's version. It was so called by John Rogers, superintendent of the English churches in Germany, and was published with notes under the fictitious name of Thomas Matthews, 1537.

The Mazarine Bible. The earliest book printed in movable metal type. It contains no date. Called from the Bibliothèque Mazurine, founded in Paris by Cardinal Mazarine in 1648.

Sacy's Bible. So called from Issac Louis Sacy (Le-maistre), director of the Port Royal Monastery. He was imprisoned for three years in the Bastille for his Jansenist opinions, and translated the Bible during his captivity (1666–1670).

Tyndale's Bible. William Tyndale, or Tindale, having embraced the Reformed religion, retired to Antwerp, where he printed an English translation of the Scriptures. All the copies were bought up, so Tyndale printed a revised edition. The book excited the rancour of the Catholics, who strangled the 'heretic' and burnt his body near Antwerp in 1536.

Wycliff's Bible, 1380, but first printed in 1850.

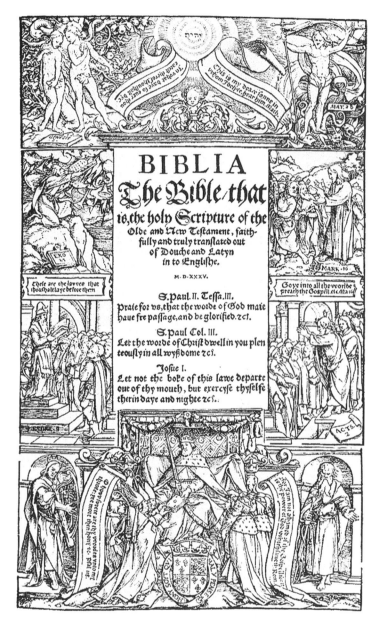

24. *Coverdale's Bible.* Published in 1535–6, the first complete Bible in English. The blocks for the title-page were made by Holbein. *Coverdale's Bible* was displaced by other versions notably the *Great Bible* issued in September 1539.

Versions

The Authorised Version, 1611. See **King James Bible**.

The Revised Version. Published in May, 1885. The work was begun in June 1870 by 25 scholars, 10 of whom died before the version was completed. The revisers had 85 sessions, which extended over 14 years.

Saints' Days and Festivals

Agnes	21 January
Aidan	31 August
Alban	22 June
All Hallows, All Saints	1 November
All Souls' Day	2 November
Alphege	19 April
Ambrose	4 April
Andrew	30 November
Anne	26 July
Anselm	21 April
Anthony	17 January
Augustine of Canterbury	26 May
Augustine of Hippo	28 August
Barnabas	11 June
Bartholomew	24 August
Benedict Abbot	21 March
— Translation	11 July
Benedict (Benet)	12 January
Bernard of Clairvaux	21 August
Blasius	3 February
Boniface	5 June
Botolph	17 June
Bridget	1 February
Candelmas	2 February
Cecilia	22 November
Chad	2 March
Christopher	25 July
Circumcision	1 January
Clement	23 November
Columba	9 June
Crispin	25 October
Cuthbert	20 March
Cyprian	26 September
David	1 March
Denys	9 October
Dominic	4 August
Dunstan	19 May
Edward, King and Martyr	18 March
Edward – Confessor	13 October
Epiphany	6 January

Etheldreda	23 June
Fabian	20 January
Francis of Assisi	4 October
Faith	6 October
George	23 April
Giles	1 September
Gregory the Great	12 March
Hilary	13 January
Hilda of Whitby	25 August
elsewhere	17 November
Holy Innocents Day	28 December
Hugh of Lincoln	17 November
James	25 July
Jerome	30 September
John the Divine	27 December
John the Baptist	24 June
John Baptist	29 August
Lambert	17 September
Leonard	6 November
Lucy	13 December
Machutus	15 November
Mark	25 April
Margaret	20 July
Mary Blessed Virgin	
— Annunciation	25 March
— Assumption	15 August
— Conception	8 December
— Purification	2 February
Mary Magdalene	22 July
Martin	11 November
Matthias	24 February
Matthew	21 September
Michael	29 September
Nicholas	6 December
Patrick	17 March
Paul	25 January
Peter and Paul	29 June
Perpetua and her companions	7 March
Philip	1 May
Polycarp	26 January
Richard of Chichester	3 April
Samson	28 July
Scholastica	10 February

Simon and Jude	28 October
Stephen, Martyr	26 December
Swithun, Deposition	2 July
— Trans.	15 July
Thomas	21 December
— Trans.	7 July
Thomas Aquinas	7 March
Thomas Becket	29 December
Transfiguration of our Lord	6 August
Twelfth Day	6 January
Valentine	14 February
Willibrord	7 November
William of York	8 June
Winifred	3 November

Movable Feast Days

Easter Day is always the first Sunday after the Full Moon occurring upon or next after 21 March; if the Full Moon occurs on a Sunday, Easter Day is the following Sunday. Easter Day governs the following feasts:

Septuagesima Sunday is the ninth Sunday before Easter Day.

Sexagesima Sunday is the eighth Sunday before Easter Day.

Quinquagesima or *Shrove Sunday* is the seventh Sunday before Easter Day.

Quadragesima Sunday is the sixth Sunday before Easter Day.

Mid Lent Sunday is the third Sunday before Easter Day.

Passion Sunday is the second Sunday before Easter Day.

Palm Sunday is the first Sunday before Easter Day.

Good Friday is the first Friday before Easter Day.

Low Sunday is the first Sunday after Easter Day.

Rogation Sunday is the fifth Sunday after Easter Day.

Ascension Day is forty days after Easter Day.

Whit Sunday or Pentecost is the seventh Sunday after Easter Day.

Trinity Sunday is the eighth Sunday after Easter Day.

Corpus Christi is the Thursday after Trinity Sunday.

Holy Thursday is the day on which the Ascension of our Saviour is commemorated.

Ash Wednesday is the first Wednesday after Shrove Sunday, and the first day of Lent.

Advent Sunday is the nearest Sunday to the feast of St. Andrew, (30 November) whether before or after.

Relic Sunday is the first Sunday after St. Thomas's Day (7 July).

Sittings of the Supreme Court

The following are general dates for guidance. For a current year, consult *Whitaker's Almanack*.

The sittings of the Court of Appeal and of the High Court shall be in every year, that is to say:

The Michaelmas sittings which shall begin on 1st October and end on 21st December.

The Hilary sittings which shall begin on 11th January and end on the Wednesday before Easter Sunday.

The Easter sittings which shall begin on the second Tuesday after Easter Sunday and end on the Friday before Spring holiday.

The Trinity sittings which shall begin on the second Tuesday after the spring holiday and end on 31st July.

In this rule 'Spring holiday' means the bank holiday falling on the last Monday in May or any day appointed instead of that day under section 1(2) of the Banking and Financial Dealings Act 1971.

Bank Holidays

Bank holidays were first established in 1871 by the Bank Holidays Act. Previously up to 1830, the Bank of England closed on approximately 40 saint days and anniversaries but then it was reduced to 18 days.

In 1834 they were reduced again to include just four: Good Friday, May 1, November 1 and Christmas Day.

By the Act of 1871 Easter Monday, Whit Monday, the first Monday in August and Boxing Day were constituted Bank Holidays, joining Good Friday and Christmas Day which were holidays by common law.

The act also made it lawful for any day off to be officially proclaimed a Bank Holiday in the UK.

Weights and Measures

Avoirdupois Weight

16 drams	=	1 ounce
16 ounces	=	1 pound
14 pounds	=	1 stone
28 pounds	=	1 quarter
4 quarters	=	1 hundredweight (112 pounds)
20 hundred-weights	=	1 ton (2240 pounds)
100 pounds	=	1 cental
2000 pounds	=	1 short ton
2240 pounds	=	1 long ton

Wool Weight

A pack of wool was made up as follows:

7 pounds	=	1 clove
4 cloves	=	1 todd
6½ todds	=	1 wey (182 lbs)
2 weys	=	1 sack
12 sacks	=	4368 pounds (29 cwt)
240 pounds	=	1 pack

Hay Weight

A statute of William and Mary for 1693 laid down that a truss of dry hay should weigh 56 lbs, but of new hay (that is hay sold between June and August) should weigh 60 lbs.

A truss of straw weighs 36 lbs.

A load was 38 truss.

A bushel of wheat on an average weighs 60 pounds; of barley 47 pounds; of oats 40 pounds.

10 sacks	=	1 coom
1 coom	=	4 bushels

Capacity

Used for liquids

4 gills	=	1 pint
2 pints	=	1 quart
4 quarts	=	1 gallon
1 gallon	=	10 lbs avoirdupois of distilled water
4½ gallons	=	1 pin
2 gallons	=	1 peck
9 gallons	=	1 firkin (for ale or beer)
18 gallons	=	1 kilderkin
36 gallons	=	1 barrel (for ale or beer)
42 gallons	=	1 tierce
54 gallons	=	1 hogshead (for ale or beer)
72 gallons	=	1 puncheon (for ale or beer)
108 gallons	=	1 pipe or butt

Used for dry goods

4 pecks	=	1 bushel
8 bushels	=	1 quarter
5 quarters	=	1 load
36 bushels	=	1 chaldron

Linear Measure

12 inches	=	1 foot
3 feet	=	1 yard
5½ yards	=	1 pole, rod or perch
4 poles	=	1 chain
10 chains	=	1 furlong
8 furlongs	=	1 mile (1760 yards)
3 miles	=	1 league

Other Linear Measure

3 barleycorns	=	1 inch
3 inches	=	1 palm
4 inches	=	1 hand
7.92 inches	=	1 link
9 inches	=	1 span

18 inches	=	1 cubit
30 inches	=	1 pace
37.2 inches	=	1 Scottish Ell
45 inches	=	1 English Ell
5 feet	=	1 geometrical pace
6 feet	=	1 fathom
608 feet	=	1 cable
10 cables	=	1 nautical mile
6080 feet	=	1 nautical mile
6087 feet	=	1 geographical mile
22 yards	=	1 chain
100 links	=	1 chain
10 chains	=	1 furlong
80 chains	=	1 mile
1 knot	=	speed of 1 nautical m.p.h.

Square Measure

144 square inches	=	1 square foot
9 square feet	=	1 square yard
30¼ square yards	=	1 square pole
40 square poles	=	1 rood
4 roods	=	1 acre
640 acres	=	1 square mile

Yarn Measure — Linen

300 yards	=	1 cut
2 cuts	=	1 heer
6 heers	=	1 hank
4 hanks	=	1 spindle

Yarn Measure — Cotton

120 yards	=	1 skein
7 skeins	=	1 hank
18 hanks	=	1 spindle

Cloth Measure

2¼ inches	=	1 nail
4 nails	=	1 quarter (9 inches)
4 quarters	=	1 yard (36 inches)
5 quarters	=	1 ell (45 inches)

Paper Measure — Writing Paper

24 sheets	=	1 quire
20 quires	=	1 ream

Paper Measure — Printing Paper

21½ quires (516 sheets)	=	1 ream
2 reams	=	1 bundle
5 bundles	=	1 bale

25. A selection of Medieval lead trade weights. From left to right: large shield weight with uncertain heraldic device, possibly two clarions (8 oz); circular weight with central shield and uncertain inscription (2½ oz); small shield weight with crowned lion rampant within a border, the arms of Richard, Earl of Cornwall (4 oz); lozenge shaped weight with large fleur-de-lys device (4 oz).

Latin Words and Phrases

This word list represents Latin most frequently encountered in parish registers; it is not intended to be comprehensive. Latin found in registers is not usually classical and meanings vary often from dictionary definitions. Words and phrases should be taken in context and in relation to the nature and original purpose of the manuscript. Translations given here reflect this.

Researchers should note that spelling variations abound in registers and other manuscripts. Certain letters were frequently interchanged — c and t, c and k, i and j, u and v. Substitution is also common — w for v, for example. The doubling and undoubling of some consonants and vowels is also frequently encountered.

a, ab, abs. From, by.

ac. And.

ad. To, at, in.

advenae. Stranger, foreigner.

aetatis (aet). Of age.

alias, aliud. Other, another, otherwise.

annus, anno. Year, in the year.

ante. Before.

antedictus. Aforesaid.

anus. Old woman.

apud. In, near by, at.

atque. And.

baptisatus, baptisata. Baptised.

bonus, bona. Good, goods.

caelebs, coelebs. Single or widowed.

capella. Chapel.

capellanus. Chaplain.

capias. Warrant for arrest.

carta, charta. Document.

circa. About, around.

civis. Citizen.

clericus pacis. Clerk of the peace, the principal legal officer of the county authority.

clericus Parochialis. Parish clerk.

cognatus. Kinsman, blood relation.

cognomen. Name, nickname.

comitatus (Comt.). County.

compatres. Godparents.

conductio sedilium. Pew rents.

conjug. Married.

conjuges. Married couple.

conjuncti fuere. (They) were married.

contra. Against, opposite.

coram. Before, in presence of.

cuius. Whose, of which, of what.

cum. With, when.

curia. Court.

de. Of, from, concerning.

decimae. Tithes.

defunctus, defunt. Deceased, dead.

Deus. God.

dictus. Named, the said.

die. Day, on a day.

dies, diem. Day.

dominus. Master, lord, judge.

domus. House.

ecclesia. Church.

ego. I.

eius, ejus. Of this, him, her, it.

eodem. To, at or on the same (place, person, time).

eodem die. On the same day.

est. It is.

et. And.

etiam. Also, even.

ex. From, out of.

extra. Outside.

fidejussores. Godparents.

filia. Daughter.

filius. Son.

frater. Brother.

fuerunt. (They) have been, were.

fuit. (He, she, it) has been, was.

gemelli, gemini. Twins.

genitores. Parents.

heredito. To grant in fee or inheritance.

hic/haec/hoc/hac. This.

huius, hujus. Of this (place).

ib, ibid, ibidem. In the same place.

idem. The same.

ignotus/ignoti. Of unknown father or name.

ille de. He was from.

ille fuit. He was.

imprimis. Firstly, at first.

in. In, on.

initiatus(a) fuit. He (she) was baptised.

incola. Inhabitant.

infans. Child, infant.

infantula. Little girl, infant girl.

infantulus. Little boy, infant boy.

infra. Within, below.

inter. Between, among.

ipse. Himself.

ipse dixit. As he said.

item. Also.

jam, iam. Already, now.

junior (jun. or iu.). Junior.

jurator. Juror.

juvenis. Young (man or woman).

lanatus. Bewoolled, i.e. buried in woollen.

levant et couchant. (Common right for cattle) for as many in summer as the produce of the land in question will maintain during the winter.

locus, locorum. Place, of the place.

magister. Master.

masculus. Masculine, male.

mater. Mother.

mater meretrix. Mother by reason of being a fornicatrix.

matrimonium solemnizat. Marriage was performed.

mendicus. Beggar, beggarly.

mensis (mens.). (Of the) month.

mensis prohibitus. Close season (marriage).

meretrix. Harlot, prostitute.

minoris. Junior.

mortuus, mortua. Deceased, dead.

nata. Born (a female).

natalis. Birth, of birth.

nativus. Native.

natus. Born.

natus et renatus. Born and reborn (i.e. baptised).

necnon. And also.

nihil. Nothing.

nomen, nomine. Name, by name.

numquam, nunquam. Never.

nunc. Now, at present.

nuper. Lately, formerly, the late.

nupt fuerant. Were married.

obiit (ob.). Died.

obiit eodem anno. Died the same year.

obiit sine prole. Died without issue.

oeconomus(i). Steward(s), churchwarden(s).

olim. Formerly.

parochia. Parish.

parva. Little or small.

passim. At random, far and wide.

pater. Father.

pauperum supervisor. Overseer of the poor.

per. Through, by.

peregrinus. Traveller, wanderer.

placea. Residence, place, site.

post. After.

predictus. Aforesaid.

pridie. The day before.

procuratores ecclesiae. Churchwardens.

proles. Offspring.

pro tempore. Before, in the time of.

puella. Maiden or girl.

puer. Boy.

puta. Reputed, supposed.

que. And (used as a suffix).

qui, quae, quod. Who, which, what.

quidam. A certain.

quietus. Receipt.

quondam. Formerly.

quoque. Also.

quorum. Whose.

relicta (rel.). Widow, separate wife.

relictus. Widower.

renatus. Baptised.

senex. Old.

sepultus, sepulta. Buried.

sequens, sequenti. Following.

sic. Thus.

sigillum. Seal.

sine prole. Without issue.

sive. Or, if.

spurius, spuria. Illegitimate son, daughter.

sub. Under.

supra. Above.

taberna cerevisiae. Church ales; the phrase is also used sometimes (and more properly) to mean simply alehouse.

tempus. Time.

trigemini. Triplets.

trinoda necessitas. The three fundamental obligations attached to land holding in the Dark and Middle Ages — military defence, and the maintenance of roads and bridges and the upkeep of fortresses.

tumulatus. Buried.

ultimus, ultima. Last, on the last.

ut dicitur. As is said.

uterque. Both.

uxor, uxoris (ux). Wife.

uxoratus. Married man.

uxoratus (-a -i) fuit (fuerunt). He/she was (they were) married.

vade mecum. Go with me. A handy reference book or indispensable pocket companion.

vel. Or.

vetura, vetus. Old.

viciatus. Bastard.

vicus. Village or district.

visus franci plegii. View of frankpledge.

votive. 1. Offered or consecrated by a vow.
          2. Given in fulfilment of a vow.

yconomus. Guardian.

zabalus. The devil.

zourus. A four-year-old buck.

zygostata. The clerk of a market.

Days of the Week

Monday	*dies lune* (on the day of the moon)
Tuesday	*dies martis*
Wednesday	*dies mercurii, dies wodenis*
Thursday	*dies jove, dies iovis*
Friday	*dies veneris*
Saturday	*dies saturno, dies sabbatina*
Sunday	*dies sole, dies domini* (day of the Lord)

Months of the Year

January	*Janarius*
February	*Februarius*
March	*Martius*
April	*Aprilis*
May	*Maius*
June	*Junius*
July	*Quintillis*
August	*Sextilis*
September	*September*
October	*October*
November	*November*
December	*December*

Seasons of the Year

Spring	*ver*
Summer	*aestas, aestivus*
Autumn	*autumnus*
Winter	*hiemalis, hiems*
Spring time	*vernum tempus*
Spring tide	*malina*
Lent	*quadragesima*
Lenten	*quadragesimalis*
In the future	*de futuro*

Latin Days of the Month

The information on this page is duly acknowledged as being supplied by Father Hilary Costello, Monk of the Cistercian Abbey of Mount Saint Bernard, Leicestershire.

1 *Dies Prima*
2 *Dies Secunda*
3 *Dies Tertia*
4 *Dies Quarta*
5 *Dies Quinta*
6 *Dies Sexta*
7 *Dies Septima*
8 *Dies Octava*
9 *Dies Nona*
10 *Dies Decima*
11 *Dies Undecima*
12 *Dies Duodecima*
13 *Dies Decima Tertia*
14 *Dies Decima Quarta*
15 *Dies Decima Quinta*
16 *Dies Decima Sexta*
17 *Dies Decima Septima*
18 *Dies Decima Octava*
19 *Dies Decima Nona*
20 *Dies Vicesima*
21 *Dies Vicesima Prima*
22 *Dies Vicesima Secunda*
23 *Dies Vicesima Tertia*
24 *Dies Vicesima Quarta*
25 *Dies Vicesima Quinta*
26 *Dies Vicesima Sexta*
27 *Dies Vicesima Septima*
28 *Dies Vicesima Octava*
29 *Dies Vicesima Nona*
30 *Dies Tricesima*
31 *Dies Tricesima Prima*

There were three chief days in each month:

1   *Calends* — 5   *Nones* — 13   *Ides*

but "in March, July, October, May the *Nones* fall on the 7 day", and the *Ides* eight days later, on the 15.

Currency

Farthing	*quadrans, quadrantis, quarta, as,*
	ferlingus
Penny	*denarius, nummis*
Penny worth	*denariata*
Penny weight	*nummata*
Silver penny	*sterlingus*
One shilling	*solidus*
One shilling's worth	*solidate*

Roman Numerals

I	=	1
II	=	2
III	=	3
IV or IIII	=	4
V	=	5
VI	=	6
VII	=	7
VIII	=	8
IX	=	9
X	=	10
XI	=	11
XII	=	12
XIII	=	13
XIV	=	14
XV	=	15
XVI	=	16
XVII	=	17
XVIII	=	18
XIX	=	19
XX	=	20
XXX	=	30
XL	=	40
L	=	50
LX	=	60
LXX	=	70
LXXX	=	80
XC	=	90
C	=	100
CC	=	200
CCC	=	300
CCCC or CD	=	400
D	=	500
DC	=	600
DCC	=	700
DCCC	=	800
CM	=	900
M	=	1000
MM	=	2000

Old Style Dating – Julian Calendar

Throughout the Middle Ages, and in some countries for much longer, the calendar in use was that known as the Julian, because it was originally introduced by Julius Caesar in 45 B.C. This way of reckoning is now known as the 'Old Style'. The New Style or Gregorian Calendar was introduced by Pope Gregory XIII in 1582. The Julian calendar set up a common year consisting of 365 days, while every fourth year was to contain an extra day, the sixth calends of March (24 February) being doubled and the year therefore being described as *annus bissextilis*. This latter device was intended to rectify, at regular intervals, the accumulated discrepancy between the calendar year of 365 days and the solar year, calculated by the astronomers at 365¼ days. The mistake was made, however, of counting in the current year when deciding which was 'every fourth year', and in practice the bissextile years occurred in what we should call every third year. Thus an error rapidly accumulated, until the Emperor Augustus removed it by ordaining that twelve successive years should consist of 365 days only. The next bissextile or leap year was A.D.4, and thereafter, as long as the Old Style lasted, every fourth year, in the modern sense, was a leap year.

New Style Dating — Gregorian Calendar

In Great Britain and Ireland the change was effected by Chesterfield's Act 24 George II, c.23 (March 1751), which decreed that throughout the dominions of the British Crown the following 1 January should be the first day of 1752, and that 2 September 1752 should be followed by 14 September. Until 1752, 25 March was the civil and legal New Year's Day.

Bibliography

Adams, I.H., *Agrarian Landscape Terms: A Glossary for Historical Geography* (1977).

Barley, M.W., *English Farmhouse & Cottage* (1976).

Blagg, T., and Wadsworth, F. (eds.), *Nottinghamshire Marriage Licences*, Volume I (1930).

Bourne, T., and Marcombe, D. (eds.), *The Burton Lazars Cartulary*, Department of Adult Education, University of Nottingham, Centre for Local History Record Series No. 6 (1987).

Brewer, E.C., *The Dictionary of Phrase and Fable* (1988).

Brooke, G.C., *English Coins* (1955).

Burnett, J., *A History of the Cost of Living.*

Butler, D. & G., *British Political Facts 1900–1994.*

Chaundler, G., *Year Book of Saints* (1978).

Cheney, C.R., *Handbook of Dates for Students of English History* (2000).

Collins' *National Dictionary and Encyclopedia* (nd).

Cook, C., *Macmillan Dictionary of Historical Terms* (1990).

Cox, J.C., *Parish Registers of England* (1974).

Cox, J.C., *Churchwardens accounts from the fourteenth century to the close of the seventeenth century* (1913).

Dartnell, G.E., *Glossary of Words*, English Dialect Society, No. 69 (1893).

Emmison, G.F., *Elizabethan Life, Home, Work & Land*, Essex Record Office Publication No. 96 (1976).

Fisher, J.L., *A Medieval Farming Glossary of Latin and English Words* (1968).

FitzHugh, Terrick V.H., *The Dictionary of Genealogy* (1988).

Ford, T.D. and Rieuwerts, J.H. (eds.), *Lead Mining in the Peak District* (1983).

Fussell, G.E. (ed.), *Robert Loader's Farm Accounts 1610–1620* (1936).

Gooder, E.A., *Latin for Local History* (1990).

Green, V.J., *Saints for all Seasons* (1982).

Gregg, P., *A Social & Economic History of Britain 1760–1963.*

Grose, F., *Provincial Glossary 1787* (1968).

Halliwell, J.O., *A Dictionary of Archaic and Provincial Words* (1960).

Hartley, D. (ed.), *Thomas Tusser: 1557 Floruit: His Good Points of Husbandry* (1931).

Hartley, D., *The Land of England* (1976).

Heslop, R.O., *A Glossary of Words used in the County of Northumberland*, English Dialect Society, No. 68 (1893).

Hibbert, C., *The English, A Social History 1066–1945* (1987).

Homas, G.C., *English Villagers of the Thirteenth Century* (1943).

James, A., *Money* (1973).

Kennedy, P.A., *Nottinghamshire Household Inventories*, Thoroton Society Record Series, Volume XXII (1963).

Kiernan, D., *The Derbyshire Lead Industry in the Sixteenth Century* (1989).

McLaughlin, E., *Simple Latin for Family Historians* (1986).

Mitchell, S. and Reeds, B. (eds.), *Coins of England & the United Kingdom*, Seaby Standard Catalogue of British Coins (1988).

Moore, J. S., *Goods and Chattels of our Forefathers* (1976).

Morris, C. (ed.), *The Illustrated Journeys of Celia Fiennes* (1982).

Morris, J., *A Latin Glossary* (1989).

Munby, L., *How Much Is That Worth.*

Needham, S., *A Glossary for East Yorkshire and North Lincolnshire Probate Inventories*, University of Hull, Department of Adult Education, Studies in Regional and Local History, No. 3 (1984).

Newman, O. & Foster, A., *The Value of a Pound 1900–1993.*

Northall, G.F., *A Warwickshire Word Book*, English Dialect Society, No. 79 (1896).

Palliser, D.M., *Tudor York* (1970).

Parker, R., *The Common Stream* (1975).

Perkins, E.R. (ed.), *Village Life from Wills & Inventories, Clayworth Parish 1670–1710*, Department of Adult Education, University of Nottingham, Centre for Local History Record Series No. 1 (1979).

Priestley, H., *The What it cost the day before Yesterday Book.*

Ravensdale, J.R., *History on your Doorstep* (1982).

Richardson, J., *The Local Historian's Encyclopedia* (1974).

Rogers, A. (ed.), *Coming into Line, Local Government in Clayworth 1674–1714*, Department of Adult Education, University of Nottingham, Centre for Local History Record Series No. 2 (1979).

Simpson, E., *Latin Word List for Family Historians* (1985).

Simpson, J.A. and Weiner, E.S.C., *The Oxford English Dictionary*, Second Edition (1989).

A Sixteenth Century Notts Village — Upton near Southwell, Department of Adult Education, University of Nottingham and Nottinghamshire County Council Education Department (1979).

Stuart, D., *Manorial Records* (1992).

Supreme Court Practice 1999. Vol. 1.

Tate, W.E., *English Village Community and the Enclosure Movement* (1967).

Tate, W.E., *The Parish Chest* (1969).

Taylor, A.J.P., *English History 1914–1945* (1977).

Trent Polytechnic, Clifton, History Division, *Glossary* (1977).

Trinder, B. and Cox, J., *Yeomen & Colliers in Telford* (1980).

Trotter, E., *Seventeenth Century Life in a Country Parish* (1919).

Walters, R.E., *Parish Registers in England* (1887).

Warren, W.L., *Henry II* (1973).

Webster, W.F., *Nottinghamshire Hearth Tax 1664–1674* (1988).

Wilson, A., *Latin Dictionary* (1965).

Wood, B.A., Watkins, C. and Wood, C.A. (eds.), *Life at Laxton 1880–1903, Childhood Memories of Edith Hickson*, Department of Adult Education, Centre for Local History Record Series No. 5, University of Nottingham (1983).

Further suggested reading

Cole, J. and Titford, J., *Tracing Your Family Tree* (2001).

Hey, D., *The Oxford Dictionary of Local and Family History*.

Richardson, J., *The Local Historian's Encyclopedia*.

ILLUSTRATION CREDITS

1. *Open chimney.* From a drawing made by J. J. Hissey in 1887. From *The English Countrywoman*, G. E. and K. R. Fussell (1981). Reproduced by permission of Little, Brown and Company (UK).

2. *Blacksmiths.* Woodcut from Roxburghe Collection of Ballads, I, 250, 251. Dept of Printed Books, British Museum. From *The Illustrated English Social History* Vol. 2, G. M. Trevelyan (1950). Reproduced by permission of The British Library and Longman Group UK.

3. *Practising at the butts.* The Luttrell Psalter. B. M. MS. Add. 42, 130 ff 170v and 147v. From *The Illustrated English Social History*, Vol. 1, G. M. Trevelyan (1949). Reproduced by permission of The British Library and Longman Group UK.

4. *Churning butter.* From *The Oxford Illustrated History of Britain*, edited by K. O. Morgan (1985). Reproduced by permission of Oxford University Press.

5. *Ducking chair at a village well.* From *The English Countrywoman*, G. E. and K. R. Fussell (1981). Reproduced by permission of Little, Brown and Company (UK).

6. *Spinning and carding wool.* The Luttrell Psalter. B. M. MS. Add. 42, 130 ff 193 and 166v. From *The Illustrated English Social History*, Vol. 1. G. M. Trevelyan (1949). Reproduced by permission of The British Library and Longman Group UK.

7. *Cloth being dipped in a dye vat.* B. M. MS. Royal 15E. iii. f269 Flemish, late XVth century. From *The Illustrated English Social History*, Vol. 1, G. M. Trevelyan (1949). Reproduced by permission of The British Library and Longman Group UK.

8. *Great Fire of London, 1666.* An engraving by W. Hollar. From *A Social History of England*, Asa Briggs (1983). BBC Hulton Picture Library. Reproduced by permission

of Weidenfeld and Nicolson, Hulton Deutsch Collection Ltd and Orion Publishing Group Ltd.

9. *Transporting Portland stone in 1790.* From a drawing by Swiss artist Samuel Hieronymus Grimm (1790). B. M. MS. Add 15, 537, ff 158 and 198. From *The Illustrated English Social History*, Vol. 2, G. M. Trevelyan (1950). Reproduced by permission of The British Library and Longman Group UK.

10. *Hackney coach.* Woodcut from Roxburghe Collection of Ballads I, 546, 547. Dept of Printed Books, British Museum. From *The Illustrated Social History*, Vol. 2, G. M. Trevelyan (1950). Reproduced by permission of The British Library and Longman Group UK.

11. *Hearse.* From the David Marcombe collection.

12. *Lazy keufs.* From the Joy Bristow collection.

13. *Ordinary or meal at an inn.* Roxburghe Collection, I, 18, 19. Dept of Printed Books, British Museum. From *The Illustrated English Social History*, Vol. 2, G. M. Trevelyan (1950). Reproduced by permission of The British Library and Longman Group UK.

14. *A pedlar and ballad-monger.* Woodcut from Roxburghe Collection of Ballads, II, 404. Dept of Printed Books, British Museum. From *The Illustrated English Social History*, Vol. 2, G. M. Trevelyan (1950). Reproduced by permission of The British Library and Longman Group UK.

15. *Double-wheeled plough.* John Fitzherbert, *Newe Tracte for Husbandmen*, c.1525. From *The Oxford Illustrated History of Britain*, edited by K. O. Morgan (1985). Reproduced by permission of Oxford University Press.

16. *Post mill.* From the Joy Bristow collection.

17. *Ridge-and-furrow, Watford.* From *Medieval England, an Aerial Survey*, M. W. Beresford and J. K. S. St. Joseph, Cambridge University Press (1979). Cambridge University Collection of Air Photographs AWI 81, copyright reserved. Reproduced by permission of the University of

Cambridge Committee for Aerial Photography.

18. *Shaft climbing.* From *Lead Mining in The Peak District* (1983). Reproduced by permission of the Peak District Mines Historical Society.

19. *Trenching tools.* From *The Illustrated English Social History* Vol. 2, G. M. Trevelyan (1950). Originally from *The English Improver Improved, etc.*, by Wa. Blith (1652). From the copy in the Cambridge University Library. By permission of the Syndics of the Cambridge University Library.

20. *Vagrancy.* From *A Social History of England*, Asa Briggs (1983). Reproduced by permission of Weidenfeld and Nicolson Ltd and Orion Publishing Group Ltd.

21. *Whipping post.* From the Joy Bristow collection.

22. *Milk delivery in the eighteenth century.* From *The English Countrywoman* (1981), G. E. and K. R. Fussell. Reproduced by permission of Little, Brown and Company (UK).

23. *Some English silver coins.* From the David Marcombe collection.

24. *Coverdale's Bible.* From *The Oxford Illustrated History of Britain*, edited by K. O. Morgan (1985). Reproduced by permission of The British Library.

25. *A selection of Medieval lead trade weights.* From the David Marcombe collection.